"F"-IT-LESS

"F"-IT-LESS

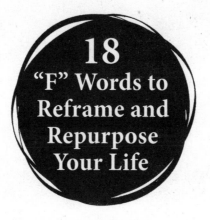

18
"F" Words to
Reframe and
Repurpose
Your Life

SHAUN RAWLS

with LAURA MORTON

Forefront
BOOKS

DEDICATION

The dedication of this work goes to those whose inner compass pulls at them, whether it be a subtle or not-so-subtle pull, and points them towards something bigger and better . . . something great.

TABLE OF CONTENTS

INTRODUCTION

I BET, IF YOU'RE ANYTHING LIKE ME, YOU WERE RAISED BY YOUR parents, teachers, and local religious leaders never to say, "F-it!" or any other curse word, for that matter. Especially not in mixed company. Too bad our well-mannered, well-intentioned elders couldn't raise us never to *feel* that way—never to be so fed up, frustrated, stuck, or defeated in at least one area of life that tossing in the towel or folding up shop and never trying again seem like viable options. Despite my upbringing, I did cuss, and I suspect you did or do too. I worked my way up to saying the F-word—or, I should say, I worked my way down, as circumstances have to get pretty low for us to just throw our hands up and wave a white flag in an act of defeat or sheer defiance..

F-it! may be the mother of all F-words, but there are plenty of others. As I've discovered, there are lots and lots of F-words, some leading to a state of F-it!, and—here's the good news—some leading out of it.

That's right: On the road to being fed up, frustrated, stuck, or defeated, you'll find yourself being fractured, flawed, and fearful, among other things. But there are mindsets you can adopt and actions you can take to help you move to a state of being fantastic, formidable, fun-loving, free, and so much more instead!

When you think about it, there's an F-word for just about every exasperating experience you can face. And there are also F-words to help pull you off that dangerous road and put you back on the right track—the track to what I fondly call a "F-it-less life."

Are you with me? Want to trade in a few of those choice words you've been muttering under your breath or—worse—shouting at the top of your lungs? Want to abandon the places they drive you mentally, physically, emotionally, and spiritually to live a life far more fulfilling than you ever dreamed of? You can, you know. This book is designed to help you do just that.

If you're ready to reframe and repurpose how you see life, *"F"-It-Less* tells the story of an existence completely transformed by some very powerful F-words, and, more important, it shows you the step-by-step process to transform your own life as well. I invite you to read on. Your journey is about to look and be so much more promising than ever before.

CHAPTER ONE
F-IT!

. . . .

Things Change
—WILLIAM EDGAR RAWLS
MY DAD

. . . .

"I've had it."

"I'm done."

"It's over."

"That's it."

"No more."

Sound familiar?

I've been a corporate trainer and a life and business coach for years, so I've heard all of this (and far worse) before. I've seen people throw up their hands, push themselves back from the table, and cry, "I can't take it anymore!" We've all been there.

We all know that point of sheer frustration and exhaustion—the point where we're tired of swimming upstream against the current, tired of settling for something less than we deserve, and tired of resisting forces that seem larger than us, whether they are mounting bills, pressures at home, school, or work, or even the sameness of our everyday routine.

"F-it! I'm out of here, I'm done, I don't give an F what happens anymore."

I get it. I've been there too. More times than I care to admit.

And while that's true, I also understand that walking away as though you don't give a damn always seems a lot better in fantasy than in reality. At the end of the day, we've all got real-world responsibilities, financial obligations, and people counting on us to show up.

Don't get me wrong—I've made my share of mistakes, and if I could go back in time and do some things differently, I would. Yet at the same time, I can never forget or discount the fact that the choices I made—as difficult as some of them were—got me all that I have today.

No regrets.

Why?

Because over the years I've recognized that I can't live my best life weighed down by remorse. It's wiser to live it with forgiveness for the times when I should have consulted WAZE before making a sharp left turn or two, and with gratitude for the bumps in the road that landed me where I am now, in a life I truly love.

What would you say if I told you I had a formula—a secret of sorts—that could help you hit a mental reset button before you ever got to the corner of "F"-It and "I'm Done"? A formula that allows you to push past being pissed off, past all your emotional baggage, past your fears, and past the so-called rules? A formula that compels you to take worthwhile risks? One that leads to what I call a truly "F-it-less life"? A life without all the resistance. A life that works with you, not against you.

What if there was a way to reframe how you see the F-word? A way to perceive better prospects for yourself whenever you get to that point of no return?

Would you want to know more?

Of *course* you would. And, even more important, you should.

Hey, there's no doubt that there are times when saying "F-it!" feels like the only way out. In fact, during those times, thinking or even saying "F-you!" can make you feel better for a moment. I'm from the South, where we usually choose to say something subtler, such as "How nice" or "Bless your heart" because we're far too polite to actually say, "Go F-yourself!" But you can rest assured that, in the right situation and circumstances, we're thinking it.

A lot of people believe that an F-it mentality means giving up or giving in, not caring, or being indifferent.

And for some, that approach works—for a while. But soon enough, you have to pay your bills. You have to go back to work. You realize that the carefree, I-don't-give-an-F attitude that felt so good at first has lost its luster. And when that happens, reality sets in.

You see, when life throws us a curve, its purpose is to sepa-rate the weak from the strong. And if you're paying attention, it will actually reveal your weaknesses and strengths to you. Rather than standing up to challenging circumstances, most people use them as crutches. They start blaming everyone and everything but themselves for how disappointing their life is. They take zero responsibility for the choices they've made—the choices that got them to this point in the first place. The kind of F-it mentality I'm talking about doesn't suggest that you forget whatever's going wrong in your life. Nope—that won't help you. The kind of F-it mentality I mean is constructive. It's actually about taking responsibility for the things that have happened, learning from them, and applying their lessons going forward. I call it "*F-it-less.*"

F-it-less is about getting unstuck.

It's about recognizing that there's nowhere else to go but up. It's about rebuilding—allowing yourself to actively define how you want to live and love, and how you're going to pursue that vision.

Okay, that's easier said than done, I know. But it's not impossible.

In fact, learning to live an F-it-less life is easier than you may think.

When you get to the place where you want to say "F-it," that's the time to pause, take a breather, and hit the reset button. That's the time to reframe your thoughts. The time to use a whole new set of F-words as fuel for change. Some of the F-words we'll explore together will help you identify where you are in the moment. They're words such as "fragmented," "frustrated," "fractured," "failed," and, on a good day, even "fine" or "fantastic." Other F-words, such as "family," "faith," "fun," and "freedom," remind us of our goals, while "find," "forgive," "forget," "fix," "float," and "foxhole" help us plan and take action. All the guiding F-words we'll employ have the potential to draw you back into alignment with your goals and to set you on the path of living a truly F-it-less life.

One thing I know for sure is that life is going to challenge us. It's going to present unexpected obstacles along the way, and it's up to us to navigate past those stumbling blocks. Some people seem to meet these challenges with ease and confidence, while others tend to buckle under the stress.

As the creator of your life's choices, and, hence, your reality, you hold the ability to overcome daily pressures, tests, and confrontations. Seeing these encounters as opportunities instead of obstacles is a great way to start adopting an F-it-less mindset.

Have you ever wondered why certain challenges seem difficult for you while other people appear to breeze right through the same situations? Or why you put off for weeks a task that can be done several times in a day by someone else?

It's not because they have anything over you or are better than you. And it has nothing to do with possessing a particular skill set or some special know-how.

It's all about perception.

In my experience, those who successfully move through challenging tasks have either found a way to avoid seeing those activities as challenges to begin with, or they value what's on the other side of the challenge highly enough that the challenge is worth taking on.

Making difficult decisions doesn't have to be a burden, either. Many people spend their time looking for ways to avoid an issue, hoping it will simply go away. They seek other avenues to get around it. They pray for guidance. And worst of all, some tend to wallow in their fear, angst, worry, and despair far longer than it would have taken them to confront the matter, deal with it, and move beyond it. When we look back on our lives, we see that the biggest, toughest, and scariest decisions frequently have the most rewarding outcomes.

All too often we pray for life to get easier when we should be praying for us to get better, smarter, and stronger.

Life has taught me that putting off the inevitable doesn't make it go away. In fact, procrastinating usually just makes things worse. It's like letting your dirty laundry pile up until the mound becomes so daunting that you postpone the chore even more. It's usually desperation—the lack of a single pair of clean socks or underwear when you need them most—that ultimately makes you give in. In the end, what would have taken you less than an hour to do up front now takes you an entire day to complete!

Getting to the point of utter despair before you make a move is not how you want to contend with important life decisions. It's simply not wise or fun. Besides, you're better than that. Let's face it: living a life you *have* to live is very different from living the life you *want* to live.

And regardless of how many people you poll for thoughts and opinions on what you should do about your situation, no one else can truly solve your problems. No one else's opinion should matter more than your own. You must value your voice, your thoughts, and your beliefs above those of all others. When you finally decide that your thoughts don't control you but, rather, *you* control your thoughts, you'll be ready to take your first real step toward living an F-it-less life. You must be willing to take action and deal with concerns head-on. If you're ready for positive change, you'll do whatever it takes to rid yourself of the self-doubt, limiting thoughts, negative energy, people, and environments that hold you back.

I hate to state the obvious, but we all know that old habits die hard. Sometimes, *really* hard. Unfortunately, there's no easy way around that truth. You simply have to do the work to bring about lasting transformation. Wisdom can guide you only so far before action is required. It's up to you to determine how to respond to the hurdles you encounter and to put your plans into effect. In business, entrepreneurs and leaders generally like disruption. It forces them to refocus and realign their company goals. However, most people despise any type of disorder or conflict in their lives, especially when it appears to be overwhelming, intimidating, or perceived as impossible.

Anyone who has ever built a company and made it successful has done so because they had unwavering passion and because they believed in their ideas more than anyone else's. Moving through the world with this kind of energy is bound to create massive amounts of conflict. Not all the time, but certainly, sometimes. How you deal with the challenges of going about doing what you know to be right for you impacts everything, just as it does for that determined business leader.

Some people prefer to deal with the conflict that often comes from making changes head-on. Others—myself included—tend to wait things out, hoping the Universe will sort through it all and make any lingering problems quietly go away. When that approach doesn't work, things eventually erupt. Then, whether you want to or not, you have to face the inevitable. You have to wrestle with the monster. By that time, however, you're on the defensive. Sure, the path of least resistance may feel safer, but be forewarned: anything less than a committed approach to change can yield collateral damage.

One of the things I love about the Bible is that it teaches us to not avoid conflict. It tells us that God wants us to experience challenges—that there's a reason for and a purpose behind our struggles. As I've gone through my own experiences and helped others through theirs, I've come to understand that more often than not, there is value in facing conflict. As Mahatma Gandhi said, "Peace is not the absence of conflict, but the ability to cope with it."

I know a guy who was thought of as "a real company man" by everyone in his workplace. He had been with his firm for most of his career, and by all accounts, he seemed very happy. He was known to be loyal and reliable, and he held an institutional knowledge that was invaluable because of his long tenure there. One day he told his boss that he was taking a position with their competitor. His boss was flabbergasted, as was everyone else. Despite his boss's attempts to keep him, no counteroffer would do. Apparently, over time this man had built up resentments that only he knew he had. If he had shared his concerns in earnest along the way—at lunch with his boss, in a well-thought-out memo, or during his annual review—his complaints could have been addressed and rectified at any number of junctures. But now he was at a point where he felt that only a do-over in a completely new environment could give him the fresh start he was looking for. So, he left.

Most people think that by the time you are on the brink of an epic "F"-it moment you've given voice to your rage countless times—that you have even screamed them from the rafters. But as this man's example proves, that's not always the case.

Many people get to "F"-it through silence—by a sheer lack of communication with others, and oftentimes by lack of communication with themselves. To keep from getting to that point, you have to periodically check in with yourself, take the temperature of your surroundings and your happiness in them, and be totally honest about how you are doing. And you must be willing to risk conflict in order to make the necessary changes that improve your life while the conflict is still manageable for all parties involved.

How do I know this to be true? After working in real estate for more than twenty-five years and being married for seventeen, I had gotten to a place where I was ready to make some big changes. The problem was, I didn't know it. I didn't realize that I was at that fork in the road because I hadn't been taking the time to assess my life or to have the conversations with myself that I needed to have. I was too busy working in and on my business that I forgot to work on me and my marriage properly.

At the time, my wife, Jean, and I had built Atlanta's number one residential real estate firm. I was the owner and operator of The Rawls Group, part of Keller Williams Realty. Our Sandy Springs location not only made a lot of money for us, it was also a lucrative and popular office for Keller Williams. Because of our stellar performances, I was asked to teach and train others. As a result, I had become well known among many of the brokers and agents in the organization throughout the country. By late 2004, five years after starting The Rawls Group, I was getting a lot of pressure from the larger corporation to step out of my day-to-day role as Team Leader in Sandy Springs to focus my energies instead on growing the business even further. It was evident that, to do this properly, I would have to hand the reins of my office over to someone else. The idea of replacing myself was a tough pill to swallow, but I understood that it had to be done. To give you an idea of how worthwhile that risk eventually was, The Rawls Group of Keller Williams currently has over 2,000 agents producing nearly $5 billion in annual sales. It consistently ranks among the best-performing companies in the Keller Williams system.

The results of replacing myself turned out to be immeasurable for me. I thrived on the expanding responsibilities and opportunities that were unfolding for me and my family. I had found a new gear professionally. And I loved it. I was busy and making a difference in the lives and businesses of countless numbers of great real estate professionals in Atlanta and all over the country.

With all of this fun and success, what I didn't realize—or rather, what I did realize on some level but didn't acknowledge, address, or work to resolve—was that I had lost some of the essential balance that makes a person, and more importantly, a marriage, whole. The problem was that I didn't communicate my feelings properly, much less work on them in a purposeful way. I naively believed that our ship would somehow right itself over time. I was foolish and wrong. I buried myself in the other things that brought me joy: my two sons and my work. They were my distraction, my escape. Unfortunately, this became a pattern; I had backed myself into a corner. Somehow, I'd convinced myself that if I could lift the tide in one area of my life, then all of my boats would float.

Remember the guy I mentioned earlier? The one who shocked his boss and colleagues by abruptly, though not really so abruptly, leaving his company for another? I was on a path to becoming that guy. Somewhere along the way I had fallen out of love with my life as it was, and the Universe was about to make sure that I realized and reconciled it.

In this era of over-sharing, I will spare you and my loved ones of all the details. But suffice it to say, I precipitated what turned out to be a painful divorce for all involved. In the process, I relinquished my positions in the company we built together. I won't sugarcoat it: it wasn't easy or pretty for anyone. It was an "F-it!" moment for me, and I take full responsibility for all aspects of it. However, out of this period of intense change, soul-searching, and transformation came this very manifesto that you are now reading for living an F-it-less life, and a checklist of what to do to be sure that I veered as far away from the path that led me there to begin with.

I'm sure you've heard the phrase "no pain, no gain" used as a motto promising greater rewards for intense training. As the saying implies, competitive professionals, such as athletes and artists, are required to endure a degree both of physical and mental stress in order to achieve their desired level of excellence. While exercise guru Jane Fonda may have brought this catchphrase into the mainstream in the early 1980s with her popular workout videos, the sentiment had been expressed in various forms for centuries before then, most especially as a spiritual teaching. Religious leaders, poets, and social influencers throughout the ages have all offered up some variation on this saying. Even Poor Richard, the pseudonym under which Benjamin Franklin often wrote, echoed this theme with the words, "He that lives upon hope will die fasting. There are no gains without pains."

Of course, I don't use this expression in this context lightly. It is one thing to inflict pain on yourself as a means of self-growth and quite another to inflict it on others in the process of your growth. The hope is that when pain occurs, everyone affected will be strengthened by the experience in some way over time. I do, however, share this expression here because the fact that this phrase repeatedly resurfaces in our cultural history suggests that the road to achievement really does run through hardship. While not every road you venture down will be paved with bricks of adversity, there's no question that you'll be met with a few bumps and twists along the way. Sometimes those curves will lead to unexpected changes. It may not even be clear why you're going down a certain path until you make it past the hardship and can see its purpose from a totally different perspective.

As I've discovered on my own journey and in coaching others on theirs, getting to "F-it!" can happen in many ways: losing a job, learning that you have cancer, a car accident, burnout, the loss of a parent, child, or spouse, getting a divorce, or just from sheer boredom in your life. You can also get there through inspiration. Falling in love, traveling encountering books or speakers that expand and reframe the vision you have for your life, or experiencing a spiritual awakening are other such pathways to "F-it."

Whatever the options are, it only takes one.

Without question, my "F-it!" moment and what it has taught me has brought about the biggest and most rewarding growth curve in my life. It has yielded a much greater perspective on events and on myself. I'm happier, clearer-minded, more purposeful, and I embrace all the love in my life more fully than ever before. I'm now married to the woman who I am convinced was my destiny to find and fight to be with in this lifetime. She and I thoroughly enjoy the life we've created together as a family that includes her sons, Andrew and Jacob, and daughter, Sarah, and my sons, Noble and Steel.

While I used to live a life focused on making so many other people happy, I now realize that the only people I need to be critically concerned about making happy are Jeri, our five children, and myself. This alone makes me a better version of myself.

This life of ours is a marathon, not a sprint. If there is a finish line, it's beyond our sight. You have to trust that your decisions—when made for the right reasons and certainly with the right intentions—must be acted upon as hard as they may be for others to accept. You may not be able to sell the world on the merits of those choices at the time, but the proof of those merits will be in living your best life, one day at a time.

On this amazing journey of self-discovery that I've been on, I have failed, focused, fixed, forgiven, forgotten, and flowed myself to freedom. I'm the best version of myself that I've ever been. In fact, I'm in the best shape of my life, both physically and mentally, and I have more peace in my heart than I've ever known. And believe me, I want the same things for all of you who read this book. As you take in all this information, understand that I'm not asking for your approval or acceptance. I am, however, asking that you examine your own life—the life you've created, and the life you've allowed to unfold—and decide whether you're living the one you really want. I'm asking you to be honest with yourself, to listen to your heart, to follow your gut, to acknowledge the areas of your life where you've compromised your own happiness for money, safety, security, or, worse, fear. I'm asking you not to let your best life pass you by. I'm asking you to take a more proactive approach to the life you want to live. And in doing so, I'm giving you the opportunity to stop ignoring, compromising, and sweeping important things under the rug, so you can avoid stepping on a land mine, like so many people before you have. I've learned so much both from my successes and my failures, and I hope that by sharing some of my greatest lessons, you, too, can live what I now refer to as an F-it-less life—the life you're entitled to discover, explore, and fulfill for yourself.

One F at a time...that's all it's going to take.

CHAPTER TWO
FROM F-IT! TO F-IT-LESS

• •

Open your eyes and look within: Are you
satisfied with the life you're living?
—BOB MARLEY, "EXODUS"

• •

VERY OFTEN, EXISTING IN A CONSTANT STATE OF CHAOS IS WHAT pushes us to say "F-it!" But once we're able to rid ourselves of all that pandemonium and anxiety, we can begin to enjoy a new sense of freedom. And freedom is what allows us to live a truly F-it-less life.

I know a lot of people who think that they're functioning at their optimum level when they're in perpetual motion. In fact, some even believe that they can't be at their best unless they're engaged in a dizzying number of projects, activities, events, and interactions. They actually think they're thriving at this pace, that somehow, they're being all things to all people. But I've never known anyone to truly flourish in this sustained state. Crowd-pleasing is a major source of chaos. Under certain circumstances, some people actually learn to ride chaos like a powerful wave. Some of them assume that it's a required part of their journey to success, or, worse, that it's a given in life. They wear their turmoil like a badge of honor, sometimes bragging about it as though the more chaos they create, the more successful they are. They eat fortified chaos for breakfast, lunch, and dinner, believing it's good, productive, character building, and even necessary.

Guess what? That's BS.

Chaos creates a lot of thick smoke, which eventually leads to total and complete burnout. Because you can't clearly see what's right in front of you, you might not even know you've hit bottom—but believe me, when you live in a chaotic state, that's where you are.

You see, humans are an incredibly adaptable species. We quickly learn to yield to our environment, all too often lowering our expec-tations and desires by adjusting to unhealthy relationships, stifling jobs, poor finances, and a host of other things that result from a steady stream of stress. Most of us will try whatever we can to make the best of such situations, even if doing so is to our detriment. Over time, we get to a place of complacency—a level of acceptance that things in our lives are exactly where they should be and where they'll likely remain, no matter what. Adaptability is a great trait under the right conditions, but it can also be very damaging. *Most people learn to adapt to things that are less than ideal when they ought to be adapting to things that are more than ideal.* I remember hearing my great-grandmother say to my mom and other family members, "You can fall in love with a rich person just as easy as you can fall in love with a poor one. It's just that one of them is harder to find."

There's a gravitational pull toward mediocrity that's tugging at us at all times. Mediocre is nothing more than average, and the word *average* can often be substituted by the word *most*. Most people live mediocre and average lives. It's difficult to change—or even see the need to change—when everyone else around you is caught up in the same vortex. Looking to the right or to the left of you reveals people whirling around in the same circular fashion, spinning so fast they can't possibly see or reach for a better lifestyle than the one they have. No wonder it's easier to live a mediocre life than to live a great one. But if you don't exert your own directional momentum, mediocrity's gravitational pull will wear you down and force you to give up on your ideas and dreams, ultimately leading you to a place where saying "F-it!" seems like the only way out. Anti-gravitational adaptation, on the other hand, helps you live a better, more rewarding, F-it-less life.

Don't get me wrong: adaptability is often a great asset. Charles Darwin is often credited with saying, "It is not the strongest of the species that survives, nor the most intelligent that survives. It is the one that is most adaptable to change." I've always prided myself on my ability to adapt. Whether it was my capacity to adjust to changing conditions in my family, school, sports, or business, I've always looked for an opportunity to make something work enough to succeed. Somewhere along the way, I learned that nothing (and no one) is all good or all bad. Embracing what's good about something or someone while managing what's bad is a gift that has always served me well. However, adaptability can have its limits, and it's important to know when you are reaching yours.

When we adapt to circumstances in order to help us achieve our goals, that's great; but when we find that we have intrinsically changed ourselves in the process of adapting—that we've actually conformed to the less desirable aspects of the life around us—that, for me, is crossing a line. That's adapting to something that's less than ideal. I'm grateful that an internal sense of knowing alerts us to this tendency. We just need to listen to it. Trusting that alarm and having enough faith to understand that it is time to change directions is essential. There's no shame in revising one's plans. That's adapting to a life that's more than ideal.

That's certainly what I discovered after working in real estate for 25 years and finding myself at a personal and professional fork in the road. My businesses were running well, but I was feeling oddly frustrated with some important parts of my life. I suspect that the Universe wanted to redirect my path because I hadn't been in touch with or communicated my feelings properly, much less worked on them in a purposeful way, for a while, and it was definitely time to do so.

It's unwise to naively believe that your ship will right itself over time. It is also unwise to distract yourself with anything other than fixing—not just patching over—what's damaged or out of order and charting your way to a happier place. When the signs are writ large and you have the power to do something about it, do it. Many people tend to throw themselves into work, a favorite pastime, or other distractions, but those things become a pattern more often than a solution. Lifting the tide in one area of your life does not mean all boats will float. Lift the tide where it is most needed. If any of this sounds remotely like it is easy or clear, it isn't—not by a long shot.

As I know from running my own business and consulting with others who do the same, the best business leaders have practices we can all learn from. The ability to make tough decisions, for instance, is the hallmark of an effective leader, especially when dealing with situations for which there isn't a precedent. Many people, whether they are in positions of authority or not, struggle with the fear that they will make mistakes when executing decisions that will either embarrass them or hurt other people. Strong leaders know that is not the time to pull back, but, rather, that is the time to move ahead in a different manner than usual. Trial and error is a tremendously powerful process for solving problems in a complex world, and you will find this to be true when you are seeking new approaches and new opportunities to improve and move your life forward too.

During my period of upheaval, I was certain that there would be failure along the way. After all, I was stepping out of my comfort zone. I was headed into terrain I hadn't yet explored, let alone understood. Hence, my goals were simple: make the failure survivable and learn from my mistakes. I knew I would stumble occasionally in this uncharted territory, and I was okay with that, because by then I was optimistic that some good would come from each fall. Wherever this blind journey was taking me, I was committed enough not to let any obstacles I encountered or mistakes I made prevent me from moving forward.

Colin Powell has a rule about making tough decisions that I believe is helpful when you are at such crossroads. I came across a reference to it years ago, and the minute I read it, I loved it. It changed my life in that it taught me how to make the best call in the absence of complete certainty. I call it *Leading with Faith*. He says that every time you face a tough decision, you should have no less than 40 percent and no more than 70 percent of the information you need to make the decision. If you make decisions with less than 40 percent of the information you need, then you're shooting from the hip and will make too many mistakes. The second part of Powell's decision-making rule, though, surprises many leaders. They often think that they need more than 70 percent of the information before they can make a decision. But if they've gathered more than 70 percent of the information needed to make that decision, then the opportunity has likely passed because someone else has beaten them to the punch. A key element that supports Powell's rule is the notion that intuition is what separates great leaders from average ones. Intuition is what allows us to make tough decisions well, but many of us ignore that feeling in our gut. We want certainty that we're making the right decision, but that's not possible. In my experience, people who want *complete* certainty before taking action end up leaving opportunity on the table and living mediocre lives. I'd taught this concept for many years, and even had to follow my own (and Colin Powell's) advice at times.

When I did it, I believed that doing so would bring me closer to the concept I now understood as *living my truth*. I gave myself the necessary space and permission to recalibrate my internal compass. I realized that saying "F-it!" doesn't have to mean throwing your hands up in the air, pushing others away, or giving up. In fact, it could mean something so much more—something better. I was inspired by the thought of changing people's mind-sets, turning their thoughts from negative to positive, and having a little fun in the process by changing the very way we perceive the phrase "F-it." Everything in my gut told me I was on to something. It resonated with me. And if it spoke to me, then I thought it would speak to others as well.

Too many people seem to be in the same place I was in—unhappy, discontent, and living a life that no longer excited them. They know something's wrong, that things are out of alignment, but they can't articulate what it is. Even worse, they aren't doing what needs to be done to make their lives better. They're standing at the precipice of an F-it moment, not knowing how to back away from the edge of the proverbial cliff.

We don't need to look any further than our own bodies to understand how important alignment is. There's a thriving medical industry dedicated to maintaining it. A chiropractor's focus, for instance, is on the relationship between structure and function and on maintaining the balance between the two to preserve and restore our health. They can identify the single little vertebra in our spine that's ever so slightly misaligned. They understand that when one thing, no matter how tiny, is out of alignment, *everything* is affected. Being out of alignment affects our ability to walk, stand, sit, sleep, breathe, properly digest food, and concentrate or think clearly. It's the ultimate disruptor. If you've ever suffered from back or neck pain, then you know exactly what I'm talking about.

Our outside world works in much the same way. When our relationships are in alignment, life is good. If just one of our relationships gets out of whack, the ripple effect can cause stress in every other relationship, and in every other aspect of our life. An argument with a coworker, your boss, your best client, your children, your parents, your partner, or your best friend can disrupt your energy, thoughts, and behavior until the only way to resolve the problem is to get aligned again.

Whether we know it or not, we're always seeking alignment in our lives. There's something beautiful about the notion of swimming in the same direction as everyone and everything else in our world. Most people believe that life will be perfect when they achieve all the things they want to— when everything is finally going their way. They see happiness in terms of the future, a goal to be worked toward, reached for. The truth is, if you're anything like me, once you get to this fantasized place, new desires, bigger goals, and more wants and needs will arise. There is always work to be done. What does this tell us? That it's an illusion to believe the perfect life exists somewhere "out there," in another time and place. Your perfect life doesn't happen at a certain point in time. It happens when you're aligned with your highest purpose. It happens the moment you step onto that path and start to live the life you desire—an F-it-less life. It's instant. It's not about the future—it's about being in the present.

When you live an F-it-less life, the things you want and truly wish for, such as happiness, fulfillment, and joy, emerge because you're aligned with your higher self. You're moving in the right direction. Now, we all veer off onto the wrong path sometimes, which can bring disappointment and unhappiness. But that's how we grow, learn, and keep ourselves moving forward. Sure, when we take a tumble, we find ourselves out of alignment and start to feel bad, lost, frustrated, or stuck—but once we get back on the path, man, life is good again!

Admittedly, some of us are better than others at creating life-improving alignment, but all of us are capable of achieving and maintaining it. It simply requires believing in your vision, living by your standards, and making an F-it-less life a priority. It takes passion, planning, and courage. It also takes practice!

Whether creating alignment comes naturally or is learned behavior for you, you'll inevitably find yourself out of alignment from time to time. But remember, you don't have to wait until the pain is so excruciating that a trip to the metaphorical emergency room is necessary. If you have the right tools at your disposal, you can easily recognize and stop the disruption and pain before it progresses any further. Catching the misalignment early and correcting it helps you to quickly get back to the place that rewards you with all the energy and peace you desire and deserve.

Of course, there are times when a fall out of alignment sneaks up on you slowly; for example, the way a marriage can deteriorate over time if it isn't protected and treated as a priority. Other times the fall can happen suddenly, the way an unexpected loss of a job or a loved one takes you by surprise. But either way, when you're misaligned and find yourself stopped in your tracks, unable to move, remember to remain calm. Try to imagine that the obstacle you're facing is nothing more than an illusion. Remind yourself that you can work around it. In fact, sometimes the best way to do that is to simply get out of the way. Some of life's strongest currents are futile to fight against. When you push back, they create more chaos and lack of alignment. If you can step aside or take an alternate route, you can actually allow things to flow as they should. When that happens, those obstacles will miraculously disappear, and your path will open up. If things are still standing in your way, it just means that you're not on the right path or that it's not the right time. It's really that simple.

So what else can you do to weather the storms that a lack of alignment causes? You can learn to strengthen yourself on the inside. You can get really clear about who you are and what you want your life's priorities to be. And you can build a true founda-tion from those goals.

That's really what this book is about—focusing, finding, fixing, forking off in a new direction, forgiving, forgetting, and floating your way to peace, love, and happiness. You can start cleaning up the fragments of your life right now by creating clarity and align-ment around the areas you deem most important to you. You can forge a new way of living and working that will help you become the very best version of yourself that you can be. I'm certain that the difference between You 1.0 and You 2.0 is a simple engage-ment with the process I'm outlining for you here. Think about it: if you're living your best life—a life in complete alignment with all the things that are meaningful to you—then you're supporting my efforts to do the same. All of us are connected by the energy and effort with which we live our lives. I'm living my chosen life, filled with passion and purpose; by sharing this book with you, I'm hoping that my energy will be contagious—that I can inspire and help you and others all over the world to live an F-it-less life too. If each of us is happier and more aligned with our purpose, we may very well be able to eradicate the circumstances that cause us to say "F-it!" in the first place!

CHAPTER THREE
FEEL

· ·

What you think, you become. What you feel,
you attract. What you imagine, you create.
—BUDDHA

· ·

WHEN I FIRST CAME UP WITH THE IDEA FOR THIS BOOK, I couldn't stop thinking about all the F-words that have such a powerful impact on us. I thought about how meaningful it might be if I could find a way to string those words together to create a disruptive change in how we view and deal with the challenges we face in our everyday lives. I actually got out of bed in the middle of the night and wrote down all the F-words that came to mind. I knew there had to be a way to communicate how I was feeling in a clear and connective way—in a manner that also resonated with other people. If this was tapping something deep inside of me, I was certain it would touch others too.

That night I found my thoughts wandering to a book by Jack Canfield and Mark Victor Hansen called *The Aladdin Factor: How to Ask for What You Want—and Get It*, which, among many other salient points, states, "The size of your questions determines the size of your answers." BAM! This quote seemed to speak directly to my thoughts on how to begin living in alignment. If you haven't asked yourself, "How do I live a great life?" then you've automatically defaulted to the far weaker question, "How do I live the most mediocre life possible?" If you want better answers and better results, you've got to ask bigger questions of yourself, your friends, your spouse, your employees, your employer, your children, your God, and so on. Whatever it is you want more from, you have to ask more of. You can't just hope that what you want will magically show up.

Whenever I'm preparing for a big meeting, getting ready to speak in front of an audience, or even having an important discussion with my wife, I get really clear about how I want those in attendance to feel when we finish our talk. Do I want to leave them feeling happy? Inspired? Pumped up? Comforted? Less overwhelmed? More focused? Do I want to give them a sense of urgency? If I'm able to lock into a desired outcome, then I can always find the right words. By doing this, I can help determine the results in advance.

I relied on this mode of communication often when I was building my real estate business, especially during tough times. Our industry always has its ups and downs, but it's far less stressful when the economy is flourishing than when it's suffering, as it was from 2007 to 2011. Back then, agents who were trying to sell houses were under more pressure than ever before. They felt as if they were walking on thin ice. While employees of the industry such as office managers and receptionists can count on getting a biweekly paycheck whether the market is good or bad, real estate agents are self-employed. They work on commission so they don't have the luxury of a steady income. If sales are slow, they're riding an emotional roller coaster, waiting for their next influx of cash.

During these years, members of our staff were getting frustrated by the angst some agents and brokers would exhibit around the support team. Sometimes pressure has a way of exposing who people really are and for bringing out the worst in them. Because the support staff was bearing the brunt of the agents' worries, they began to resent having to help those agents out, and the rift became noticeable, to say the least. I needed to figure out how to get those with steady incomes to have some compassion for the agents, who were genuinely enduring hard times.

What aggravated the circumstances further were the rumors floating around about competitors who were either letting valued employees go or closing their offices altogether, so I thought it might be a good time to bring everyone into our conference room for a meeting.

"We all know what's going on with the economy," I began. "These are hard times. While we're doing well compared to our competition, we are not without our own issues. So I just want all of you to know we're going to be fine—but, that being said, we aren't going to make payroll this week. You will get paid, but it won't be for another three weeks, so please, just hang in there." Everybody in the room started looking around to see if what I had said was real.

Then the panic set in.

I saw it in people's eyes. While nothing in my speech was true, it could have been. Before I let everyone in on my ruse, I stood at the head of the conference room table for a few minutes and let the group think about what it would mean if this really were to happen.

"Okay . . . everything I just told you was a lie. Payroll is not going to be interrupted. You will all get paid as you normally do. But for a few moments there, you undoubtedly felt the way all the agents who work with us feel every day when they get out of bed. I don't ever want you to forget how you just felt."

And I meant it.

My actions were intentional, and they served a purpose. My agents got up every morning and got their hustle on whether they had the opportunity to close a deal or not. They hoped to. They wanted to, but there were certainly no guarantees. My support staff never had to think about that. This exercise helped them understand that if an agent seemed a little testy or snapped a little more often than they ought to, it was because that agent felt *every F-ing day* the way the support staff had felt for just thirty seconds. I knew that if I could get the support staff to experience the angst and stress my agents felt, the problem would correct itself. Thankfully, everyone understood why I'd done what I did. And it all happened because I asked myself, "How do I get these people to understand what my agents feel?" It was a big question that naturally elicited a big answer. And the method really worked: everyone got back on track, and we went on to win a string of "Atlanta's Best Place to Work" awards, beating out some of the top corporations in America.

All of us have feelings. I like to think of them as our internal compass, giving us feedback and direction, delivering emotional messages to our brains in the hope that our brains can strategize ways to unlock more of the feelings we like than those we don't.

When our feelings and our brains work well together, life tends to be good. But sometimes our feelings and brains don't communicate well. Sometimes our brains don't have the where-withal to come up with those needed solutions, or even some simple next steps. When this happens, we tend to get stuck in an emotional loop. That's when we find ourselves doing the same things over and over and expecting different results. This can feel like the human equivalent of trying to start your car with a dead battery: "I *want* to go, but nothing is happening." Before we know it, we've wasted precious time spinning our wheels in unproductive jobs, relationships, mindsets, and lifestyles.

One of the most powerful lessons I've had to learn in my life has been this: "Whatever is bugging you is holding you back." As a parent who's always trying to instill mental and emotional toughness in my children, I see examples of this more clearly than ever. It's so simple once you get it, but until you do, it can be extremely complicated to comprehend and put into daily action.

Did you know that your body retains every one of your fears, insecurities, and limitations in the equivalent of a password-protected database? It knows what you think you're worth, why you can't change, and whether you'll succeed or fail. It saves your emotional responses to virtually every situation you encounter. Each response is produced by a chemical reaction in your body, borne out of events that occurred previously. In other words, we don't always have fresh, discrete responses to events happening in the current moment. Instead, our brain is programmed to connect each new experience to a prior, similar situation from the past. In a split second, these experiences combine, and the new one prompts the same unconscious reaction to the old one, influencing the way we behave accordingly. In this way, "emotional baggage" from a single, seemingly insignificant past event can residually impact our behavior in the present, instantaneously building "safe" boundaries for what we say is possible but also ultimately disempowering us and limiting our full potential.

I've talked to many people in my time and I can tell you that nobody plans to enter into a violent marriage. Nobody plans to ruin his or her finances. Nobody plans to struggle with an addiction or anger issues. We want to believe we have control over everything—particularly our own behavior, emotions, and feelings. And while most of us want to see the best in ourselves, we spend much of our time seeking validation for our feelings of inadequacy instead of building up our self-esteem. If only we could stop, look at our wiring, and see what circuits are crossing to trigger automatic and often seemingly unrelated responses. Then we could have greater command over our emotional life.

The good news is, we can.

If you've ever ventured to a large shopping mall you've never been to before, then you've likely stood in front of a map that shows you the schematic of the place, with a star symbol next to the words, "You are here." The only way to get to where you want to go is to first identify where you are and then plot the best course to your destination from there. The same is true in life.

A necessary part of figuring out your direction is breaking down your feelings. In the rawest sense, it's taking a naked look in the mirror. If you want to get the best results, you'll need to be real, blunt, and unabashedly honest. Where are you? And why are you in this unhappy place, this unfulfilling career or whatever other state you want to change? The answers don't all have to be negative. For instance, you may be in an okay place, but you want to get to a great place. Either way, you need to be pure and truthful about your circumstances. How did you contribute to being in this place? What can you change to get yourself onto a different path? What emotions are coming from old experiences instead of present ones? These are the kinds of big questions you need to ask yourself to go from where you are to where you want to be.

The point is that each of us is responsible for our own happiness, our own sadness, our own anger, and so on. No one gets to determine how content, depressed, or irate we are except us. Sure, people do things to provoke us. Circumstances arise that we don't necessarily like or want. Things happen that we didn't ask for and never would have. However, our reactions to these people and events—particularly our reactions to how they make us *feel*—can become completely voluntary on our part once we do this introspective work. All our feelings are things we allow ourselves to have. We can choose to have more power and control over the negative forces and events that occur in our life, or we can allow them to have power and control over our thoughts and feelings—and, therefore, *us*. As simple as it sounds, it's always a game of Rock, Paper, Scissors. The more defined and resolute you are about the way you choose to be, the easier it is to put external forces and events into proper perspective. I've found it to be extremely important that I not give away the power to determine my personal peace and happiness.

Anything that attracts your attention attracts your energy.
Anything that commands your attention commands your energy.
And furthermore, anything that holds your attention and energy
is sending its energy right back to you. So when you find yourself mentally, emotionally, and physically dragging, it may be
the consequence of having given your power away to the wrong
people, circumstances, or things. Likewise, when you feel positive, excited, and optimistic, it's probably because you've been
giving your attention and energy to the right people and the right
things. In fact, sharing your attention and energy with the right
parties automatically steers you toward a life of peace, happiness, and alignment and away from the kinds of things that don't
support that lifestyle.

My friends Peter and Sarah Chatel sort people into one of
two categories they refer to as *lifters* and *leaners*. Their goal is
to limit or eliminate people who lean on them without lifting
them up. I love this concept. Do you spend significant time
with lifters or leaners? An even bigger question is, are *you* a
lifter or a leaner? Lifters raise you up. They lift your energy
and raise your emotions. Leaners take your energy and use it
for their own well-being. How does that make you feel? Stop
for a moment and take inventory of the lifters and leaners
in your life. Think about the impact each has had upon you.
(And just so you know, the people who immediately come to
mind as leaners are not necessarily your problem. You already
know their tendencies and can separate yourself from them.
The challenge comes from all the people in between those
two categories—all those you aren't sure about. You could be
spending time with leaners and leaking energy without even
knowing about it!)

This is all to say that your energy and your emotions are a reflection of who and what you allow into your life. The clearer and more resolved you are to be a happy, peaceful, and positively energetic person, the easier it is to identify and resist the unwanted energy that negative people and circumstances inflict on you. If something's bugging you or holding you back from being the person you want to be, it may very well be because you're exchanging your good energy for someone else's bad energy. Gary Keller, the founder of the real estate company Keller Williams has often said, "If you say yes to something, you are automatically saying no to something else." Take stock of those to whom you are saying *yes* and be sure they are the right people to be sharing your personal energy with.

All parents have seen this at some point in their child's development process. When a toddler's emotions outweigh their brain's ability to properly handle them, a meltdown ensues. In adults, it's typically harder to see this coming because we tend to present ourselves as being in control of our emotions even when we're not. If we don't examine our emotions on our own or with help, then we're doomed to experience a version of what happens to Bill Murray's character in the movie *Groundhog Day*, until we throw in the towel or someone stops the fight for us. Either way, humans are emotional creatures, and our feelings can often run circles around our brains, making it hard for us to figure out our next move. What's important is to be aware enough of our emotional patterns to recognize when this chase is happening to us. Awareness of our propensity for emotional tangents allows us to arrest them long enough to make choices that will lessen our frustrations and help us move into a more positive and healthy space, where greater personal development can occur.

Growing up, I fell in love with the game of tennis. While I played fairly competitively, I ultimately realized that the best and most profitable use of my time and talent in the sport was as an instructor. I started teaching kids in summer camp and coached a few teams in Atlanta. By the time I was a junior in college at Georgia Tech, I had become the assistant coach for the women's tennis team, which was something I really loved. College tennis is the last level of competition that allows on-court interaction between players and their coaches during changeovers in match play, which is not allowed in the professional game. I greatly enjoyed that aspect of working with my players.

During one of our matches against another Atlantic Coast Conference (ACC) school, I went down to the court where our number-one player, Kristi, was playing our competitor's number-one player. They were only in the first set, but Kristi was losing because she was missing her first serve, giving her opponent too many opportunities to tee off on her slower second serve. When I asked her what was going on, her answer was, "I don't know. My serve's just not working for me today." Her answer amazed me. It was startling, because she was a very talented athlete who had probably been playing tennis competitively since the age of four or five, and she was telling me that her serve "just wasn't working" that day.

I began asking Kristi some questions, hoping to show her that there were more logical responses to the situation than her emotional one.

"Where's the ball going?" I asked.

"It's hitting the net."

"And what are the two biggest reasons for a serve hitting the net?"

"A low toss or I drop my shoulder," she said.

"Or maybe *both*," I replied. "All you've got to do is *reach* for it. Get your toss up there and reach for it, and you'll be fine. You can win this match!"

And she did. It might have taken her all three sets to do it, but she won.

I had successfully interrupted her downward emotional spiral. It was important to keep her from emotionally resigning in that moment, so I invited her to outthink her feelings—and she did.

In real life, we don't have a coach watching our performance every day. We don't have someone who can call us out when we let our feelings get the best of us—someone who can offer a logical solution to help us win the day. We have to learn to manage ourselves in this regard.

Therefore, it's critical that we get in touch with our feelings, our patterns of behavior, and the things that drive our optimal performance so that we can coach ourselves to be the best we can be. Our feelings control our thoughts; our thoughts control our behavior; and, in circular fashion, our behavior validates our feelings. Very often these feelings come from our attachment to things. Therefore, all we have to do is attach ourselves to the things that produce the feelings, thoughts, and behaviors we most want and detach from all the feelings, thoughts, and behaviors we don't want. That's it. Like many things in life, it's not complicated; it's just hard.

If we truly want to live an F-it-less life, then recognizing our feelings is the very first step toward creating that life. Our feelings tell us not only that we're happy, sad, mad, or confused, but also that we're frustrated, satisfied, or thrilled with where we are. Our feelings provide the first indication that we might need to change some things about ourselves internally or about our environment externally. They tell us if we have some work to do or not. They help us formulate standards, boundaries, and expectations. Feelings are awesome sources of information and guidance, if we pay attention to them and what they're trying to tell us.

Whether you tend to be in touch with your feelings, bury them until you find yourself against the ropes and fighting for another round in the ring, or are simply oblivious to them, getting to know and understand them better is an essential part of living an F-it-less life. And because sorting and then divesting old feelings from new ones is so integral to determining direction and change in your life, it only makes sense that "Feel" is one of the first F-words you should explore when pursuing an F-it-less life.

CHAPTER FOUR

FINE VERSUS FANTASTIC

• • • • • • • • • • • • • • • • • • • •

Change your thoughts and you change your world.
—NORMAN VINCENT PEALE

• • • • • • • • • • • • • • • • • • • •

I ONCE HEARD COMEDIAN CRAIG SHOEMAKER TALK ABOUT THE differences between men and women, particularly regarding things women say and how guys should interpret them. He said if you ask your girl if she's okay and she says, "I'm fine," do not assume that means she's okay. In fact, in any relationship, including the one you have with yourself, the correct interpretation of "I'm fine" is, "You're f*cked."

Any variation on the answer "Fine" means pretty much the same thing. "I'm fine," "We're fine," "It's fine"—they're all inter-changeable. They're all bald-faced lies.

You are *not* fine.

When anyone, including you, says, "I'm fine," let's be real—it usually means we haven't processed the quality of our life in a while, or if we have, we just don't feel like sharing the details of our current frustrations. It certainly doesn't mean our life is perfect. Far from it. And because it's one of the most overused phrases in the English language, the words *I'm fine* can trick us into believing that they mean *all is well* or *life is great* when fine is far from the fantastic we all seek.

Think of the response *fine* as acceptable and think of the response *fantastic* as desirable. If you really want to live an F-it-less life, then clearly the answer *fine* is *not* desirable. To reach true F-it-less, you have to cross the bridge from fine to fantastic. You have to believe that fine is not an option anymore and fantastic is the goal.

Over the course of sixteen years, I built the largest and most productive real estate firm in Atlanta. When I stepped away from operations at the end of 2014, we had over 1,400 agents and sold nearly $3.5 billion in real estate that year. My schedule was packed every day. There was rarely a minute between meetings, classes, or interviews. I loved being busy morning, noon, and night. At the time, I believed I was thriving. It was exhausting work, but I found meaning and purpose in what I was doing. I loved the fast pace, and, more important, I loved the impact I was having on so many lives, from those of my team to our customers. Though I didn't recognize it at the time, my role as company leader and my repetitive daily routine led me to develop more of a *fine* mentality than a *fantastic* one—perhaps not so much from a business perspective, but certainly from a personal one. While our company was flourishing, I was not. Every time someone asked me how I was doing, I would answer, "Fine!" with gusto. After all, things were great, right? The reality was that I didn't have time to really process what was lacking in my life, nor did I want to get into that with anyone. My role was to lead my team to the promised land, to show them the way to success, period. So without any thought, I answered, "Fine" so often that I truly believed I was.

I suspect that this is where some of you may be now or you wouldn't have picked up this book. We've all been there.

In *fine* mode.

But the good news is that we don't need to stay there.

The truth is, most of us wear our *fine* mask to cover up how we really feel, which is usually frustrated. We'll say we're good when we feel bad. We lie to others and even to ourselves, and oftentimes, we don't even know we're doing it. It's an impulse. A habit. And a bad one at that.

I'll bet there are important areas in your life where you've been accustomed to *fine* for so long that you can't even remember what fantastic feels like—or whether you've ever felt it at all. Remember, human beings are the most adaptable species on the planet. We get so accustomed to what we're used to that we forget to think about what would be better, or even best, for us.

In his book *Good to Great*, Jim Collins provides one of my favorite takeaways from any business book I've ever read. He says,

"Good is the enemy of great." As you read that, you might have thought, *Isn't bad the enemy of great?*

No, it's not.

Good is the enemy of great.

That's because when things are bad, we want them to change—and if you're anything like me, you're willing to do whatever it takes to change them. However, when things are good, the need to change or improve becomes less of a priority for us, and we tend to accept the mediocre rather than strive for the excellent. While this idea that "Good is the enemy of great" was intended for business leaders, the same concept holds true for us as individuals, as people, as human beings.

One of the most impactful things I ever heard is, "Stop fighting for your limitations." Another way of saying this is, "Stop trying to be right all the time." It's sad but true that people all too often look for ways to be right, digging in to their positions and defending them at all costs. They close doors that could lead to something better over time, all for the sake of being right. In the best-case scenario, they're *fine*. In the worst-case scenario, they're *f*cked*. Neither are great options.

I recently read that there's one attribute Jeff Bezos values above most others: a person's willingness to make and admit mistakes. As I understood the statement, people who like to be right are not the people who will help him change the world. People who like to be right are people who protect their ego and the status quo. That's why Bezos hires engineers and other people who like to question theories and ponder possibilities—people who aren't afraid to try new things, even if they don't work out. People who aren't afraid of mistakes, who see failure as a part of success. It's pretty interesting, isn't it?

This concept is at the core of our parents' concerns about who our friends were when we were growing up. Those of us who are parents now have the same concerns for our kids. Parents innately know that who you spend your time with and what you spend your time doing shape what you consider normal, good, and acceptable. If you're involved with troublemakers, drug addicts, alcoholics, or abusive partners, that kind of behavior can and often will become normal to you. Likewise, if you hang out with the best students, athletes, and performers; if your relationships with your spouse, parents, and children are full of love, support, and laughter; and if your friends are successful, healthy, and happy, then that's normal to you. I've learned that our lowest acceptable standard in all aspects of our life *is* our standard—the bar we choose to live up to, or down to. The surroundings we deem acceptable are more often than not what determine the quality of our lives.

Where does *your* bar hang?

That sense of simply being "fine" actually develops from years of bottled-up frustration. Maybe you feel hampered in your job, your relationships, or your general situation. When there's a lack of communication—*authentic* communication—between yourself and others, this frustration tends to fester. We skirt the issues, we avoid confrontation, we dance around what's really bothering us without expressing our true feelings. And that's if we even know the true root cause of our frustration in the first place.

The sense of being fine is a culmination of things that gets us to where we want to say "F-it!" It's a slow build that bubbles up inside us until we can't take one more layer of stress, anger, resentment, dissatisfaction, and (you fill in the blank).

I don't know about you, but living in a world of fine doesn't seem all that fine to me.

Why?

Because just as good is the enemy of great, fine is the enemy of fantastic.

I want fantastic.

I want fan-f*ing-tastic. Don't we all?

Don't *you*?!

Isn't it time to rip off the mask and face reality? Isn't it time to address the ten-thousand-pound elephant(s) in the room? Isn't it time to finally move from fine to fantastic?

All you need to get there is a willingness to share how you really feel and to not be attached to what outsiders may think. Those who really care about you will want to hear your thoughts, help you however they can, and love you regardless. And those who don't, won't.

Look, even after you take the necessary steps to move from fine to fantastic, there will be days when you still experience frustration. It's natural and completely okay. Those days will be fewer and far between, though. When they happen, let your family and friends know. Saying, "No ups, no downs today. Just feeling chill," helps assure them that you're not sending any other message. Frankly, it will also keep you from falling back into the habit of saying, living, or accepting *fine* again.

As most of us know, it's not just *what* we say that matters, it's *how* we say it. In fact, we often convey the most important messages without speaking. So, yeah, those Facebook and Instagram posts may help you appear to have an ideal existence, but they can also reveal that you're sad, pissed off, pensive, or more contemplative than you may say in person. I have a friend who posted inspirational quotes on Facebook for a week, and several people privately reached out to her to make sure she was okay. When I asked how she was doing, she said, "Fine." But was she? I wasn't convinced, that's for sure. The thing about all those inspirational quotes we post is that sooner or later we're going to have to live up to them. Or not.

Most people portray themselves as being far more put together than they really are—especially when it comes to social media. I see it all the time in social circles too. At first you think, *Wow, they've got it all.* But when the ribbons start coming off the pretty packaging, you can see that perhaps they don't. They're doing everything they can to keep up with the Joneses without realizing that the Joneses can't keep up with themselves. If this is something you find yourself doing, it's time to hit the pause button and appreciate where you are without worrying about where everyone else is. Stop and take a good, hard look at your life. Acknowledge that there are things to work on, and that maybe the other person has some things that you'd like, too, but also be grateful for what you have. Just know that you can always do more. Use that other person as inspiration to get you from fine to fantastic.

Are you with me?

Although tennis is my game of choice, I've also played golf all my life. In tennis you can serve the ball harder to overpower your opponent, but what I love about golf is that it requires you to hit the ball well, one stroke at a time. Whether the wheels fall off the other person's bus or not, the only way you're going to win is by hitting your ball better than anybody else hits theirs. There's nothing else anyone can do to affect your stroke. It's all up to you. If you can focus on each and every shot for eighteen straight holes, you might just be the leader at the end of the game. Golf is about being the best *you* can be; it's not about being as good as or better than others. I've stopped worrying about what other people are doing, what they're thinking, or what the conditions are on the course and simply play my best game. In the process, I've found a rhythm and a comfort level that has served me well. It's helped me be more realistic about who I am as a golfer, but, more important, it's provided a philosophy that works off the golf course too.

All we can do is see the world and the people in it realistically. We often miss so much in life trying to keep ourselves from ever getting hurt. We spend our time worrying or trying to protect ourselves from something that may or may not ever happen.

There's a longtime favorite real estate saying of mine that applies here: "Getting screwed is in the brochure...and it's not in the fine print." If you're going to sell real estate, expect that at some point you're going to get screwed. Somebody is going to take advantage of you. Someone is going to sell a house to one of your clients and try to cut you out of the deal by not paying you your share of the commission. Stop trying to protect yourself from it and just find a way to do business in a manner you enjoy. You can't build a successful company while constantly worrying about protecting yourself from the many ways you could get cheated. You'll never grow your business if you're spending all your time stressing out over things that could happen, might happen, but haven't happened . . . yet. Instead, you've got to go out there and focus on all the things you love doing.

And the same holds true for us outside of our working life. Look, we all have bad days. And when you think about it, there are varying degrees of bad:

A bad day in real estate is not getting that listing. It's getting screwed.

A bad day for a pilot is losing an engine.

A bad day for an airline is losing a plane in a crash.

A bad day for a doctor is losing a patient.

A bad day for a parent is losing a child.

A bad day for a marriage is losing a spouse to cancer. Perspective is everything.

As a parent, my job is to keep my kids from putting their hands on a hot stove or from crossing the street when there's oncoming traffic. It's not to keep them from falling down and scraping their knees. That's how they learn. Of course, I want to keep my kids from dying, but getting hurt happens. It's a part of life. Everything in this book is a part of life. It's about love, loss, pain, gain, excitement, disappointment, failing, succeeding, and the experience of achieving miserable, mediocre, and magnificent results. The key is having the proper perspective when all of these things occur.

As a business leader and coach, I've learned that many people either overcomplicate the simple or oversimplify the complicated. They tend to focus more on what makes them unhappy than they do on what's going well for them. That can be massively overwhelming. When we choose to look only at the things we don't like about our life, it feels damn near impossible to drum up the energy, courage, resources, and actions necessary to change them.

One of my favorite sayings is, "The only way to eat an elephant is by doing so one bite at a time," which is also the only way to tackle the stuff in your life that has you feeling stuck in a perennial state of *fine*. Nothing worth having or doing comes easy.

Ever.

But it's usually worth the effort in the end. Am I right?

What if I told you that creating your version of fantastic isn't all that complicated? That it can begin now by focusing on the things that make you happy? Really. Manifesting your version of fantastic can be that easy.

Once you envision something, the real version isn't that far behind.

To help you go from living a *fine* life to living an *F-it-lessly fantastic* one, I've created a three-question exercise that I guarantee will give you an immediate sense of relief and hope.

But before we get to the questions, I must tell you that I'm a big fan of making to-do lists. Whenever there are things I want to get done, I make a list. Interestingly, my wife is a big fan of doing this as well. It seems to work for her too—I get everything on her list done before I tackle mine. 😊

All kidding aside, making a personal to-do list is a vital part of this exercise. It will help you formulate answers that will easily convert into an action plan later. I would like you to create a to-do list of all of the things you innately know you have to do, or start doing, in order to feel better about yourself and to move the needle from *fine* to *fantastic* in your life. Maybe you need to eat better, exercise more, meditate, attend religious services more, find a therapist, show more appreciation and gratitude, save more money, get more sleep, or finish that novel you've been reading or writing. Write down whatever thoughts and feelings come to you. This is an exercise, not the final plan, so don't panic and don't overthink it. This part of the activity and the following one are just to prime the pump. It's intended to get you thinking about you and what you need to live your best life.

When you write some of these thoughts down the same way you might write a grocery list, you'll start to see how once-jumbled feelings turn into clear and concise points you can reflect on and refer to later. The act itself helps you acknowledge how you really feel.

When most people are fearful, overwhelmed, or nervous about something, they tend to shut down. They think of things they're contending with as being *a lot*. The term *a lot* is used in association with numbers, money, steps, tasks, and so on. People think, *It would take* a lot *of time, money, energy, and so forth for me to do that*—when in reality, *a lot* is a vague concept. It isn't quantifiable. Once people can see that *a lot* is akin to the boogeyman, they feel as if they've lost twenty pounds. What is *a lot*? Ten thousand dollars, twenty hours, one month? Examining what you fear—or what I call "landing some of the planes flying around in your head"— helps you move from fiction to fact. It also helps you move from *fine* to *fantastic*.

Try it.

Stop reading right now and write down some stuff on your to-do list. Land some planes.

Now think about one thing from your to-do list that you'd like to improve and jot down some actions that you believe would help you move in that direction. Any number of things on the list is fine right now. One, two, three, ten—it doesn't matter.

Just do it.

Now.

So, how was that? Easy, right?

Okay—for the next exercise in priming the pump, let's make a *stop-doing* list.

That's right—I'm talking about a list of things to *stop doing* so you can make time and room for all the things on your to-do list. Or you can write down things that you know you need to stop doing in order for you to live the fantastic F-it-less life you know you want and deserve. What's cool about the stop-doing list is that it's often easier to check things off this list than it is to check things off your to-do list. Even better, once you check things off of your stop-doing list, the things on your to-do list become even easier to complete. Maybe you need to stop talking down to yourself or others, stop eating poorly, stop drinking or doing drugs, stop procrastinating, stop wasting money, or stop sabotaging yourself or your relationships.

Only you know which bad habits you've grown accustomed to and which you wish you would stop. This is your chance to list them, face them, and see them for what they are:

Destructive.

Try it. Pretend I'm a magic genie who's appeared to you and said, "I can make all of the things you want to stop doing in your life go away with the snap of finger. All you have to do is give me a list." What would be on your list?

Do it.

Do it now.

Start a stop-doing list.

Go.

Again, it's not a plan yet. It's a brainstorming exercise that only you will see. Don't overthink it. Just write down whatever comes to mind, as fast as you can. Land some more planes.

Now that you've got your lists, you're ready for the fun part. Let's create a simple, visual map to guide you from *fine* to *fantastic*. I've taught this system all over the country to thousands of people over the years, and I love it.

Why?

Because it works!

You can use this format to solve problems, develop business plans, and, well, for almost anything. And best of all, it's really, really simple.

Take a blank sheet of paper. In the middle of it, mark down the one part of your life that you most want to improve. Is it your job, your marriage, your weight, your dependency on drugs or alcohol? It's your choice. Write it down small enough so that you can draw a circle around it.

Next, note the three most important things you believe need to happen to move you from *fine* to *fantastic*. Feel free to peruse your to-do and stop-doing lists for possible answers.

Put one answer directly below your first circle, then circle it. Put another above your first circle to the left, and circle that. Then put your third answer above your first circle to the right, and circle that as well.

Ta-daaaa!

You're halfway home.

You've successfully identified an area of your life that's just *fine*, and you've listed the three things you believe need to happen in order to make *fantastic* a reality.

The last part of this exercise is all about making these goals actionable.

As you might have guessed by now, you'll be drawing more bubbles on your paper. Every supporting action you write down gets its own bubble.

Try to come up with five things you can do that collectively will make each of first three bubbles a reality. You might think of only two or three, you might come up with five, or you may even list ten. It doesn't matter. What matters is that you *think* about all the possible things that can be done to support the three bubbles surrounding the center bubble.

You're almost done with your F-it-less plan!

Now, look at your paper. See all those planes you landed? Can you believe that all these circles—these ideas—were just a jumbled mess in your mind at one time? They seemed like *a lot* (aka, *too much*) to manage before. Now what do they look like? I'll bet what once seemed like *a lot* now seems quite doable. So let's finish it, shall we?

Look at each of the action items you wrote down. Using a highlighter, mark the things that can be done in one week or less. Then, using a different-colored highlighter, mark the things that can be done in a month. Take a third highlighter and mark the things that would take three to six months to complete. If there are any action bubbles left, they're likely to take a year (or more) to complete. Give them their own color as well.

That's it.

You're done.

It's that simple.

Sitting in front of you is a tiered plan that actually helps you visualize what you need to do clearly and precisely.

In my life, I've learned that what's easy to do, *is easier not to do*. This little exercise certainly makes that point. The hardest part about it was opening the closet door and peering in at all that's been hiding there.

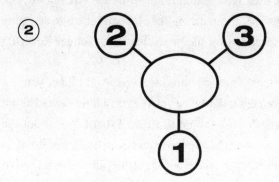

But wasn't it worth it? Doesn't it feel *good* to clean out that closet? To look at that accumulated stuff in a simplistic way? To see its lack of power over you once it had landed on paper?

Living in *fine* mode is actually the hard part. F-it-less living, on the other hand, is about being clearer, happier, more confident, and more creative. It's about allowing less stress and resistance in our lives. It's about eating the elephant one bite at a time or landing those planes on paper so they're no longer hovering in your head.

Congratulations! I'm really proud of you. And I'll bet you're a little proud of yourself too. Maybe you're even a little excited about the positive changes you're about to make. What I love about the F-it-less plan is that it can be used over and over. It's almost limitless in its application. So after you've accomplished all you've set out to do and are fantastic in this one area of your life, you can use the same process in as many other areas as you'd like.

F-it-lesstastic

Name the category in your life you wish to work on.

Where do you rate yourself in this category?

Frustrated

Fine

Fantastic

What would fantastic look like for you? _____
_____
_____
_____

What two or three things would need to happen/change to achieve fantastic?
_____
_____

What actions do you believe you need to take in order for each of those things to happen? _____
_____
_____

What time frame are you willing to commit to achieve each action you've listed?
_____
_____
_____

CHAPTER FIVE
FRACTURED

....

Better to do something imperfectly
than to do nothing flawlessly.
—ROBERT H. SCHULLER

....

TO BE ALIVE IS TO BE FRACTURED. FLAWED. NO ONE ON THE planet is perfect (though my wife, Jeri, comes pretty darn close). For most of us, the moment we're born marks the time in our life when we're as close to perfect as we will ever be. Why? We're clean slates, yet to be subjected to any disappointments, injustices, pain, small-mindedness, judgment, family drama, poor parenting, accidents, sickness, broken hearts, questionable personal choices, broken relationships, and loss of loved ones.

It's a moment when we teeter on the brink of flawless-ness. Once we take that first breath and then let out that

65

high-pitched scream, everything changes. The process of living our lives begins, and each of us starts our own personal, and therefore unique, journey. With every passing moment, we create and accumulate individual life experiences. We become branded by the traits we see as flaws, even when others don't necessarily view them as we do. We go out of our way to disguise those habits, those characteristics. You know the ones I'm talking about—indecision, OCD, neediness, excessive partying, incessant organizing, controlling ways, messiness, lying, confrontational mannerisms, undisciplined spending habits, frugality, cheating, and sarcasm, just to name a few. Imagine if we wore those inward flaws outside ourselves, around our necks like jewelry or neckties so people could easily spot what we so desperately try to hide. In an instant they could decide so much about us. In many ways, that wouldn't be such a bad thing, right? Think about how many bad dates or relationships you could have avoided. Except for one thing: everyone is fractured. You are. I am. How do I know this? We're breathing. As long as we're alive, we will be flawed. And that doesn't have to be bad. Really. It's impossible to live without being fractured by time and the circumstances of life. If we know and accept our flaws, learn to embrace them as parts of who we are, they can actually make us stronger.

Years ago, my brother, two great friends, and I rode motorcycles from Phoenix to the Grand Canyon, Zion National Park, Bryce Canyon, and back. As an avid motorcyclist, I'd always wondered what it would be like to ride my bike through the desert along one of those vast and endless two-lane highways. Our trip enabled me to experience, firsthand, what I'd seen on

TV and in magazines. The breathtaking images had inspired me for many years. But there's not a picture in the world that can replicate what it feels like to ride those open roads through hot, dry, desert air.

As I punched the throttle, I took in my surroundings. That's when it occurred to me that I was driving along what must have been the floor of an ocean thousands of years ago. The walls of the canyons and cliffs all around me bore the marks where water once lapped against the boundaries of these giant stone structures. It was as spiritually mesmerizing as it was visually stunning. It was almost impossible to absorb the beauty and magnitude of it all. The imperfections were especially poignant—the jagged edges, the discoloration on the mountains. And still, I could see only the beauty in those flaws. In fact, that's what made each of those mountains—those stone monuments—unique and special.

So when I think of *fractured* as it pertains to living an F-it-less life, I immediately conjure up an image of a giant, natural beige mosaic, absent of any other color—just like what I saw when we rode our steel horses along the bone-dry desert floor in Arizona. The endless array of fissures created by hundreds and thousands of years of wind and sun and (lack of) water is one of the aspects that makes the desert so interesting and beautiful. It's beautiful because of its imperfections—just like we are. The cracks and wrinkles that exist in and on us are no different. Individually and up close, you see the imperfections; zoom out and you can't help but appreciate the beauty, character, and interest they create as part of the whole. Just like those imperfections on the desert floor, our cracks can be tiny hairline fractures or big, crooked, deep ones. It just depends on what life events caused them in the first place. The good news is that if you look back at each splintering, there's a point of origin and a point of termination. So when we face fractures in life, they're really just challenges, lessons, or experiences that ultimately make us who we are. They're meant to give us the wisdom to make a difference in the world when the time is right.

From the moment a fracture begins to occur until it reaches its end, it can and often does consume our lives. (This is true for some of us more than others!) Active fractures make it hard to concentrate on anything else. It's easy to get caught up in the deep emotional drama, pain, frustration, and difficulty they tend to cause. In fact, some people actually thrive in fractures. And when active fractures come at us, usually fast and furiously, they're hard to make sense of in the moment. Oftentimes, we don't know why they're happening or how they started, and we certainly don't yet know how or when they'll end. All we know is that we didn't plan on such disruptions in our life, and it can feel like the world as we knew it is crashing down all around us. It's certainly the last thing we need or want to be dealing with on top of everything else we have going on.

There's no doubt that we're supposed to go through fractures. While we're always moving through life according to our own free will, the Universe has a way of making sure we don't miss certain destinations it has planned for us along the way. This can be a gentle nudge or something that feels like an abrupt turn made at one hundred miles per hour. Either way, we have to trust that there are certain parts of our story that are being written, or have already been written, by something or someone greater than ourselves. We can see only as far as our earthly headlights shine, but the Universe knows more than we'll ever be able to glimpse or make sense of. It's imperative that we learn to trust this knowledge during times of fracture.

We almost always understand why we had to endure a fracture once it's over. Think about it—everything in our past looks clearer in the rearview mirror. Everything. How many times have you said, "Oh! If *that* hadn't happened, then I would never have met so-and-so . . . or found this . . . or done that . . . or become this"? It's the rearview mirror that allows us to find the logic in all the emotional chaos that fractures cause. Whether it's immediately after a fracture or years later, looking back can give us closure and allow us to move on, having made sense of what we went through.

Finally, fractures tend to make us better. Once we've sorted out the how, what, and why of a fracture, we not only see how it moved us along the spectrum of our life, but we also realize what it helped us accomplish. We faced a challenge and we overcame it. We were stronger than we thought we were. When we needed more patience, intelligence, courage, assertiveness, faith, or whatever, we came up with it. That's the power of experience. That's the power of *fractures*. We can be taught all day long about life, but until we truly live it, we can't possibly know the satisfaction of slaying a fire-breathing dragon on our own.

Fractures get a bad rap. The things we perceive as imperfections often hold us back from believing in ourselves. When we overfocus on the things we think are our flaws, we end up telling ourselves that we're undeserving of a better life, that we aren't worth more. We feel weak, beaten down, and bad about ourselves. Some people take it to extremes, spending gobs of money to fix their outside appearance, when it's their fractured emotional state and mindset they ought to be focusing on.

Years ago, I was driving late at night. In an effort to find something engaging on the radio to keep me awake, I came across Dr. Laura. Little did I know that Dr. Laura would provide a massive aha moment about the simplicity and power of our inner voice. During the show, a young lady began telling Dr. Laura about putting up with a man who didn't treat her very well. She was lamenting one frustration after another. Not long into the call, Dr. Laura interrupted her and said, "Fat, dumb, or ugly?"

"What?" the lady asked.

"Fat, dumb, or ugly. Which do you think you are?" "I don't understand," said the caller.

"People who make these kinds of choices in their life make them only because they see themselves as either fat, dumb, or ugly. So, which one do you think you are?"

I couldn't believe what I was hearing. At first, I was offended by Dr. Laura's audacity. I was both shocked and amazed at this in-your-face accountability session. It was like listening to someone have a breakdown in slow motion. Though I wanted to, I simply couldn't turn to another station. I was hanging on every word—every *breath*—waiting to see how this radio intervention was going to turn out.

After a pause that seemed to last for minutes on end, Dr. Laura repeated her question, only this time she said it even slower. *"So ... which ... one ... do ... you ... think ... you ... are?"*

And after a moment, in a soft, weak, and defeated tone, the woman said, "Fat."

My heart sank for the caller. But at the same time, I was awestruck by the clarity that this admission provided to the situation.

Dr. Laura began to explain the importance of what she had just gotten the caller to self-discover, saying that most people make poor personal decisions due to a lack of confidence stemming from the deep-rooted conviction that they're either fat, dumb, or ugly.

Wow.

We've all let our flaws define us in some negative way. Who hasn't felt fat, dumb, or ugly at some point in their lives? All of this is completely normal—it's part of what makes us human—but knowing that doesn't make it easier.

Hearing this late-night caller's revelation made me think about my own life, and as much as I didn't want to believe it, I realized that what Dr. Laura was saying was also true for me. You see, I've always been a little pudgy. I haven't been fat per se, but I've had enough of a belly to be considered chubby, at least compared to most of my friends and to my brother, whose ribs could be precisely counted at any given time.

In junior high school, I played on the basketball team. Coach Williams, our coach, was fun, funny, and a good mentor. We all loved playing for him. One of the things Coach Williams was known for was giving his players nicknames. And because I was the pudgy kid on the team, he affectionately called me "Jelly Roll" at practice one day; as you might imagine, the name stuck with me throughout my high school years.

At the time, the guys and I all thought it was a funny name. After all, it came from a person I liked and respected, and in a safe environment among my best friends, so being called Jelly Roll didn't particularly bother me. Besides, in my mind, I knew it fit. Being a little heavier than most of my friends was never really a problem, except for the fact that my inner voice constantly reminded me of it . . . and I listened.

While I heard my inner voice's comments, they never affected me to the point of depression or anything. That's not to say that they didn't have a negative impact. They did. The notion of being fat stayed with me as if it were my shadow. In fact, it *was* my psychological shadow. It kept me from enjoying things as much as I could or should have. When the other guys were wolfing down milkshakes, cheeseburgers, and fries after practice, I was cautious about joining in. I made up excuses about having to go help my mom with something or needing to do homework so I wouldn't have to eat with them. As a result, I lacked confidence in certain situations throughout my life. I remember not wanting to take my shirt off at pool parties when I was young and thinking that certain girls were "out of my league" solely because of what I allowed my inner voice to tell me about my body. Looking back, I can't help but wonder if I was always pudgy because I accepted or believed I was pudgy, and therefore never really tried too hard to change the situation. Could it merely have been an adolescent phase? I'll never know for sure, and I suppose it doesn't matter much now. But that's the thing about our inner voice: we can't get back what we lose by listening to it.

From a medical point of view, there's no difference between the words *fractured* and *broken* when it comes to bones. However, I believe that there *is* a distinction between the two words when talking about people. There's no question that we're all fractured beings, but I don't believe we're all *broken*. As fractured people, we have the capacity to heal—to be fixed.

If we can embrace that possibility and understand our fractures, then those bothersome flaws can actually serve us well. They can help us to grow, learn, and become stronger. When you think about it, they're one of the most important aspects of the story we tell about ourselves. They're the events that ultimately lead to pivotal forks in the road. They set our new direction and help us define our new path. They teach us more about what we want, what we don't want, what we're willing to do, what we won't do, and what we're truly capable of more than almost anything else. They make us more complex, more interesting, more lovable, more celebrated, more experienced, and more attractive, too. Face it—a life without fractures would be boring. And, to be certain, a life without fractures doesn't exist.

There are three great things to remember about fractures. One, for whatever reason, we're supposed to be going through them. Two, we almost always understand why we had to endure a fracture only after it's over. And three, fractures tend to make us better, bringing us closer to the very best version of ourselves. Learning to appreciate and accept your fractures helps you realize how amazing a person you really are and how your flaws helped you get to where you are.

It's those faults and occasional failures that allow other people to see themselves in you and therefore connect with you. If you made mistakes, said the wrong thing at a party, told an off-color joke, or forgot your boss's spouse's name, guess what? You're human! You screwed up. You can't do everything perfectly, and if you did, I'd have a really hard time wanting to be around you, because I know *I* mess up from time to time. What would you possibly know about my struggles or challenges if you've had none of your own? Our fractures connect us to one another.

When you realize that your fractures are not marks against your character so much as traits that make you unique, you can begin to accept the places where you fall short. When you acknowledge this "humanness" and admit that you're not perfect and never will be, you can begin to heal from any past pain you've suffered as a result of holding yourself to this impossible standard in the first place. Instead of beating yourself up over things that didn't happen, goals you didn't achieve, or plans you never followed through on, you can hit the reset button and start anew. Embracing our fractures allows us to be reflective and decisive, which often gives us the opportunity to set our sails for a different direction, taking us places we might never have contemplated or seen had the fractures not occurred. Doing this allows us to reformat and reformulate our course, and, consequently, the life we're living.

If you're in the middle of a fracture right now, take heart from something my preacher, Andy Stanley, said: "Whatever you're going through right now, in five years you will talk about it in thirty seconds or less." Wow! That's worth repeating: Whatever you're going through right now, in five years you will talk about it in thirty seconds or less. Since the first time I heard that, there hasn't been a fracture in my life that this statement didn't help put in perspective. It's such a sobering and powerfully enabling tidbit of wisdom—and even better, it's true.

Think about a fracture in your life. Remember how hard it seemed at the time? Remember how you felt as though it would *never* end? Remember how mad, sad, frustrated, confused, or alone you felt? Now look at you. Look at where you are today. Look at how you might mention that period in your life at a cocktail party with relative ease. "That was when I was going through my divorce" or "When I lost my job" or "When I hit rock bottom and went to rehab." And that's it! Then you move on in the conversation because you've moved on in your life. You can appreciate the fracture for being the conduit you needed to get you where you are right now.

Unfortunately, the only way get to this level of comfort and confidence regarding fractures is experience. My hope is that this F in the F-it-less plan can provide support to you until you can find that comfort and confidence on your own.

To live an F-it-less life, you must be able see your fractures as important ingredients in the very best version of yourself. You don't have to enjoy those fractures, but you cannot allow yourself to be debilitated by them either. You have to keep reminding yourself of this until you feel it in your bones—until you know for certain that fractures are bridges to better places. Fractures show you what you're capable of.

I have a close friend who lived her life in typical Type A fashion. Always in control, always in charge. Then in 2015, she was diagnosed with breast cancer. Wham! The Big C. When we spoke about her journey, she said that her biggest takeaway was, "You can't control the uncontrollable." She thought she could outsmart, outmaneuver, or outwit cancer. Not so much. Every time she took one step forward, cancer kicked her in the ass and knocked her two steps back. Happily, today she's cancer-free, and has a very different outlook on life than she did before her diagnosis. There's so much in this life that you can't control, won't make sense of, can't fix, can't replace, can't change the direction of, even if you move mountains on a regular basis. If you can embrace the thought that you're not in control of all things—that you don't always hold sway over every aspect of your life—you can learn to relax and let things unfold. That's really the idea behind acceptance, isn't it? Tony Robbins says, "The Universe always unfolds exactly as it should." Who are we to get in the way? Imperfections do not make you inferior. Your mistakes and failures do not make you inadequate. Your fractures and flaws do not make any area of your life empty. Who you are, now and going forward, is a whole person shaped by your uniqueness and your decisions.

One of the most profound secrets to living an F-it-less life is learning how to use our fractures as ways to move us forward, to heal us, and make us better without allowing them to break us. Whether we like it or not, our fractures ultimately help us find our way to a better formation.

Fracture is not necessarily failure, although it can be. Either way, whether it's to fracture, to have fractures, to have been fractured, or to be fracturing, it's all a part of this amazing thing called life.

If you want to fix your fractures, you must first acknowledge them, and then own who you are and the life you're living. The root of resilience and change is the willingness to take responsibility for your progress and outcome. If you're not willing to do that, stop reading. I mean it. Just stop. You're not ready to live an F-it-less life.

CHAPTER SIX
FIX IT!

············

Only the wisest and stupidest
of men never change.
—CONFUCIUS

············

WHENEVER I TEACH A CLASS, BEFORE WE GET STARTED, I'LL often ask, "Who in here can draw?" Keep in mind that I've posed this question to thousands of people in my career. Invariably, for every hundred people in attendance, no more than five hands ever go up. I'm always able to count the number of hands raised out loud.

"One, two, three, four, five. Only five of you can draw? Really? I'm in disbelief. I didn't ask if you were *good* at drawing. I didn't ask if you've ever won a drawing contest. I didn't ask if you make a living drawing, or if you could make a living by drawing if you had to. All I asked is, can you draw? That's it. And almost everyone, by *not* raising your hand, said no."

In an effort to connect the people in the room, I'll say something like, "Let's try that again, although this time I want everyone to pretend that you're four or five years old and that you're in kindergarten. Can you do that? Can you remember being young and full of excitement and believing that you could actually be a superhero when you grew up? Let's see: Good morning, boys and girls! How are you today? You know what? We're going to do something super fun today! Who wants to do something super fun? Okay! Now, first we're going to need to draw! Who in here can *draw*?"

And with that, *every single hand* shoots up in the air.

"The question is, what happened between the age of five and your current age that made you change your answer to the question 'Can you draw?' When did you *decide* that you can't draw, when the truth is that *everybody* can draw? Even if you can only draw crooked lines, you can draw. Who determined that drawing can only be called 'drawing' if what you draw is actually good enough to be liked by others, or even yourself? What shifted? Did the criteria change in your mind? Did someone laugh at something you once drew? Did someone tell you that you couldn't draw? Did someone say that your brother or your sister or your friend draws better than you, and therefore it was determined that you could no longer draw? What happened? And why are we even talking about this? Why is this even important right now?

"Here's why: Although drawing isn't a big or financially rewarding part of life for those of you sitting in this room, the reason it's important is because you're telling yourself that you can't do something, or that you suck at it so strongly that you're willing to admit it in public. And what's worse is that this thing you've determined you can't do doesn't even matter!

"So, if you're sending yourself the message that you suck at stuff that doesn't make one bit of difference in your life, I can only imagine the terrible things you're telling yourself about the things that actually do matter. Things that make you a better businessperson, a better leader, a better friend, a better father or mother, a better son or daughter ... or simply a better person."

The truth is, all of us have that voice inside our head that likes to tell us that we're not good enough, that we're not welcome, that we can't or won't have the brains or guts to figure things out or pull things off. While imaginary, it often seems so real and credible that we allow it to occupy valuable space in our mind. We let it nag us like a twisted partner. It haunts us, taunts us, and bullies us, trying to separate us from our true potential and our greatest desires. For some, the voice is a quiet murmur; for others it's a shout that stole the keys to their car and drove off with the life they could have had, if only they hadn't listened to it. Either way, this voice is as loud and powerful as we allow it to be. It's been called our "inner voice" or "inner critic." Call it anything you want, but don't call it "right."

An article I once read about this inner critic recommended that we try to separate the voice from ourselves, with the intent of seeing it as something other than ourselves entirely. If we can successfully separate ourselves from this negative, degrading voice, then it can be easier to challenge and overcome it with better, more empowering thoughts. The article cleverly suggested that we give the voice a name. And, even better, it said that the sillier and/or dumber the name, the easier it would be to discount or ignore what it says to us. If that's the case, I should have given my voice one of those all-too-clever job titles, such as Chief Destruction Officer or the VP of Self-Sabotage. After all, who would listen to *that* guy at work?

I actually started to call this inner voice my "Mediocre Hoodlum" so I could quickly recognize and then dismiss any self-defeating messages it was sending me before it robbed me of my self-esteem. Once I had given the voice that name, it was simple to recognize the mediocrity coming from it as bad advice. I love using the word *mediocre* because I absolutely despise it. It's the last thing I want to be in life. Likewise, *hoodlum* is defined as a "thug or a person engaged in crime, violence, or gang activity"— the type of person all of us need to steer clear of and whom none of us wants to be.

When your Mediocre Hoodlum, or whatever you call it, talks to you, you have to find a way to outsmart it. You have to find a way to put what it's saying into perspective. You have to find a way to break down its false statements and replace them with the truth. You have to find a way to stand up to that destructive voice and call BS on everything it's saying, because most of the time that's exactly what it is: BS. So, if you're tired of being bullied by your inner voice, perhaps it's time to say "F-it!" and *Fix It*.

I once heard someone say, "There are people who've had more difficulties and worse circumstances who've achieved more than you." The minute I heard that, l loved it. Why? Because it's true. And because it reminds us that everything that determines how well we live, how much we achieve, how much we love, and how much peace we experience rests inside us. It doesn't come from an outside source. It's not about how much money we grew up with, the kind of parents we had or didn't have, the physical abilities we were or weren't blessed with, or the intelligence we do or do not possess. It's about what's in our heart and head. That's it. When our heart wants something bad enough and our head stops placing obstacles in our way and allows us to develop the necessary confidence and tools, there's no limit to what we can do.

How do we get there? By fixing the way we listen, adjusting our internal sound system, and tuning out the Mediocre Hoodlum.

To fix it, you have to fight back. Be louder than that stupid voice. When your Mediocre Hoodlum talks to you, can anyone else hear it? No! You're not repeating what it's saying out loud, are you? I didn't think so.

When it comes to fixing your head, you have to talk more and listen less. That mediocre-minded voice in your head has only the amount of power you give it. The more you listen to it, the more power it has. The less you listen to it, the less power it has over you. This is why I suggest you listen less and talk more. You have to say what you want, preferably out loud. You have to debate this voice. You have to counter it. You have to remind it that *you* are the boss. You have to put what your heart wants and what you're capable of having back in charge. You have to tell that voice to go F-itself! The more you tell yourself what you want, the more you believe it. The more you believe it, the more likely you are to get it.

The good news is that your self-defeating thoughts are nothing more than programs. You allowed other people and circumstances to program you instead of programming yourself. And when it comes to you, *you* are the only one with the power to make the changes you need to make.

What else is your Mediocre Hoodlum saying you suck at? What other limiting remarks is it making? Maybe you can't paint like Picasso or sing like Sinatra, but that doesn't mean you can't be great at something else. We will never know how good we can be at anything if we don't learn to talk more to ourselves and listen less to our Mediocre Hoodlum.

CHAPTER SEVEN
FIND

....

Being lost is worth the coming home.
—NEIL DIAMOND, "STONES"

....

*F*IND IS A SIMPLE BUT IMPORTANT WORD IN THE PROCESS OF F-ing our way to an F-it-less life. *Find* provides direction, much like a lighthouse guides ships to the shore. *Find* doesn't mean "to look for problems" or "to hunt down the people responsible for them." It doesn't mean rummaging through what you've got. *Find* means to figure out what you want. When you figure out what you want, whether that's the complete opposite of what you have now or more of it, you naturally begin to discover ways to heal your feelings and fractures.

When you stay in a hotel and look up toward the ceiling in the rooms and hallways, you will inevitably see exit signs. They're universal signals required by law to be installed so that people can easily locate the elevators, stairs, and doors. Almost every exit sign has an arrow that points in the direction of a way out. Exit signs show people how to quickly and efficiently go from inside the building to outside, particularly in emergencies. All you have to do is follow those arrows from exit sign to exit sign until you've left the building and arrived at safety or freedom, whichever you're seeking.

When we find the exit signs, we trust that there's a plan that will lead us where we want or need to go. Exit signs allow us to focus on the solution, not the problem. If we're stuck, they show us how to get out. If we're scared, they show us how to get out. If we don't know where we are, they show us how to get out. There's no confusion. Without exit signs, we would waste a lot of time and energy opening every door that we see, thinking, *Is this the one that will get me out of here?* Without their red lights and arrows, we would work ourselves into an emotional frenzy.

Find is our exit sign.

I've given a lot of thought to Find and its importance in our formula for living an F-it-less life. Most important, I've thought about *where* to best introduce Find in this book. Mind you, there's no set order to the F-words that guide us. They all hold equal importance, and you should feel free to use them whenever they apply. But this particular F-word helps us set our compass, so I think encountering it sooner rather than later is important.

Find tells us what we want. Find shows us where we want to go. Find is the destination we want to reach. Find declares the end result we're seeking. Think about it: When you want to go on a vacation, the first step is deciding where to go. Do you want to travel to the beach? The mountains? A bustling city? Do you want to sit, relax, and do nothing on your trip? Or do you want to ski, snowboard, or hike trails? Is a meditation retreat your thing? Or do you want to sightsee? Are you into pyramids or roller coasters? You can't do a single thing until you've decided where you want to go. Once you do that, you can determine your mode of transportation, where you'll stay, what you'll do, where you'll eat, the order of your itinerary, and who will go with you, among other details.

I used to teach a class about this, though it wasn't called Find. It was a class about creating results that matter in your life and business.

One part of the class was designed to help students experience the differences between dwelling on a problem and focusing on a solution to it. I loved this part because there were always so many different aha moments for the students. When we reached this section of the class, I would walk students through an exercise that consisted of a series of questions they had to think about and respond to in the space provided. The questions went something like this:

What is your problem?

How long has this problem existed? Who is responsible for this problem?

What obstacles is this problem creating in your life? What other aspects of your life is this problem affecting?

By the time the students reached the last question, the energy in the place was terrible. An entire roomful of people had to identify a problem and focus on it with no solution in sight. I would then ask them how they felt.

"Not good" was always the predominant answer.

"That's because we just wallowed in our problems without a solution," I would say. "More specifically, how did that exercise make you feel?"

"Like a failure."

"Like I couldn't breathe."

"Sad."

"Angry."

"Worthless."

Next, I would show them a more empowering way of thinking, one that focused on the results they wanted rather than the situation they were in. Looking back, I can see that this part of the class was all about the F-word *Find*.

"Let's try looking at things in a different way," I'd say. "Turn the page and answer the questions you see there, please." This time, the questions were:

What do you want? When do you want it?

How hard are you willing to work to have it? How will you know when you have it?

Is there anything you can think of that could get in the way of you getting what you want?

Do you know what you need to do to achieve it?

If not, do you know where you can learn what you need to know?

Who can help you achieve what you want? Make a list of these people.

When you achieve what you want, what else in your life will become easier and/or better because you achieved the result you wanted?

When you achieve what you want, how will that make you feel?

Even as I write this it makes me smile. I loved watching those people progress from feeling sad, angry, deflated, and worthless to feeling excited, energized, fearless, and unstoppable. Before anyone even said a word, you could feel the potential in the room. It felt lighter and more focused. This happened because everyone found an exit sign that led to where they wanted to go, instead of a stop sign that kept them mired in their problems.

This is why Find is critically important to introduce now. The sooner you create a clear vision of the change you want to see, the better. Paying attention to what your feelings are trying to tell you and putting your fractures into perspective are important steps toward living an F-it-less life, too, or I wouldn't have begun with them. But if you want to move forward and actually create the change you're hoping for in your life, then *finding* a vision that inspires you and that will pull you through any and all obstacles you might face on your journey is the only way you'll ever fulfill your desire for change.

The more attached you are to the vision you find, the less distracting, stressful, and painful the hurdles along the way will be. If you don't find and hold on to that vision, then any obstacle along the way will likely stop you in your tracks. Therefore, Find must be established as your highest priority from this point forward. If your vision is your priority, then nothing can stop you.

When I was in elementary school, I learned how to water-ski. I wasn't very good at it, at least initially, but I loved it. Water-skiing always gave me a refreshing rush of exhilaration and a true sense of accomplishment. There's something about sitting in the water behind a boat, holding on to a rope, giving the signal to go, and getting pulled up to glide across the surface of the water. Certain things about learning to water-ski, however, can be terrifying.

If you've ever been on a boat or water-skied behind one, then you know that the propeller leaves a V-shaped wake in the water, one that widens as it gets farther away from the boat. When you're water-skiing, you're positioned in between the edges of the wake. I can remember getting up on water skis the first few times and steering close to the wake on one side, looking at the gigantic hump of water before me, and then steering myself back to the safety of the calmer water in between. I can remember everyone in the boat yelling excitedly and signaling for me to work my way over the wake to get outside of it, but I wouldn't dare. I was too scared. To me, the wake looked like something that would end my life prematurely. Besides, I was water-skiing, for God's sake; what difference did it make whether I was inside the wake or outside? I was fine.

However, the more I watched other people water-ski— people who crossed the wake and lived to tell about it—the more it piqued my curiosity. When I asked what was so special about going outside the wake, I got a number of responses:

"It's smooth as glass out there."

"You can go faster."

"It's so much fun to jump from one side of the wake to the other!"

I finally asked, "What's the secret to getting over the wake?" The answer to my question surprised me.

"The secret is to not look at the wake. Don't focus on it. If you focus on the wake, you'll fall. Focus on where you want to go. When you do that, the little bump between there and where you are will be barely noticeable. You might not even feel it. Crossing the wake is one of the best parts of water-skiing. You'll see. That thing you fear is the very thing that's going to make you *love* water-skiing. All you've got to do is cross it once and you'll be hooked."

And guess what? They were right!

Finding and focusing on your vision is no different than finding that spot outside the wake. It's like setting your gaze on smooth waters—like having an exit sign in front of you, wherever you go, pointing the way. When your vision is clear, the journey is easier. Find that vision—your intentional destination—and enjoy the ride.

F-It-Less Exercise: Find

Before moving on to the next chapter, take a few minutes to answer these questions for yourself. Really think about each one and write down your responses where you can easily refer to them. Make adjustments as needed.

What do you want? _____

_____

_____

_____

_____

When do you want it? _____

_____

_____

_____

_____

How will you know when you have it? _____

_____

_____

_____

_____

Do you know what you need to do to achieve it? _____

_____

_____

_____

_____

If not, do you know where you can learn what you need to know? _____

_____
_____
_____
_____
_____

Do you know who can help you achieve it? _____

_____
_____
_____
_____
_____
_____

When you get it, what else in your life will become better and/or easier? __

_____
_____
_____
_____
_____

How will it make you feel to achieve what you want? _____

_____
_____
_____
_____
_____
_____

CHAPTER EIGHT

FOCUS

••••••••••••••••••••

The secret of change is to focus all your energy
not on fighting the old but on building the new.
—SOCRATES

••••••••••••••••••••

A NUMBER OF YEARS AGO, I TOOK A MOTORCYCLE CLASS THAT taught me about target fixation, a rule of the road that states, "What you focus on, you will hit." If you focus on the wrong thing at certain times, especially on a motorcycle, it can kill you. For example, if a car pulls out in front of you and you think, I'm going to hit that car, you might indeed hit it. On the other hand, if you think, I can stop or swerve to get out of the way, then you may actualize a better outcome simply because you fixated on it.

What you focus on often becomes reality. There's science that backs this up. It's called experience-dependent neuroplasticity.

The studies examining this idea have caught fire. Why? The findings are powerful and the implications profound.

Researchers have found that experience changes the brain. Everything we do impacts how we think, process, and perform. Based on their findings, it's reasonable to believe that we have the ability to guide the changes in our brains through our experiences. Up until about a decade ago, it was thought that the adult brain stayed pretty much the same and wasn't open to influence or change. Of course, we now know that isn't true. Our brains are flexible, meaning they're open to influence—positive or negative. Whatever you feed your brain, it believes.

Here's how this works. Between the walls of your skull, billions of neurons work together to shape us into the people we are. Different neurons are responsible for different parts of our experiences, including eating, feeling, sleeping, sensing threats, getting excited, falling in love, laughing, remembering, learning, nurturing, and so much more. Every time you have an experience, the relevant neurons switch on and start firing. If you aren't consciously shaping your thoughts, other people and experiences will do it for you. Being purposeful about your thoughts and experiences, especially those you repeat often, can have a direct impact on their outcome.

If you've ever read the book *The Secret*, you'll recognize this concept as the Law of Attraction. Simply put, we have the ability to attract into our lives whatever it is we focus on. Regardless of your age, religious beliefs, or place of residence, you are susceptible to the laws of the Universe, including this one. The Law of Attraction uses the power of our mind to translate our thoughts into reality. It says that our thoughts are a potent form of energy that sets the Universe in motion,

What you focus on is powerful. Your thoughts will build on what they rest upon. What you pay attention to shapes your thoughts, and consequently your experiences, relationships, and life.

Target fixation and the Law of Attraction are real. Our thoughts are real. Both have real consequences. We have to treat our thoughts as our most important assets, for without proper focus, we end up living a consolation-prize life instead of the "f"-it-less life we're capable of.

eventually turning what we imagine into reality. "What you think about, you bring about."

There have been times in my life when I've struggled with this, and there still are. Not because I don't buy into the concept of target fixation or the Law of Attraction; no, it's because even though I'm a positive person, I still have negative thoughts. We all do. We're actually wired to notice threats and bad feelings. It's completely normal and a healthy form of self-protection. Most of us are really good at noticing the bad, analyzing it, and then hanging on to it until we learn from the experience. But, as it happens, many of us hold on to the bad more than we do the good. It's a tendency unique to humans. It's called negativity bias, and it can be quite powerful.

So while it's normal to notice the bad, it's also normal to let the good slide past us. How many times have you had a great day, yet your mind gets stuck on one negative exchange? Maybe it was an unexpected phone call, an argument with your spouse, your boss calling you out, or your kid thinking you're an idiot.

Wouldn't it be great if, on days like that, you had the capacity to hold on to all the good and let the bad slip away?

What if I told you that this power already lives inside you?

All it takes is work, focus, and determination to activate it.

If you focus on the doom and gloom, you keep living under that cloud. If, however, you focus on positive thoughts and goals, you'll find a way to get there. It takes consistent action, but it can happen. It sounds so simple, doesn't it?

Understand, though, that even the most positive people are not without negative thoughts. The difference is that genuinely positive people don't let their negative thoughts grow roots. They counter those thoughts with a nuclear dose of positive thinking.

This positivity changes the energy of their thoughts entirely and influences the outcome of their efforts.

Focus is about how you think at a core level. It's the thought-based energy that you give to your actions, and it's the energy that's going to empower the Universe to support you and give you what you want. In "Find," I showed you the importance of knowing where you want to go. "Focus" goes one step further by welding your intended destination to the thoughts required to get you there. Think of it this way: knowing what you want or where you want to go is just a *wish*, while believing you're worthy and that you're going to get there makes it a *plan*.

The kind of changes you need to make to live an F-it-less life require you to be focused and determined enough to think, feel, and believe with an energy that makes living an F-it-less life not just possible, but probable. One of the great life lessons I learned at Keller Williams is, "I can't control my first thought—but I *can* control my second."

Focus is about concentrating on your first thoughts and the thoughts that come after them. It's about putting the energy of your thoughts under a microscope and getting it right before you do anything else. Focus understands that the DNA of thought—its fundamental, characteristic qualities—has as much to do with our outcomes in life as anything else, if not more. You can't really achieve an F-it-less life if you don't believe you should have one.

Over the course of my life, I've listened to the likes of Zig Ziglar, Jim Rohn, Tony Robbins, and Wayne Dyer. These people are masters of thought, belief, and focus. You can't listen to any of them without realizing that negative, doubtful, and self-destructive thoughts are a choice, just as positive, assured, and self-em- powering thoughts are. The thoughts

and beliefs we choose to act upon are the thoughts that control our destiny. Every outcome is tied to a was Henry Ford who said, "Whether you think you can't, you're right."

One of the questions a world-leading technolog asks in order to help determine if they should hir is (get ready for this), "Do you consider yourself to person?" They found that people who think they're more positive and create better and greater changes who don't. Maybe start there. Do you consider yours lucky person? I do. I always have. My wife, Jeri, frequ about my great parking or travel karma. The truth is, I't have good karma, period. I've always felt like the Univ me to be great and do great things. I'm hardwired to b any struggles in my life will turn out in a positive wa the most part, they do.

I struggled as a young competitive tennis player. Th to coach tennis, which gave me a ton of flexibility, mc and lots of joy and experiences that have helped me th my life.

I struggled as a young Realtor. I contemplated quitt point because I felt like I was meant for something g the time, I didn't understand how great my career in could become. It turned out that I *was* meant to be the Universe wouldn't let me quit until I had started, gr presided over the number-one real estate company in C

I struggled with everything leading up to my div I knew what kind of life I wanted to live going forw focused on that. Despite all my trials, frustrations, setb disappointments, I wound up with a life I love.

eventually turning what we imagine into reality. "What you think about, you bring about."

There have been times in my life when I've struggled with this, and there still are. Not because I don't buy into the concept of target fixation or the Law of Attraction; no, it's because even though I'm a positive person, I still have negative thoughts. We all do. We're actually wired to notice threats and bad feelings. It's completely normal and a healthy form of self-protection. Most of us are really good at noticing the bad, analyzing it, and then hanging on to it until we learn from the experience. But, as it happens, many of us hold on to the bad more than we do the good. It's a tendency unique to humans. It's called negativity bias, and it can be quite powerful.

So while it's normal to notice the bad, it's also normal to let the good slide past us. How many times have you had a great day, yet your mind gets stuck on one negative exchange? Maybe it was an unexpected phone call, an argument with your spouse, your boss calling you out, or your kid thinking you're an idiot.

Wouldn't it be great if, on days like that, you had the capacity to hold on to all the good and let the bad slip away?

What if I told you that this power already lives inside you?

All it takes is work, focus, and determination to activate it.

If you focus on the doom and gloom, you keep living under that cloud. If, however, you focus on positive thoughts and goals, you'll find a way to get there. It takes consistent action, but it can happen. It sounds so simple, doesn't it?

Understand, though, that even the most positive people are not without negative thoughts. The difference is that genuinely positive people don't let their negative thoughts grow roots. They counter those thoughts with a nuclear dose of positive thinking.

This positivity changes the energy of their thoughts entirely and influences the outcome of their efforts.

Focus is about how you think at a core level. It's the thought-based energy that you give to your actions, and it's the energy that's going to empower the Universe to support you and give you what you want. In "Find," I showed you the importance of knowing where you want to go. "Focus" goes one step further by welding your intended destination to the thoughts required to get you there. Think of it this way: knowing what you want or where you want to go is just a *wish*, while believing you're worthy and that you're going to get there makes it a *plan*.

The kind of changes you need to make to live an F-it-less life require you to be focused and determined enough to think, feel, and believe with an energy that makes living an F-it-less life not just possible, but probable. One of the great life lessons I learned at Keller Williams is, "I can't control my first thought—but I *can* control my second."

Focus is about concentrating on your first thoughts and the thoughts that come after them. It's about putting the energy of your thoughts under a microscope and getting it right before you do anything else. Focus understands that the DNA of thought—its fundamental, characteristic qualities—has as much to do with our outcomes in life as anything else, if not more. You can't really achieve an F-it-less life if you don't believe you should have one.

Over the course of my life, I've listened to the likes of Zig Ziglar, Jim Rohn, Tony Robbins, and Wayne Dyer. These people are masters of thought, belief, and focus. You can't listen to any of them without realizing that negative, doubtful, and self-destructive thoughts are a choice, just as positive, assured, and self-em- powering thoughts are. The thoughts and beliefs we choose to act upon are the thoughts and beliefs that control our destiny. Every outcome is tied to a thought. It was Henry Ford who said, "Whether you think you can or you can't, you're right."

One of the questions a world-leading technology company asks in order to help determine if they should hire someone is (get ready for this), "Do you consider yourself to be a lucky person?" They found that people who think they're lucky are more positive and create better and greater changes than those who don't. Maybe start there. Do you consider yourself to be a lucky person? I do. I always have. My wife, Jeri, frequently talks about my great parking or travel karma. The truth is, I think I just have good karma, period. I've always felt like the Universe wants me to be great and do great things. I'm hardwired to believe that any struggles in my life will turn out in a positive way. And for the most part, they do.

I struggled as a young competitive tennis player. Then I began to coach tennis, which gave me a ton of flexibility, more money, and lots of joy and experiences that have helped me throughout my life.

I struggled as a young Realtor. I contemplated quitting at one point because I felt like I was meant for something greater. At the time, I didn't understand how great my career in real estate could become. It turned out that I *was* meant to be great, and the Universe wouldn't let me quit until I had started, grown, and presided over the number-one real estate company in Georgia.

I struggled with everything leading up to my divorce. Yet I knew what kind of life I wanted to live going forward and focused on that. Despite all my trials, frustrations, setbacks, and disappointments, I wound up with a life I love.

What you focus on is powerful. Your thoughts will build on what they rest upon. What you pay attention to shapes your thoughts, and consequently your experiences, relationships, and life.

Target fixation and the Law of Attraction are real. Our thoughts are real. Both have real consequences. We have to treat our thoughts as our most important assets, for without proper focus, we end up living a consolation-prize life instead of the F-it-less life we're capable of.

CHAPTER NINE

FORGIVE

••••••••••••••••••••

Forgiveness is about empowering yourself
rather than empowering your past.
—T. D. JAKES

••••••••••••••••••••

ALONG THE WAY TO LIVING AN F-IT-LESS LIFE, YOU WILL
certainly encounter a number of obstacles, and one of the
biggest and toughest of them all will most likely be yourself.
As we go through life, we often collect unnecessary baggage,
which we inadvertently project onto others for things they
did or didn't do to or for us. I'll often refer to this baggage
as garbage, because that's how I see it. It's emotions like
anger, frustration, disappointment, disgust, resentment, jeal-
ousy, and others that hold us back. This emotional garbage
is so powerful that it has kept empires from being built and

fortunes from being made. It has torn apart families, friends, and coworkers. It can ruin the most promising of relationships. Not only can it keep you cemented where you are, it will stop you from finally living the F-it-less life you want. Worse, it can also push you backward by trapping you in a negative, *Groundhog Day* version of life simply by preoccupying you with your self-defeating emotions while everything truly important to you waits idly on the sidelines.

Sounds awful, doesn't it?

That's because it is. The harm we do ourselves by carrying around this negativity is extremely damaging.

It's natural to feel those emotions, especially if you've been wronged. And it's equally natural to feel guilt, shame, or pain if you've caused a loved one, a coworker, or even yourself, hurt. I've always loved this quote: "It's not the load that breaks you down, it's the way you carry it."

Finding a way to deal with those feelings and then moving forward has long-term benefits well beyond the initial sense of relief. It can actually lower your stress levels and keep you from becoming depressed.

Hanging on to all that negativity is like leaving a knife in a wound. By doing that, we're refusing to give ourselves the chance to heal. In the end, we hurt ourselves the most.

I know what you're probably thinking: *I'd love to let go of this garbage, but I don't know how.*

It's easy. Really.

Let . . . it . . . go.

If you truly want to go where you say you want to go, then understand that your emotional garbage is too heavy to be carried with you, and from this day forward, it must be left behind. And there's no better time to unpack it than right now.

Author Jon Kabat-Zinn, the father of mindfulness, defines letting go not as forgiving or forgetting but as *acceptance*—acceptance of things for what they are.

We have a tendency to want things in life to be the way we want them, and when they fall short of our expectations, we find ourselves in conflict.

Learning to let go is a process of forgiveness.

It's a process of moving on from disappointing, challenging, unwanted, or unexpected situations.

So much emphasis has been placed on learning to forgive others in life that sometimes we forget the most important person: ourselves.

The behaviors we're most critical of in ourselves are often coping mechanisms or attempts at what psychologists refer to as self-regulation. These might include various forms of self-soothing or efforts to deal with high levels of anxiety.

While it's important to forgive yourself for the harm you may have caused others, it's just as important to forgive yourself for the harm you've caused yourself. Maybe you didn't love or respect your body, your spirit, or the image you have of yourself. Maybe you spent money you didn't have or got wrapped up in some type of debt through gambling or partying too much. Perhaps you strayed outside your relationship, engaging in behavior that pushed away the people who loved and believed in you.

Here's what you need to know: it's time to forgive yourself for these things.

Perhaps some of you were only doing what you'd been taught to do.

For others, maybe it was the best you could do at the time.

Did you push away people because you didn't know how to trust or love, or because you believed you didn't deserve to be loved yourself?

Did you feel bad about yourself because no one believed in you when you were growing up?

These feelings are not your fault. Forgive yourself.

I mean it.

Let it go.

Stop allowing these actions to hold you back from living your best life from this day forward.

Write yourself a letter asking yourself for forgiveness. It won't be an easy letter to write, but it's an important part of the process. Take your time and let your feelings flow. Allow yourself to include all the ways you've hurt yourself, and as you write, find self-compassion. Don't waste another moment feeling sorry for yourself. Feel empathy and understanding for why you acted the way you did. Research shows that those who have high self-compassion exhibit significantly lower stress responses, while those with low self-compassion have higher baseline stress levels. What this means is that people lacking self-forgiveness get more stressed in the first place, and they also hold on to that stress for longer periods of time than those who forgive themselves. And, as you might suspect, with higher stress levels come more health problems.

When we forgive ourselves and others, we feel better.

Most people want to feel good. Forgiveness is the key to doing that.

We're all human. We all make mistakes. The fact is, mistakes are inevitable. How we manage our lapses in judgment, screwups, and plain old botched decisions matters more than the outcome of those mistakes. This means you must forgive yourself at some point for being human.

Forgiving yourself brings catharsis. It moves you out of the past and into the present, while showing you a clear and walkable pathway for the future. And it's the first step toward forgiving others.

As the saying goes, "We can't give what we don't have." We can only forgive others once we've forgiven ourselves. In the same way that we're guaranteed to make mistakes, so are those we have relationships with. When we can forgive them for being human, the result is healing. Forgiving others engenders peace.

Look, forgiveness is a challenge. It's not a quick solution. It can sometimes take months or even years to get there. But it's worth it—especially when it comes to forgiving ourselves, which is something most people find harder to do than forgiving others.

Both matter.

Holding on to that garbage ultimately creates more garbage. It builds more anger, resentment, and stress, and can even lead to physical fallout. What someone else did to us can become so ingrained in our thoughts that we actually repeat that behavior with others.

All of us have experienced anger toward another person in our lifetime. It's believed that chronic anger can put individuals into an ongoing state of fight or flight. This, in turn, can raise the heart rate and blood pressure, and even impact the immune system. Anger toward another is one of the most detrimental voluntary transfers of energy that exists. If life is too short for this and too short for that, then life is surely too short to harbor anger toward another person. Sure, you've been hurt, and sure, you've been wronged, but harboring those feelings in a way that creates anger toward the person or persons who wronged you hurts only yourself. In the most intentional of circumstances, allowing your anger toward someone to eat away at you only gives them what they want, as they likely intended to get under your skin all along. In other cases, an offender's lack of awareness that they even did anything wrong can be equally frustrating. Either way, you have to find a means of reconciling situations that spark anger within you quickly and effectively.

When you get angry, you give your power to that which has angered you. It may not seem like it at first, because anger gives you a sudden burst of emotional energy that momentarily makes you feel as if you're in command of the situation. But this only tricks you into holding on to negative energy. Unfortunately, that little voice inside us that tries to justify our smallness helps create misguided and self-destructive behavior patterns.

I've always told my children, "No one can make you angry but you." Anger is a choice; it's something that you *choose*—or *not*. Don't ever give someone that kind of control over you. You're better than that. The world is filled with people who've learned to love the false sense of power that anger gives them. Don't be one of them. Life is too short for that.

Try feeling sorry for the person instead of being angry at them. Look for all the reasons he or she might have done what they did. Perhaps they lack good judgment, or knowledge, or emotional intelligence, or empathy, or maturity, or an ability to see the big picture. Maybe their environment or upbringing gave them a warped sense of reality. Maybe they haven't been able to develop a concern for others' wants and needs the way you have. It could be that they're selfish. Maybe they're surrounded by others who condone or encourage their behavior, and they just don't know any better. Perhaps they're compensating for their own fears and insecurities. Maybe they're angry or unhappy with themselves in some way. Maybe they just haven't developed the capacity for wisdom, maturity, or self-control that you have.

The point is that if you try to look at something differently and ask enough questions, you can neutralize your anger with sorrow, compassion, or sympathy. Doing so can keep you in control of your emotions and energy and allow you to move forward positively, without permitting negative distractions to thwart your inner peace and happiness. More important, it will allow you to realize that you're *bigger* than the problem or the problematic person. Life is a constant game of Rock, Paper, Scissors, and we have to ensure that we're always more powerful on the inside than anyone or anything that we face on the outside.

Many people hold grudges—deep ones—that can last a long time. Some even harbor them for a lifetime. There are people who simply can't or won't let go of the anger they feel toward those who've wronged them in the past. Some carry these grudges without even realizing it, while others use them as a crutch, all the while wishing they could get rid of them because they feel as heavy as thousand-pound weights.

When we find it difficult to forgive, it's often because we aren't living in the present and are giving more importance to something that happened in the past. We waste too much of our daily energy and attention on complaining about something that happened years ago. We even use that as the reason we can't be happy or fulfilled today.

Why do we do this to ourselves? Why do we allow wounds from our past to control our present, and worse, our future? What keeps us stuck where we are when we'd like to move on and let go?

The answer is relatively simple.

Grudges, anger, and resentment—these come with an identity. They reflect who we are and what we've been through.

As much as we don't like seeing ourselves as someone who has been wronged, that label helps to explain us to ourselves in some way. If we've been wronged, then we must be *right*. If we've endured offense, then we must be strong. It's not an ideal definition of who we are, but for a lot of people, it's one that feels familiar, and therefore it works. It's an identity that gives us a sense of purpose and has some value. It may not carry a lot of weight out there in the world, but it's a history that matters to us. The sad truth, however, is that it only fuels our anger and our sense of victimhood. It's a vicious and unrelenting cycle, one that's almost impossible to break unless we're ready, willing, and able to let go of that identity. In doing so, we have to also be willing to give up whatever strength, comfort, sympathy, and compassion we receive because of it. Think of this release as stepping out of the past and into the present.

There's a proverb that's often attributed to Confucius that says, "If you're going to pursue revenge, you'd better dig two graves," which means your resentments will eventually destroy you. Have you ever heard the saying, "Resentment is like taking poison and waiting for the other person to die"? That's exactly what holding a grudge is like. As it happens, most grudges start as misunderstandings that people never talk through. They're based on a pool of wrong assumptions and judgments. Before you know it, you're wallowing in an ocean of resentment. The longer you remain at sea, the more bitter you become.

What most people, especially grudge holders, don't understand is that resentment and anger never serve their supposed purpose. They don't make us feel better, and they certainly don't take our hurt away. If anything, both build to higher levels. It takes a lot of energy to keep a steady stream of hostility and aggression going. At the end of the day, carrying a grudge around is really nothing more than proof that you've suffered. It's an ongoing reminder of your own pain. The person you're mad at rarely feels what you do, if ever. Over time, the story grows, and somehow a pebble becomes a boulder that blocks your heart and mind from experiencing the one thing you truly seek: healing.

When I stepped away from my leadership role at the company I founded, I was in the midst of a divorce and was taking bold steps to craft a new life. Not only was this process difficult for me, it was difficult for other people too. My choices were disappointing and hurtful to many. Up until that point in my life, my decisions and actions had been designed to make people happy. I had no idea how others' disappointment, hurt, and anger toward me would affect me until I experienced it. The funny thing is, I felt betrayed by them. I was, in turn, disappointed in them. I got angry. I found myself spending a great deal of time looking for—and making up—evidence to support my negative emotions. Thankfully, I realized that the more negativity I looked for, the more I found. I had to forgive those who couldn't forgive me. And I did. Don't get me wrong—we didn't become friends again. But just because I felt wronged in some way didn't mean that I had to add that feeling to my daily playlist. I realized that if someone wasn't going to be in my physical life going forward, then they shouldn't be in my mental or emotional life, either. I accepted my human tendency to make mistakes. I forgave myself for hurting others. I gave all the people who hurt me credit for reacting to my decisions in a way that worked for them (although not for me), and I released them from the energy of my life. It was the most successful weight-loss program I've ever tried, and I will never put on that kind of weight again.

The path to freedom doesn't start with forgiveness of others so much as it does with loving yourself. Allowing self-love to conquer whatever suffering you may have endured at the hands of others is what ultimately heals the pain and allows your anger to slowly melt away. So few people have the capacity to sit inside their pain, to really touch it, to feel it. Most people need time to understand and accept it. Then, and only then, can they release it by directing their thoughts away from those who wronged them, away from the story of their suffering, and away from the memories of what they lived through. This is how acceptance and letting go work.

Forgiveness takes more than words. It's an active process. It's making a conscious decision to put all negative feelings behind you whether the person deserves it or not. It's finding soothing kindness and compassion for oneself and others. It's taking responsibility for the hurt you may have caused someone else and knowing that it matters. And it's being accountable for your own healing.

It is, as Kabat-Zinn suggests, total acceptance of things, people, and situations as they are.

Whatever happened to you, the actual act that hurt or offended you will likely always remain in your memory—but forgiveness loosens its grip on you and helps you redirect your focus onto other, more positive areas of your life.

Bear in mind that you can forgive without excusing the act.

Forgiving doesn't justify or minimize the wrongdoing.

It's important to remember that forgiveness is a personal choice, not an obligation. Offering an olive branch to someone before you're emotionally ready won't automatically bring you peace or satisfaction. It's like being told to sit at the table until you've eaten all your food. If you can't do it, you can't do it. In the end, you'll feel worse, not better. And for many, forgiveness isn't an all-or-nothing proposition, either. There's some middle ground, a space between being hurt and forgiving where progress is made but the goal hasn't yet been reached. That's also forgiveness, even if it's not complete. We've all been there. We move forward but keep what happened in the back of our mind, as if it could happen again at any moment. Think about a time in your life when this may have happened to you. Maybe your partner wasn't faithful, a friend let you down, or a coworker took credit for work you did. If true forgiveness can happen only at 100 percent, it's less likely to happen at all. An imperfect forgiveness may be a better goal, or at least a more realistic one.

Forgiveness is one of the great pathways to finding peace and happiness. Perhaps that's because it's one of the most difficult paths to take. True forgiveness requires time. If it's genuine, more often than not, it's something that you must earn. Forgiveness isn't something you can simply request, because if you do, it's doubtful that you'll receive the real thing. It's better to have authentic forgiveness than some superficial version that comes with ill feelings still attached.

Finally, we don't need a reason to forgive. We can forgive "just because." You might say, "But what about the fact that he or she did or said such and such?" And I would say, "It doesn't matter—unless you allow it to." We can forgive others without any reason other than just to forgive. We can forgive others because we don't want them to take up valuable real estate in our head or our heart anymore. We can forgive others because we want to be free. We can forgive others because they have no place in our present or future life, and it makes sense to leave them and everything about them in our past. We can forgive others because we love ourselves too much to poison ourselves with negative emotions that serve no real purpose. We can forgive others just because we can, because we want to, or because we should. We don't need any better reasons than those.

F-It-Less Exercise: Be a Giver of Forgiveness

Wherever you are, whenever you feel strong emotions stirring within you and notice yourself feeling the need to be right, silently recite the following words from the Prayer of Saint Francis:

"Where there is hatred, let me sow love; where there is injury, pardon . . . where there is darkness, light." _____

_____

_____

_____

_____

_____

_____

_____

_____

_____

_____

_____

_____

_____

_____

_____

_____

_____

_____

_____

_____

CHAPTER TEN
FORGET

. . . .

What other people think of me
is none of my business.
—Dr. Wayne Dyer

. . . .

The expression "fuhgeddaboudit" became a pop cultural reference around the time of the 1997 film *Donnie Brasco*. Johnny Depp's character, an FBI agent who infiltrates one of the major New York Mafia families, is living under the assumed name Brasco. He develops a relationship with mob hit man Benjamin "Lefty" Ruggiero, played by Al Pacino, in order to get deeper under cover, but he ends up becoming actual friends with the Mafioso. As their relationship develops, Brasco must decide whether to complete his job, knowing that it will lead to the murder of his new friend. At one point in the film Brasco explains the meaning

of "fuhgeddaboudit" to his fellow FBI agents. The term was often
used in Mafia culture as a way to agree with an emphatic statement, such as "My wife is a beautiful woman." "Fuhgeddaboudit"
would be the response.

If you're not in the Mafia, "forget about it" likely has a
completely different meaning. It could mean, "Don't worry, I've
got this," or, "Let it go. Move on," depending on how it's used. I
chose *Forget* as one of my key F-words because, as an entrepre-
neur, there have been many times throughout my career when I
had to do just that. I had to either agree or forget about it, let it
go, and move on. I have a friend whose aunt wears a T-shirt that
reads, "Everyone is entitled to my opinion." Why? She genuinely
believes that to be true. Most people are prone to offer their opinions, whether you want them or not. And while opinions can be
helpful in some situations, they are, after all, just that—opinions.
For this reason, they shouldn't be the deterrents that keep you
from moving toward your goal, whether it be starting your own
business, getting out of a negative relationship, or just having a
good idea.

Oftentimes, opinions can feel more like criticism. As
they say in Hollywood, "Everyone's a critic." There are often
valuable takeaways from criticism, even when it might hurt.
Sometimes a covert little criticism that makes you feel small,
weak, or *less than* can sneak up on you and stop you cold, para-
lyzing you with fear and worry. It can be a virtual punch to
the gut, especially if you feel attacked or belittled. When that
criticism is unnecessarily harsh, it may elicit emotional reactions you'd prefer to avoid. Whenever any of us feels verbally
attacked, whether the other person intended their comments
as an affront or we just took their comments that way because

the subject was personal to us, we're bound to have an emotional response. It doesn't matter if that person is being critical or just opinionated. While feeling your emotions is important, especially when it comes to tapping into your gut, there are times when you need to keep emotion at bay. That's why it's important to understand the difference between criticism and opinions. General criticism isn't meant to tear you apart as much as provide a different perspective or angle on what you're saying, thinking, or working on.

The real issue isn't what's said as much as how we respond to it. And for most of us, those responses are rooted in our emotional triggers. People can judge only on their own experience, and most are led by their bad experiences. A lot of the time, negative feedback comes from negative people. It's a rare person who can support you unconditionally without judging.

People love to share their negativity. As the saying goes, misery loves company. Unfortunately, that point of view strengthens our fears and insecurities. But it shouldn't. We have total control over and responsibility for our thoughts, actions, and words, and, as a result, the outcome. Besides, most people don't get anything out of shutting down other people's dreams. In fact, I believe most people spend more time thinking about themselves than about others, so if they're expressing an opinion about your life, it's probably more off-the-cuff than calculated.

Real estate coach Tom Ferry talks about the addiction many people have to the opinions of others in his book *Life! By Design: 6 Steps to an Extraordinary You.* He says, "The addiction to what other people think has another significant impact; it represses us, which in turn keeps us in a sort of purgatory, afraid of the consequences of pursuing the life we really want." We've all felt judged. We worry about what others think or say about us, we have good ideas but never act on them, we spend money we don't have on things we don't need, we seek the approval of others, and, at times, we don't speak up for what we truly believe in. Think you're immune to the opinions of others? Ask yourself, why do you live in your neighborhood? Why do you drive the car you own? Why do you wear specific designer clothes, go on vacation to the places you do, or belong to clubs or your church? What memories from the past are you still holding on to that may be getting in your way?

Too many of us have fallen into this trap and ended up making the wrong choice, whether about our career, who we married, who we choose to listen to, who we aspire to be most like, or even who we compete with. Maybe you became an accountant instead of pursuing a career in advertising because your parents expected you to go into the family business; or perhaps you married your high school sweetheart, and thirty years later you've found that you have nothing in common anymore. When you choose to stay in a situation that you know is making you miserable, you're actually nurturing your weaknesses over your strengths. You aren't living your best or most authentic life.

I used to think that other people's opinions didn't really affect me or my decision-making.

I was wrong.

It's impossible to live up to everyone's expectations; therefore, you will inevitably let someone down, disappoint them, or fall short. And that's okay, as long as your aim is true.

There have been plenty of times in my life when I've questioned who I am and what I know because of something someone else said.

Those questions impacted my self-esteem and my self-confidence. For instance, being called Jelly Roll in junior high by my coach; that seemingly harmless nickname followed me well into my early twenties, and, as I mentioned in chapter five, I spent years questioning whether I was pudgy because I accepted or believed I was, or if it was merely an adolescent phase I could have outgrown or changed with some concentrated effort.

We've all been there.

Pursuing the approval of others is like living an imagined life created in someone else's mind. Nobody else is living your life, which means you know yourself better than anyone else. This also means that you need to learn from your own mistakes and failures. So stop asking what other people think of you. It's important to understand that we're mostly the product of the stories we tell ourselves. Those inner conversations impact everything from our behavior to its outcomes. It's only when we can let go of the old stories, the ones we carry from the past as part of our programming and self-image, that we can break free from the trap they've kept us in for so long.

I know so many people—men and women—who battled their weight as kids. And though they don't have any issues with their weight as an adult, they still see themselves as fat, unfit, and unattractive. Likewise, I know people who were bullied growing up, and are easily intimidated at work or in social situations to this day. How about those who are crowd-pleasers, constantly putting the needs of others over their own? None of those people ever changed their language—their self-talk—and let go of their former images of themselves. They carry those beliefs with them like balls and chains, oftentimes without even being aware of it.

Evaluate the validity of those opinions and ask yourself whether it's still worth holding on to them, or if it's time to forget about the past and move on.

Our reactions are learned, and show up in various situations, especially those with people who influenced us at an early age. What do you believe as a result of your mother's negative views? What have you read or heard in the news or through social media that inhibits you still? These experiences are like layers of fake news that get imprinted in our mind over the years and become stories we believe. Of course, our reaction isn't the problem; that's more of a symptom. In fact, it's the event that we experienced over and over that's the root. If you can unravel that puzzle, you can let go of those opinions, move on from the past, and start moving toward your authentic, independent, thinking self.

Independent thinking, free from the influence of the opinions of those around us, doesn't mean ignoring the accumulated wisdom of others' experiences. I often find that it's worth listening closely to those who love and care for us, but then we must use that information to feed our power, not our weaknesses. And if you're listening to others, make sure you're following the right advice. Try to find positive aspects in what others are sharing, especially if they have more experience in a particular area. Remember, if you put too much value on their opinions, you'll live in a constant state of purgatory, waffling between your vision and theirs. Focus on what matters, what's important, and think more about the big picture. Giving too much weight to what others think dilutes your focus on what you really want to accomplish; it may even impede your progress and diminish your happiness in the process. Truly independent thinkers follow their own heart, even when faced with great risk.

By nature, we all seek approval. We've been conditioned for this response since birth. Why? The approval of others helps us have a higher sense of self. It makes us feel better about who we are and what we're doing.

Whenever I made big bold decisions in my life, I knew there would be lots of opinions from family and friends about what I should or shouldn't do. Many times I worried about how those decisions would impact my children, my business relationships, and what my friends and colleagues might think. But it wasn't until I asked myself one pressing question that I realized there was really only one answer: *Why would I stay in any situation that was making me unhappy or that didn't hold the prospect of a promising future?* When I stopped placing value on the opinions of others, I was able to do what I needed to do regardless of the outcome.

We inherently know when it's time to move on, but we often don't trust ourselves to take that first step forward because we know it's a harder road to walk. Worse, when it comes to change, whether it involves our diet, habits, job, or any other aspect of our life, we always find reasons for discouragement at a subconscious level, because change makes us uncomfortable. People's arguments, when internally debating change, are based solely on their own experience, which can undermine their efforts even before they've gotten off the ground.

Why did we stop trusting our intuition or listening to our gut? Why did we stop believing we know what's right for ourselves? Who else walks in our shoes? Who else feels what we feel?

Our spouse? Our doctor? A friend? Our mother?

No. Not any of those people.

You know what's good for you, just as I know what's good for me.

Somebody else's experiences, whether positive or negative, will always be somebody else's experiences. No matter how
common the circumstances, they will never be yours.

You will never gain anyone's approval by begging for it. When
you stand confident in your own worth, you will gain the respect
of others. And isn't that so much better?

Letting go of the past isn't a ticket to write off your prior
mistakes. There's a great opportunity to learn from those blun-
ders. The ultimate goal is to not let your past affect you in the
present or future. Athletes are especially adept at this. Coaches
call this the "next play" mindset—meaning forget about whatever mistake you just made and push forward by focusing on the
task at hand. Whenever I play golf, I know one lousy swing can
set me back—if I allow it to. And whenever I've allowed it to, it
usually leads to another bad shot. What I aim for is a shift in my
mindset. I aim to not let it drag me down. Rather than getting
caught up in trying to soothe myself, I forget it ever happened
and go to the next shot. Sure, screwing up sucks. When you fail
at something, it's easy to get down on yourself and let it eat away
at your confidence. Rather than endlessly wrestling with your
failure, it's better to embrace it and move on. I like to say, "Learn
from the past, live in the present, and believe in the future."

The only way to have total freedom from the opinions of
others is to unplug your need to care about them. It takes effort to
let go of what other people think. It's a skill, and like anything we
want to excel at, we need to practice it. People are going to love
you, people are going to hate you, and, for the most part, those
opinions won't actually have anything to do with you—so why
spend one more minute worrying about them? Why would you
choose to live your life based on what others tell you to think, feel,

or want? Take back your power. Forget about what others think and act on your beliefs. Remember, others' opinions aren't facts; they may not even be truths. They're just someone else's outlook being thrust upon you based solely on personal judgment.

Successfully going through this adventure called life requires us to become expert packers. We all have a backpack that we carry around. It's an invisible backpack, but it's real, nonetheless. What we choose to put into this backpack determines how much we love our lives, how far we'll go, and how fast we'll get there, or whether we'll get there at all. This backpack consists of our hopes and dreams, joys, loves, fears, perspectives, memories, and more. Sometimes it contains a lot more. Even too much at times. Just because we experience things every day of our lives doesn't mean we have to take all those experiences with us everywhere we go. We're the boss of our own backpack. We get to choose what we put in it and what we don't. And we get to choose when it's time to unpack some things we've carried around for too long—things that will only weigh us down in the journey ahead.

Aside from the actions we take, our life's adventures and where they lead come down to two things: what we think about and what we forget about. This chapter is a critical component of an F-it-less life because it focuses on the importance of forgetting things for the sake of living the life you want and deserve.

Over time, I've found that there are two things that need to be forgotten. We've all relied on packing lists before, but this is my essential *unpacking* list. First of all, we have to forget about what people say or think about us. Second, we have to forget about the mistakes we've made up until now. Moving on in our lives requires us to leave these things behind. Toss them now, if you can.

I recommend this because many of us have spent too much of our lives trying to please others. In my opinion, this is normal. It's a part of life and a part of learning more about the world and, ultimately, about ourselves. However, there comes a time when we long to do something that, for whatever reason, feels right to us but likely won't be a hit among our friends, family, peers, and so forth. And if this longing doesn't go away—if it keeps gnawing at us—it's likely going to lead to an F-it! moment.

Let's be clear: We shouldn't wholly discount the approval of others throughout our entire life. There will be many occasions when some people's opinions will warrant consideration. However, life shouldn't be lived with an unhealthy level of concern for what others think, either. There must be a balance. Most important, when you're passionate about something, you should follow that energy to see where it leads you, even if it might be unpopular.

I have a saying: "If you help me pay my bills, then you get a vote." It's a reminder for me that people need to earn the right to influence me with their opinions. How many times have you asked yourself, *What would they say or think?* Who is this "they," anyway? Who knows? And yet, what this faceless (and sometimes even imaginary) "they" might say or think has squashed a million different pursuits of happiness, interest, curiosity, love, and who knows what else.

When my first wife, Jean, was pregnant with our eldest son, we waded into the all-too-dangerous discussion of baby names with friends and family. My wife was Catholic, which meant that biblical names were popular among her relatives. My family has always been less traditional, which means that I am too. Regardless, we stumbled upon the name Noble, and liked it a lot. I'll never forget tossing that name out to Jean's father one day, fishing for approval.

He said, "Noble?" with a weird, questioning tone. And then ... "What the hell kind of name is Noble?"

And that's when we decided to keep our ideas close to the vest from that point forward.

In the end, we did name our son Noble. I love his name, and I think he does too. Had we continued to poll our audience for a more "acceptable" alternative, however, Noble could have ended up being named something entirely different. I love that Noble has to spend the rest of his life living up to a name—his own.

In my life, it's become increasingly clear to me that being comfortable with and living out our individuality is our greatest gift to the world. It's the only way for each of us to maximize the part we play. God gave us all a sense of purpose. We each have our own internal compass to follow. Jesus wasn't sent here to be popular; He came to change the world. So were George Washington, Thomas Edison, Henry Ford, Elvis Presley, Abe Lincoln, Harriet Tubman, Mother Theresa, Martin Luther King Jr., Steve Jobs, Bill Gates—and you and me too. Big or small, our paths leave footprints and effect change. If we make choices based on popular opinion, who knows what opportunities for making an impact we might miss! Like Steve Jobs said, "If you want to make everyone happy...sell ice cream."

As we grow, we're influenced by our family and our friends. The thoughts we have, the words we use, our attitudes and actions— pretty much everything comes from the example of others. Our parents tell us we're this or that. Sometimes they tell us we'll be great at this, but *not* at that. They'll let us know in so many ways whether they think we're smart, funny, athletic, nice ... you get the picture. For the first X number of years, we live what I call an "outside-in" life, meaning that our outside influences program us to some degree about who we are. Oftentimes this outside-in programming works well, at least in part, and people live their lives on the continuum that was established for them before they could think for themselves. Other times, it doesn't work—and when it doesn't, we start to live an "inside-out" life, where we begin to question our programming and how various thoughts and assumptions about us surfaced.

Once the process of living inside-out starts, it's hard to stop it. Maybe you come from a family of athletes, yet all you want to do is sing; maybe you're gay and don't know how you're going to come out, but know you must; maybe you're a third- or fourth-generation doctor or attorney in the making, yet you know that you don't have a passion for the career you've always been told you're destined for. Once you know, you know. Then you have two choices: you either get busy living or get busy dying. Living inside-out is about following your internal compass regardless of what the people in the stands have to say about it. Whether the people you love embrace your path or hate it is irrelevant; it's just important to know who you can bring with you on your journey and who you can't. One thing's for sure—when you start living your truth, all the love and support that you need shows up. That's because the Universe is ready to reward your energy with *everything* you need in order to do *everything* you're capable of. The Universe is always conspiring to support the greatness within us all.

If you really want to live an inside-out life, you must be able to put mistakes in perspective. Mistakes exist to make us tougher and smarter. They aren't meant to leave us in the fetal position, scared to take any more risks going forward. Mistakes are part of the formula for ultimate success, happiness, and satisfaction. Without mistakes, we would have no sense of accomplishment. So don't worry about the mistakes you'll make, because you *will* make them. You're supposed to make them. No progress has ever been made without mistakes. Mistakes are life's best teachers.

Unfortunately, we live in a world where people are constantly covering up their mistakes in an effort to look as close to perfect as possible. We celebrate getting it right while booing the mistakes made along the way. This has created an epidemic of sorts—one in which people get crushed when they make a mistake. Too many people dwell on their mistakes and failures to the extent that they become depressed, angry, and emotionally and energetically likely to attract more failure.

My stepson, Andrew, was a Little League baseball player. He was good—good enough to make a summer All-Star league, in fact. His coach, however, recognized that his team was made up of a whole lot of kids who hated making mistakes. Just watch a ten-year-old at a baseball game and you'll see tears well up or a total emotional breakdown ensue when that kid strikes out, gets tagged out, or misses a play in the outfield. Andrew's coach tried to tell the kids on his team that getting out was as much a part of baseball as hitting a home run. In fact, he would say, "If you strike out two times and get on base once, you're an all-star batter!" Every time a kid made a mistake, he would yell, "Flush it!" Coach was reminding the player to forget about the error and just move on. Why? Because that's baseball, and that's life too. Crying about your mistakes after you make them only keeps you from doing better on the next play. It wasn't long before it was Andrew's turn to make a mistake. Tears welled then, too, and Coach yelled, as usual, "Flush it, Andrew! Flush it!" I saw Andrew acknowledge the command with eye contact, give a not-so-subtle forearm swipe across his eyes to "flush" the tears away, and try to focus on the next opportunity. It worked.

Flush it, forget it—it's all the same. What mistakes are you still crying about that are causing you to miss the next ball coming your way? It's time to stop it. Forget about it. Move on. Move up. You can't be an All-Star if you're playing with tears in your eyes. The game you're in right now requires clear vision and concentration on what's ahead, not on the ancient history of the last play.

CHAPTER ELEVEN
FAIL

•••••••••••••••••••••

Failure should be our teacher, not out undertaker.
Failure is delay, not defeat. It is a temporary
detour, not a dead end.
—DENIS WAITLEY

•••••••••••••••••••••

GIVEN OUR CURRENT SOCIAL MEDIA CLIMATE WHERE FAKE news abounds, I believe the world has become less honest and transparent. What do I mean by that? Look at your Instagram, Twitter, and other social media feeds. Most people are constantly posing as perfectionists. Everyone is going out of their way (and in some cases, broke!) to look better, happier, and more successful than they are. We spend our money, time, and energy going to great lengths to try to cover up our fractures, flaws, and failures. And perhaps nothing is more indicative of this less-than-honest portrayal of our lives than when we participate in the game of cover-up without even realizing it.

Botox, padded bras, padded jeans, Spanx, cosmetic surgery, hair transplants, designer clothes, Photoshop, credit cards, jewelry, houses, cars, and selfies are just a few examples of how we choose not to show the rest of the world the truth about the life we're living. We're constantly comparing our insides to everyone else's outsides. It's no wonder we get to a breaking point and finally say "F-it!" We may be the only ones to ever see our true insides, but believe me, everyone has internal struggles they battle with too.

When you're at work, how often do you hear someone say, "I really screwed this one up" or, "Boy, did I miss the mark on that" or, "I'd like to start this meeting by talking about our failures this week. I'll go first." *Never.* The people talking the loudest are the ones trying to convince the rest of us that their bag of poop smells better than everyone else's.

Putting lipstick on our metaphoric pigs and selling them as beauty queens has become an art form, if not the norm. If we can't see through that, how in the world are we supposed to get a clearer perspective on the value of failure, let alone embrace it?

Deep down, we know when we've failed. And as long as we're not bona fide sociopaths or narcissists, we feel bad about it. We may even feel guilty, remorseful, or regretful for what we did wrong, or for something we didn't do that would have been a better choice. We know the truth. We all do.

As a successful real estate broker, I've consulted with a lot of people over the years, from rookie agents to nervous buyers and sellers. I was in a coaching session once with a yet-to-be great agent. He was building his business at a painfully slow pace because he didn't want to make a single mistake. I had seen overly cautious people before. His fear of failure was not uncommon among agents, seasoned or new. "What if I mess this up? What if I offend someone? What will they say?" These were the worries halting his progress. He was clearly spending far too much time "getting ready to get ready," when he could have enjoyed quicker success by forging ahead and learning from his mistakes.

Frustrated by his pace, I called him into my office. I knew he was ready for a breakthrough, even if he didn't. All he needed was clarity, and perhaps a push. "Do you know what you remind me of?" I asked him. "You remind me of a bear that's chewing off his own leg so he won't get it caught in a trap."

The agent looked at me wide-eyed. What I'd said shocked him.

Without saying a single word, he stood up and walked out of my office. Later that day, he closed his first sale.

When you think about it, accepting failure shouldn't be so hard, but it is. After all, most of our infancy and childhood is spent falling down and getting back up—failing and trying again—over and over as we progress from crawling to walking. It's how we evolved as a species. Somewhere along the way, though, most of us are taught that failure is a bad thing, that life is about winning, following the rules, and living as we're told we should instead of how we feel, think, and believe we should.

As a business leader, I teach classes on entrepreneurship. One of the first lessons is that the sign of a great leader is a willingness to fail. On average, entrepreneurs fail 3.8 times before they finally succeed in business. It took Henry Ford three tries before he turned the Ford Motor Company into a success. James Dyson designed more than 5,100 bagless vacuums before he built one that worked.

And even famous writers have struggled to achieve their current status. For example, Stephen King's first book *Carrie* was rejected by publishers 30 times before Doubleday eventually picked it up. Before that, he had mostly written stories for a men's magazine called *Cavalier*. He was in good company there as Ray Bradbury and Isaac Asimov also wrote for the publication. At some point, a reader of the magazine challenged King to write a piece featuring a strong female character. King accepted the challenge, perhaps to prove to himself and his readership that he was up to the task. What he wrote ultimately became the book *Carrie*. It proved to be a more difficult endeavor than he expected. He threw his first attempts at the manuscript in the trash. Thankfully his wife, Tabby, who is also a writer, discovered those discarded pages, read them, and strongly encouraged him to continue.

As King was creating the character of Carrie White, he drew from the characteristics of two lonely girls he recalled from his high school days, both of whom died tragically before the book was written. It took nearly a year for King to complete the manuscript to his satisfaction and to earn a thumbs-up from his wife. It's safe to say that he met the reader's challenge and even surpassed it, having created one of the most memorable and well-crafted female characters of the genre.

Doubleday paid King a $2,500 advance, which wasn't enough money for King to quit his day job as a teacher but was certainly enough to bolster his faith in his writing career. Sometime after the paperback edition of *Carrie* was published, King began to realize just how bright his future could be. It has been said that King made *Carrie* and, in turn, that *Carrie* made King. From there, of course, he went on to become the literary icon he is today. He is one of our most prolific authors, having published more than 60 novels, a half-dozen nonfiction books, and more than 200 short stories.

Many of us have a hard time distinguishing between success and failure. We often deny failure, or sometimes we identify with it to the point that we spend too much time chasing our losses in an effort to make them back. Other times we convince ourselves that there isn't much to be learned from a mistake because the mistake doesn't matter. But as Ken Iverson, the legendary former CEO of Nucor Steel, put it, "If something's worth doing, it's worth doing wrong. Get on with it and see if it works."

The sweetest victories in life are the ones that are most diffi-cult—the ones that require us to reach down deep inside, to fight with everything we've got, to be willing to leave something, if not everything—on the battlefield without knowing until that do-or-die moment if our heroic effort will be enough.

History doesn't celebrate defeat the way it does victory, though it should because it's the failures we endure along the way that we use as stepping stones to our success. The Beatles were rejected by Decca Studios because Decca thought they had no future in show business. Oprah Winfrey was fired from her first job in television because her employers didn't see her full poten-tial. J. K. Rowling was met with rejection twelve times before UK publisher Bloomsbury acquired what became *Harry Potter and the Philosopher's Stone*. And of course, Steve Jobs was uncere-moniously dismissed from Apple, the very company he founded when he was thirty years old. None of these "failures" stopped these legendary leaders from moving forward with their lives. They simply licked their wounds and moved on.

I've always loved the way Thomas Edison framed failure. He said, "I have not failed. I've just found ten thousand ways that won't work." Innovation happens in the space between failures. The problem you solve often looks different from the one you started out with, and that's part of the journey of trial and error. You will fail, but you can learn to move forward through persistence and the right mindset.

Our ability to put failure into a proper perspective is, perhaps, *the* most important component of living an F-it-less life. The problem is that kind of perspective is hard to find, let alone live by. Why? Most people avoid the prospect of failure at all costs.

Instead, they choose to play it safe. They don't dare push the envelope. They prefer to explore within safe boundaries.

Where's the fun in that?

When people don't recognize that failure is a necessary aspect of success, they tend to sweep the failures—and the lessons that are supposed to come from them—under the rug. Hidden failures cannot possibly guide one's next attempts. This is why failure often leads to more failure. If you can't analyze your mistakes because you're too busy masking them, you cannot possibly break the cycle. When you look at the person next to you who posts only the things they do well on Facebook and Instagram, you're only seeing half the picture. These people aren't making public proclamations about how they've screwed up. They hide their poor decisions from the world, but that certainly doesn't mean they're exempt from making them. The behavior of people who are untruthful in this way only makes you anxious, because it leads you to believe (erroneously) that you're somehow inferior— or, worse, it can make you feel that you have to cover up your failures too. Now I'm not saying that you need to broadcast them to the world, especially when they involve the feelings of others. But at the very least, you should own up to them with those who have been affected by them. When you conceal your failures, the silence can be downright toxic. No wonder so many people are on antidepressants!

Here's some good news: Your failures are not supposed to cause depression. They actually have the power to make you stronger, better, and more successful at whatever you've failed at. Failures ultimately pave the way for us to become the very best version of ourselves. With this in mind, why wouldn't you grab hold of them for everything they're worth? The only difference between the failures that hold us back and the failures that propel us forward is how we view them. If you believe that failure is bad, then it's as if a two-ton concrete weight has been wrapped around your ankles. You'll sink under the burden of those beliefs until you can see and fully believe that failure is a beneficial learning experience. Then, at least, you'll have the capacity to rebuild and rebound, and ultimately land on much higher ground.

Unless and until you learn how to use each failure to your advantage—to let it fuel your future—you will be stuck in an endless self-defeating loop.

We all have a desire to feel good about ourselves, but when we fail at something, we become less confident, and that chips away at our self-esteem. It makes us feel awful, which in turn stops many of us from trying new things or taking bigger risks. It can even make us afraid to break out of our comfort zones, even if we know they no longer serve us well.

But here's a news flash for you.

If you want to reach your greatest potential, you have to take risks. You can't fear failure. You have to push yourself to accept that it's a necessary step to unprecedented growth and success, whether personal or professional.

From sports, to business, to science, "Failure is not an option" has become a battle cry for many. Yet when you really think about it, there are times in our lives when failure is not only an option, it's one of life's best teachers. When we make a mistake, our default action is to avoid owning it. We tend to gloss over it or, worse, find a way to expunge it from our narrative. If you want to know one of life's greatest secrets, here it is: The desire to never be wrong is ... well, wrong. It's crucial to the development of human cognition to err. The greatest thinkers, leaders, athletes, and mavericks of the world will tell you that failure is as powerful a tool as any training they've ever received. They'll also tell you that most failures have added exponentially to their success. If given the choice of failing before ultimately succeeding or never trying at all, which would you pick?

Albert Einstein said, "Failure is success in progress." Man, I love that quote so much.

Sure, just saying the words "I failed" means opening yourself up to criticism and self-examination, but it can also mean opening yourself up to possibility.

I know that for some people, failure equates to giving up on a goal or dream. It can feel like a heavy burden. But it doesn't have to. And it certainly shouldn't *define* you.

So why do we fail in the first place? Is it a mindset issue, or is it caused by an external chain of events and actions?

To me, they're one and the same. To be certain, failure rarely comes from nowhere; it often comes from a buildup of constricting thoughts and fears on a subject. But what if you had a buildup of positive thoughts instead? When the explosive energy of those new thoughts is released, imagine the creativity and insight that could flow. It's like solving a complicated math equation. It's tough to understand at first, but when you walk away for a short while and let it marinate in your mind, suddenly the answer just comes to you. Failure creates moments when something is finally seen, found, or understood like never before. The value in that experience is immeasurable, because its primary purpose is to prepare us for what's next. What better way to learn what we need to know? You can't really plan for failure, but you can certainly learn to accept and embrace it.

Failure can lead to two different outcomes: despair or growth. The choice is yours. When things don't go as you would like them to, it's easy to become pissed off, disappointed, or even depressed. This is the perfect time to reframe your experience and see it from a different point of view. Ask yourself some very important questions, such as, "Why did this break down? Where did things get off track? What could I have done differently to change the outcome?" Failures are necessary in our lives to shake things up, to help us see things in a new light—and to take us to the next level. There's no doubt that all those bumps and bruises will leave some type of impact. The key is to allow those experiences to thicken your skin so you can take the hits. Believe me, they'll come, but eventually they'll be easier to handle. Before you know it, you'll find that every test of your fortitude, every knock to your ego, every fall that lands you on your bum, and every teachable moment has helped you grow. A lot of things in life can be hard to take, understand, or appreciate while they're happening. They may even feel insurmountable—but, most of the time, when we persevere and work through our setbacks, we emerge wiser and more capable than ever before. Being able to admit you've failed at any point along the way may feel uncomfortable, but it's a necessary step toward moving past that failure. Admitting to failure isn't giving up, giving in, or settling for a lower standard; on the contrary, it's a way of leaning in toward your fullest potential. *Everyone* fails. That's a fact. And that's okay. If you can embrace the notion that failure is a regular part of life, then you'll ultimately be able to swing the bat without missing the ball. Failure humbles us. It helps us remember who we really are and where we came from. Allow yourself to see the opportunities that result from it.

The most successful people I've ever known talk a lot more about how often they've failed, what they did wrong and the challenges they faced, overcame, and learned from, than they ever do about their successes and the things they did right.

Go back and reread that paragraph. Really.

Because this is some of the best business and life advice anyone ever gave me, and now I'm passing it along to you.

Knowing this, and then *living* it, will change everything you believe about success. Once you understand the value of failure, you'll never fear it again.

So when you're at your next board meeting or your child's school function, look at the person on your left and the person on your right and think to yourself, *I can fail faster than you.* And be okay with that. Why? Because it's been scientifically proven that an object in motion tends to stay in motion. Follow my logic here: An object won't change direction unless it hits something. Success and failure are both "something." Once you have a successful result, you're more likely to repeat that same behavior so that you keep getting great results. Likewise, an unsuccessful result (aka, failure) causes you to do things differently so you can get better results. Either way, you're making progress. Both success and failure move you forward, as long as you don't anchor yourself to whatever spot you're in right now.

Whether you are getting the results you want or not, you are so much closer to where you know you want to be, especially if you're paying attention. Results, either good or bad, provide necessary feedback. They're data. Use them. Assess them. And then move on. One thing is for sure: More feedback is better than less or none at all.

As you go forward, saying "F-it!" because you have a warped sense of failure is absolutely forbidden. Living an F-it-less life means loving yourself through your failures and believing that your failures will only make you better, stronger, smarter, wiser, more experienced, attractive, valuable, credible, unique, and lovable to yourself and to others.

So what if you have more scars than the other people on the podium? I would take that over never being on the podium at all because I was too scared to fall down during the race. Wouldn't you?

Let's stop feeling bad about ourselves by comparing our imperfect life to everyone else's Facebook life. So we got a peek through the keyhole of their world; let's not assume that we would want to trade our whole life for theirs. We all have our baggage. We've all put lipstick on our pigs. I have. You have. They have. We don't get to live other people's lives. We only get to live our own. And that's the beauty of life: it's ours. Our path, our journey, our story. If it's not filled with highs and lows, then it would be, well, boring.

CHAPTER TWELVE
FLEXIBLE

••••••••••••••••••••••

Stay committed in your decisions, but
stay flexible in your approach.
—TONY ROBBINS

••••••••••••••••••••••

ONE OF MY FAVORITE SAYINGS IS, "THE ONLY OUTCOME I'M attached to is the best possible outcome, and I may not yet know what that is."

Living your F-it-less life requires *flexibility*. Nothing worth fighting for ever comes easy, and it certainly doesn't come via a short, straight path. Sure, you may know what you want, when you want it, and perhaps how you want to get it, but at times you're going to have to be flexible with any or all of these variables. Remember, we make decisions based on what we know at the time. As we gain more experience and knowledge, or simply learn to recognize the Universe's nudges, we may decide to alter our previously planned path or destination based on what we now believe to be true for us.

I saw a Tai Chi presentation a couple of years ago. The instructor was demonstrating Tai Chi's benefits in self-defense and showed how a rigid body posture was the worst possible posture for taking a punch. By contrast, he revealed how a flexible posture could move with the punch, thereby taking away most, if not all, of its force. Flexibility is powerful when properly used.

Similarly, pursuing a life goal or destination with a come-hell-or-high-water mindset is a lot like assuming a rigid posture. It starts off with an antagonistic mental energy. The Law of Cause and Effect tells us that "Every cause has its effect, and every effect has its cause." In accordance with this law, every effect you see in your outside or physical world has a very specific cause, which originates in your inner or mental world. This is the essence of thought power. Every one of your thoughts, words, and actions sets a specific effect in motion, which materializes over time. To become the master of your destiny, you must first master your mind, for everything in your reality is a mental creation. Know that chance and luck do not exist. These are simply terms used by people who are unaware of the Law of Cause and Effect. Living F-it-lessly in a world of cause and effect is about positively changing your energy and the way you live your life. It means assuming a happy and peaceful stance—not a rigid one that anticipates conflict. To live an F-it-less life, you must plan for happiness and peace to be constant parts of your journey. That is perhaps the only nonnegotiable factor.

When my first wife and I divorced, I was determined to keep things civil. There is hurt in the air at the dissolution of any marriage and that was certainly the case with us. The emotional toll was difficult enough; I didn't want the legal process to be mean or ugly. As odd as it may sound, I simply wanted out in the fairest, least contentious way possible. If serenity, fulfillment, and forward motion were what I wanted more of in my life, then I knew I had to approach the divorce with as much intention for that as I could muster for my new life to head in that direction. I remember discussing this idea with my father before he died. He said, "That sounds great, but you do know that there's no such thing as an amicable divorce, right?" The truth is, I didn't know that. I believed I could navigate this stage as I'd hoped to, even under the incredibly difficult circumstances I had created. I was wrong. And along the way I definitely had to be flexible so that I could move on and live the new life I was seeking.

The first meeting with our attorneys about the divorce occurred after multiple legal papers had been served, answered, and contested. It was clear, based on the life and business we had built together, that this could be a more complicated, painful, and expensive process than either of us had expected. But there we were. After seventeen years of marriage, we were sitting across from each other in a law office conference room for reasons neither of us ever anticipated. Having both been well represented, the lawyers pretty much took over from there.

Just before this meeting, a great friend and confidant of mine had advised me to ask myself a critical question so as not to lose sight of the forest through the trees. She knew that the process of divorce often throws up a zillion smoke screens that send both sides chasing less important rabbits down unnecessary holes. She said, "You're going to be met with a lot of opposition, and not just from each other. The question you have to keep in your back pocket so that you can pull it out and ask it to yourself as often as possible is: *What price peace?*"

What price peace? Wow. Hearing that was like hearing angels sing. It was sobering. It was clarifying. It was freeing. My game of Rock, Paper, Scissors had a new option: peace. And peace had to win over all else. *What price peace?* was now my guiding principle, and not just for my divorce but for the rest of my life. If the reality of our lives is actually the answer to the questions we ask, I had a new, huge question that I was going to be asking a lot. In fact, I was going to ask it in stereo because I wanted the answer to resound through every part of my world.

When all was said and done, it took nearly a year for our attorneys to divide our assets fairly. And as it is with all divorces that involve attorneys, their hourly fees had to be considered as being part of the price of peace.

If you want a lesson in being flexible, divorce will give it to you. So will battling an illness, buying a car, establishing a business, building a house, getting married, moving in together, having children, or going on a diet. The point is that being flexible in order to get what you want is a part of life. It's certainly a part of an F-it-less life. Sometimes we think we want to fight for money, possessions, or any number of things, when all we really want is peace, love, happiness, security, passion, respect, purpose, significance, or freedom. And once we focus on *those*, being flexible becomes easy—certainly easier than fighting. Putting things into perspective enough that we can make decisions we're at peace with is at the core of my F-it-less life, and it will be for you too.

A few years ago, I read a book by Michael Roach called *The Diamond Cutter: The Buddha on Managing Your Business and Your Life*. In the book, Roach discusses the Buddhist principle of emptiness, which states that nothing has value in and of itself except for the value a person gives it. When I read this, it had a profound effect on me—one that enabled me to separate myself from situations and things enough to look at them objectively without bringing any personal attachment, bias, or value to them. It allowed me to be a better, higher-minded broker for my agents. And it also helped me be a better father, friend, and leader. Understanding this concept of emptiness enabled me to see more clearly what truly mattered in confusing, chaotic, and stressful situations. I had a new tool in my bag that gave me the ability to rise above the noise and offer advice and strategies that worked for both me and those who sought my counsel. It allowed me to see and share flexible solutions that led to preferred outcomes.

There once was a simple bumper sticker that rose to fame. Its message? "Shit Happens." Truly profound, right? The fact is, shit does happen. And we can either roll with it or not. There's another saying I love that may be a higher-brow version of the same message, and that is, "We make plans, and God laughs." It means that sometimes the ideas we have about our own direction or path may be trumped by the Big Guy. Once again, we can fight those clues, or we can adjust our plans and follow them where they lead.

Most sports teams enter a competitive game with a predefined plan or strategy to win. Once the contest begins, however, reality sets in and determines whether the plan will stand up to the conditions on the field and the performance of the opponent. In my experience, the team that's flexible enough to make the best adjustments along the way wins. How many times have you watched a team go into halftime trailing their opponent, only to come back in the second half, after altering or even scrapping their game plan altogether, and change the whole dynamic? It happens all the time. That's what great coaches and players do. They pay attention and make adjustments that get them what they want—a win for the team.

Whatever it is that you want out of your life, whatever desire burns within you, whatever game plan you've been following with disappointing results, consider this moment your halftime. You're in the locker room, able to make the changes you feel are needed to clinch the game. What plays are working for you? What plays need rethinking? Do you need to change your formation? Your path? Your teammates? Your coaches? Be flexible. Look as objectively as you can at all aspects of your situation. The only value things have is the value you give them. And the only outcome you should be attached to is the best possible one. Just consider the fact that you may not know what that is yet. Remain flexible, and you'll find the way to your F-it-less life.

CHAPTER THIRTEEN
FORKING

....

Yes, there are two paths you can go by, but in the long run, there's still time to change the road you're on.
—ROBERT PLANT, "STAIRWAY TO HEAVEN"

....

I'VE ALWAYS CONSIDERED MYSELF TO BE A PRETTY ADAPTABLE guy who's fairly unattached to specific outcomes unless I set my intention on something. After twenty-five years of working in real estate, I never thought that my career as I knew it was going to change when Jeri and I decided to make a life together. In fact, I always believed that my career and relationships could peacefully coexist no matter what was going on, because I could logically separate the two. But there were quite a few people around me who were unable to do the same around the time of my divorce.

In every breakup, mutual friends tend to fall into two camps. Consciously or unconsciously, they choose sides the way the whole world seemed to choose between Team Brad and Team Jen in the famous Pitt-Aniston split. Sometimes the sides that form are even; sometimes they're not. But no matter who is in your camp, it is still a sobering reality to see loyalties shift. You can only imagine how difficult it all was in our case, since the lines that were being drawn involved "work family." My ex-wife and I both held leadership positions in the company so showing any kind of empathy toward one or the other of us must have felt like choosing between parents at times.

Some of our more prescient colleagues recognized the inherent challenges ahead of us and encouraged me to strike out on my own and establish a new real estate firm to avoid all the messiness. Many even said they would follow me. But I longed to stay in the franchise that I helped to make such a success.

Somewhere along the way, however, it dawned on me that I couldn't be *equally* attached to the world I had known and a world of hopeful new prospects at the same time. Increasingly, I was feeling as if my feet were in two different canoes. If I didn't pick a canoe and make a choice about how to proceed soon, I was going to end up in the water, soaking wet, with nothing.

I confided in a colleague and mentor within the larger organization whom I had known for many years. I had always regarded him as a friend and was hopeful he could give me some guidance. I felt like I could talk openly with him about the conflicted reactions I was receiving from people I had worked with for a very long time. He and I had a common interest in leadership styles and shared core spiritual beliefs. I thought for sure that he would understand my decision to choose greater personal fulfillment and that he would be just the person to help me sort out some of the more delicate aspects of the situation I was in.

Sadly, the conversation did not go as planned. I was expecting support from an old friend, someone I looked to as a confidant and trusted advisor. Instead what I got somehow felt more like an intervention. To my surprise, another person who knew me well and whose opinion I also respected was there as "an added voice of reason." They were very clear about what I was up against, outlining the leadership roles that I would be forfeiting if I continued on my path. Up until that point I had thought of my situation as personal—one I could keep separate from my business life. But clearly, that was not the case.

I wasn't prepared for the conversation that took place that day. However, in retrospect, I view it as a necessary and important experience because it prompted me to know exactly which canoe to firmly plant both of my feet. I could not be persuaded to row in any other direction but forward. I was more certain than ever that I had to follow a new path with all the focus I could muster.

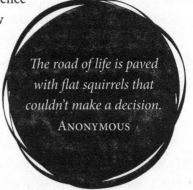

> *The road of life is paved with flat squirrels that couldn't make a decision.*
> — ANONYMOUS

Believe me, I had put a lot of thought and a great deal of energy into the changes I was making in my personal life before that conversation. I knew there would be challenges ahead for me and for others, though I didn't expect the kind of resistance I was receiving from people I had worked so closely with for so long, let alone from people I had respected and actually thought of as allies. I believed in my choice so deeply that I resolved it would be the route I took no matter what anyone else had to say.

You know that point on a roller coaster when you're climbing, climbing, climbing to the top of the first big hill, before the first big drop? The anxiety and the anticipation of what's to come is certainly uncertain. And then, you start flying. Faster and faster. So fast that you feel like you might fall off. And there's the resulting fear and comfort that all of that adrenaline will be over soon. Can you remember what that's like? That's what that day felt like for me. Everything sped up, became chaotic, bumpy and surprising. It was the beginning of the end of the ride for me as I had known it.

To be certain, I didn't leave that conversation thinking it was the best thing that had ever happened to me. It took time and perspective to see the real value of that encounter and even the sincerity of the advice that was offered, as much as I disagreed with it. But it did quickly force me to get real about my circumstances and to manifest the intention I had just put into the Universe.

It was a great moment—one I'll never forget, and, frankly, one that I'll always appreciate. At some point in your life, you'll face a big opportunity or challenge that—based on the decision you make—will likely significantly alter your future. This was definitely one of those choices for me.

I call these "forks," as in forks in the road. Why? Because we all fork our way through life, constantly making choices that lead us to one place or another—hopefully closer to where we want to be. The aim in moving forward is to create results. Sometimes, however, we create ambiguity so we won't have to make a decision. Guess what? All that does is complicate things.

Ultimately, confiding in this person I had sought reason from, and having the contentious discussion that ensued, helped me see that I was indeed at a fork in the road, and it also helped me choose my path. It allowed me to pick my own direction to fulfillment, and in the process it honed my focus, because there would be no turning back from this point onward. I couldn't control what thoughts or words anyone uttered or what actions they attempted to take to dissuade me. What I could control were my own actions based on what I believed I wanted. As a guy who grew up being a perpetual people pleaser, this was a real turning point for me. It was one of those mile markers in life where I had to make a grown-up decision that wasn't likely to please a lot of people. I could see the storm brewing on the road I had chosen, but I still dropped the top and screamed, "Bring it on!" as loud as I could.

And you know what?

It was damn freeing.

We live in a world where we constantly face forks; all day, every day we have decisions to make. We can do this or we can do that. We can make the decision to be the best version of ourselves, or not. We can choose to listen to God, or not. We can trust our God-given ideas or talk ourselves out of them. We can choose to embrace inspiration or to embrace fear. We do this *all day long*. Some of us do this more consciously than others. Either way, we do it. We fork.

This experience got me thinking about all the other forks I'd confronted and the choices I'd made that brought me to this exact point in my life. I was curious about what a map of those choices would look like if I actually drew it out on a piece of paper. I began

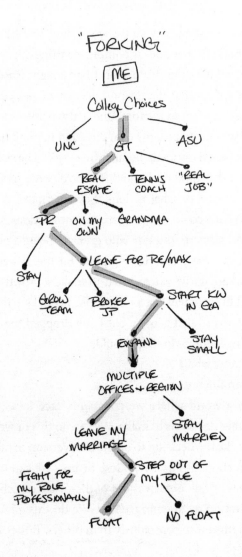

with my earliest adult decision about where to attend college and followed the trajectory to my choice of real estate over a regular nine-to-five office job. Then I traced other choices, from working for my grandmother or for RE/MAX to playing things safe or taking risks, and on and on. (See the diagram on next page.)

This was quite an interesting exercise because it showed me, in a visual way, the various directions I'd taken over the years and the times in my life when I thought I was forking one way only to find myself moving in a different direction because of unexpected circumstances. Sometimes I changed direction in an instant; other times it felt like looking for lost car keys—the moment you give up looking is when they finally appear right in front of you. Forking is nothing more than a change in direction—a recalibration. There isn't much architecture to it other than to allow the plan to unfold instead of fighting it. Ultimately accepting that it's someone else's plan for you helps you let go of that control. The less resistance you put up, the easier it is to move forward.

As a broker and owner of seven real estate offices, I've faced many forks throughout my career, including when I had to decide if it was time to grow or to stay safely where we were. Growing meant taking risks, spending money, and stretching beyond our comfort zone. There were lots of times when the security of playing things safe was more appealing. In real estate, it's easy to get to a place where offers come in and you just take them. If you do that long enough, you can forget what it's like to go back to basics or to play hardball. The fear of losing a deal overpowers the instinct or desire to take risks. And yet it's those gambles that often pay off, especially when the stakes are high. Sometimes we get so complacent that we forget what got us to where we are.

When you think about it, you typically make dozens of decisions a day, from whom you'll socialize with to whether you'll have a slice of pizza or a salad for lunch. Decisions abound in short-term planning and in long-term planning—and they definitely crop up when you start losing your grip on people, places, positions, or things you thought you'd never leave! You're either making a decision to become the best version of yourself or something less than that at all times. Granted, some choices are harder to make than others, and often for good reason. There are many variables that can impact those decisions, including mood, mindset, personal situations, financial circumstances, and career concerns, just to name a few. The specifics of the decision itself can have their own implications. Whatever choices you're called upon to make, there will always be some degree of pressure, which can result in your feeling stuck or, worse, completely paralyzed and unable to choose a path.

Earlier in the book, I talked about Leading with Faith, my name for Colin Powell's forty-seventy rule, which he devised to help him make good decisions. This rule applies to the kinds of choices we must make when we arrive at major forks in our life. Tapping into our intuition to fill in the information gap and trusting our gut more are critical components of the process, especially when we don't have all the information we'd like, or when some unexpected circumstance changes the playing field. You won't always make the right decision, of course, but hopefully you'll make more correct ones than wrong ones. If you want certainty, you'll never make a move at all. People who look for certainty fear change. They don't trust their gut feelings or listen to their intuition. They look for perfection, and by now we know that there is no such thing.

It's been said that all roads lead somewhere. Perhaps our greatest growth comes from figuring out how to be okay even when we don't know where our road is headed. I've always had a strong belief that things happen the way they are supposed to in life, so I don't try to control a lot as I move forward. I can't fathom explaining where I see myself in five years. Anyone who can answer that question is either lying or dreaming. How do I know this? Simple: The existence of forks tells us so. We must all fork our way to where we're supposed to be.

While knowledge is power in most situations, when it comes to forking, you also have to assess and understand what you *don't* know. Then you have to filter whatever information you gather so you can properly weigh your options. I once heard that the number-one trait among successful entrepreneurs was having a high tolerance for ambiguity. If you can accept not knowing what's coming next, then you are well-positioned to thrive in life and business. So while minimizing risk is important, it's fully understanding what you don't know that helps you formulate your best choices. You can't always see that from your purview. If your decision seems to be motivated by a gut reaction instead of fully rational thinking, then take your time. Sleep on it. Give yourself some space away from outside factors. Often, the answer will come before you succumb to an impulsive response you might later regret. Doing this is important in business and in life.

Everyone can learn to make better, more sound decisions, even under adverse circumstances, but it's a skill set that needs to be developed like any other. Nothing tests you more in life than your ability to assess a situation and act upon it decisively.

Why do most people fail?

They make poor choices that lead to bad decisions. And, in some cases, those bad decisions can have serious compound effects, leading to other bad decisions.

All of us know what goals and plans are. If you're in business, I'm sure that, like me, you've been asked many times what your objectives are and where you see yourself in X number of years. And, like me, you've probably come up with some pretty good answers to both questions—answers that you believed in and were committed to at the time. I bet if you were asked the same questions right now, you'd probably have no problem listing a few current goals.

But what if I told you that your answers are quite possibly meaningless just because they're *your* answers? When compared to what God or the Universe or the Divine has planned for you, they very likely are. How can we have a better answer to the question, "Where do you see yourself in X number of years?" than God does? Perhaps this is why Woody Allen said, "If you want to make God laugh, tell him about your plans."

To be clear, business goals are requirements of most jobs. They typically have to be specific and time-bound. However, when it comes to personal or life goals, perhaps it's better to be more general and conceptual than it is to be specific. All of us like to exercise—and even tout—our free will. However, specific life goals can edge God or the Universe or the Divine out of the equation by not allowing room for what He, She, or It may have in store for us.

Dr. Ihaleakala Hew Len, co-author of *Zero Limits: The Secret Hawaiian System for Wealth, Health, Peace, and More*, writes that our personal intentions and reactions can be created only by our personal memories. He believes, as I understand it, that anything created by our memories limits us compared to what the Universe wants for us. He has a simple and powerful method for cleaning and erasing our memories (just like we clean the hard drives in our computers) so that we can get to zero and allow the Divine to work through us, without us unintentionally pushing back or interfering.

If you think about it, it's our collection of personal experiences or memories that determines our free will (or *free won't*) to act upon a divinely generated impulse or idea. Once an idea comes to us, we put it through our personal filters to decide whether we'll play or pass. And it's our memories and experiences that determine how faithfully (or not) we move into our future.

The challenge is this: How do we get better at moving our limited selves out of the Divine's way so that we can live in greater alignment with our destiny and the life of inspiration intended for us? I think the key to this, in some way, is to stop pretending to be able to plan better than the Grand Planner of our life and to trust the inspirational nudges that the Universe provides for us. Joe Vitale, co-author of *Zero Limits*, may have nailed it in his response to the question, "Where do you see yourself a year from now?" He simply said, "Wherever I'll be will be far better than what I can imagine right now."

My wish for all of us is that we can be more in tune, more open, more trusting, more excited about, more in love with, and thus more in alignment with what God or the Universe or the Divine wants for us. This requires that we plan less and listen more. It requires us to be still more. It requires an acknowledgment that we currently don't have the capacity to see or comprehend what the best version of ourselves could be.

Overfocusing on the next moment of our lives only lessens our experience of the current moment. Wherever you are, *be* there. Trust that you are exactly where you're supposed to be. The better we are in this moment, the better our next moment will be, and the more likely it is that we'll fork our way to a greater version of our life than we ever could have imagined.

F-It-Less Exercise: Forking

Take a moment now before moving on to the next chapter of this book—
and the next chapter in your life—to map out your forking path so far. What
choices have brought you to where you are today? Looking back, would
you have made any different choices? If so, in what way do you think those
alternate choices would have impacted your journey?

CHAPTER FOURTEEN
FAITH

· · · · · · · · · · · · · · · · · · · ·

Those who pray, who have faith in and a relationship with God,
shall live with the fruit of the Spirit, which is love, joy, peace,
patience, kindness, goodness, faithfulness, and self-control.
—Galatians 5:22 (KJV)

· · · · · · · · · · · · · · · · · · · ·

I DON'T THINK I'VE EVER MET ANYONE WHO SAID, "I WANT TO burn in hell when I die." However, a part of being human is being imperfect and making mistakes. We've all done things that, in the absence of other good deeds and decisions, might keep us out of heaven. Living life is a process of trial and error. No one gets things right on the first try. Screwing up, in whatever capacity, is usually the best way to learn why and how we need to do better. That's because we learn more from experience than any other way. We can read about how to live a great life; we can be told how to live a great life; we can be shown by example how to live a great life; but sooner or later, it's our *trying* to live a great life that truly gets us there. Trying is a process. Trying is doing what we think is right and putting forth the effort we think is required, even though we sometimes fall short. Trying gives us results to wrestle with. It teaches us through pain, frustration, and the regret of failure. Trying shows us as much about what doesn't work as what does.

Sometimes, we try and succeed. Other times, we try and fail. Either way, we learn only when we try. As I've talked about before, mistakes are some of the biggest ingredients of success. Failing forward is very likely the most assured path to an F-it-less life. If you've been fighting progress by wanting to be right all the time, then buckle up. The road is supposed to be bumpy.

At this point, you may be thinking, *So, how do I keep my wits about me amid all of these potential failures?*

My answer?

Faith.

Faith is the firm belief in something for which there is no proof. It's a belief in something or someone bigger than you.

I realize that faith is an incredibly personal topic, so do with this F-word as you wish. However, this is my story, and I'd be remiss if I didn't share my beliefs on the topic with you, as faith is one of the most important F-words in my walk of life.

When I read Galatians 5:22, I believe it's the Bible's way of telling us that we're meant to live an F-it-less life—a life filled with love, joy, peace, patience, kindness, goodness, faithfulness, and control of ourselves.

But what if life doesn't always feel that way?

In his books *Letting Go: The Pathway of Surrender* and *Power vs. Force: The Hidden Determinants of Human Behavior*, the brilliant author David R. Hawkins delves deeply into the topic of human consciousness. He presents the theory that the human mind has a limited ability to distinguish truth from falsity until greater consciousness is attained. In fact, he presents readers with an incredible tool he created called the Map of Consciousness. It's intended to help pinpoint where you are developmentally on the journey toward achieving *total* consciousness (aka, arriving at pure truth or enlightenment). His aim is to give you the most accurate picture possible—as clear as a street image on Google Maps. No blind spots. If you can take an honest look at where you stand in the moment, then you can see how to move from there to higher and healthier states of awareness and being.

I was turned on to Dr. Hawkins's work by Mark Willis, the former CEO of Keller Williams, and I have since shared it with many people all over the country. In his Map of Consciousness, Hawkins assigns a point value to a wide range of feelings and emotions and shows how each drives our assessment of our lives; determines how we process different events, including various trials and tribulations; and even affects how we view God. For instance, Hawkins maintains that people who are consumed by shame and humiliation view God as a despising God; consequently, shame and humiliation rank as the lowest levels of energy and life on the Map of Consciousness. Much higher on the scale are the emotions of love and reverence. It's in these latter states of mind that people believe God to be loving and forgiving. Enlightenment is, of course, the highest form of spiritual energy. Those who have achieved this level see God in themselves and others and accept all things and people for who and what they are. I've always believed that God has been a part of my life, and that He has great plans for me. My grandmother was a strong Christian woman who taught me about God, Jesus, and the Holy Spirit. And while I'm not the most exemplary Christian, I am a Christian, nonetheless. But you don't need to be a Christian to have faith.

Faith comes in all shapes and sizes, is represented in all religions, and is held closely by the vast majority of people. And whether we hold Christian, Jewish, Muslim, or other beliefs, we're all just trying to get to a better place, albeit in different cars. Whether we call it the Universe, the Creator, God, or something else, we're all talking about some version of the same infinite force. We're all aware of and blessed and protected by a presence greater than ourselves, who loves us and wants the best for us.

To be certain, faith can be represented many different ways. I bought into Jesus at an early age, and as in most parent-child relationships, I've relied on Him, yelled at Him, questioned Him, left Him, and come back to Him throughout my life. And while I've gone through myriad emotions as a Christian, I've never doubted His love for me.

Faith.

When I was in college at Georgia Tech, I got away from my relationship with God. I quit going to church, and on some level, I was questioning what I knew about Him. It wasn't that I didn't believe in God anymore; it was more like I was just distancing myself from Him on some level. Maybe even testing Him. I had been a good but not great student in high school. Unlike most of the other, smarter kids who went to Tech, I had to really study in high school to get the grades I received. If you know anything about Georgia Tech, you probably know that pretty smart people go there. I would say that *only* really smart people go there, except for the fact that I did, so that statement wouldn't be true. My introduction to the rigors of Georgia Tech academics was rough. I remember studying endlessly during the first quarter of my freshman year for an accounting test only to get a D on it. I was convinced then that it was going to be a *long* four years.

One evening, I happened to drive by Trinity Presbyterian church, a beautiful house of worship on Howell Mill Road.

Its long, green front lawn, flanked by tall trees on either side, gently sloped upward to where the large brick sanctuary was perched. Its huge steeple soared toward heaven. Something in my gut told me to turn in. No one was there. I drove to the empty parking lot next to the main building. Two spotlights shined high enough to illuminate the spire at the very top. I just stared at it, mesmerized. My neck started to ache from looking straight up, so I walked to the grass in front of the church and sat down. Before long I was actually lying down, talking to God for the first time in what felt like forever. I talked out loud. I wasn't praying—I was talking. I talked for hours. I told Him how intimidated I was about being at Georgia Tech and asked for His help. I told Him about everything that was bothering me. And for some reason, I felt better, although nothing had changed. I liked the feeling so much that I came back again, and again . . . and again . . . for the four years that followed. I drove to that church at night and would lie in the grass, talking to God, until I left with a degree in industrial management.

As soon as I graduated, I thought the least I could do was actually go inside that church. So I attended a service there on a Sunday morning. Interestingly, they were expecting their new minister to arrive in the coming weeks, a woman by the name of Joanna Adams. That was somewhat coincidental, because my grandfather's sister was a pioneering female Presbyterian minister and author. I took that as a sign and came back again to see this new preacher. She was fantastic—smart, enthusiastic, and funny. She was a great speaker, and someone I knew would have a big impact on my life. I was so impressed with her that I invited friends and family to come see her preach. Joanna ended up officiating my brother's wedding, then my mother and step-father's wedding, and, ultimately, she presided over my and Jeri's wedding in 2015. Having Joanna officiate for us was like a full-circle, F-it-less faith experience for me. Even as I write this, it brings a smile to my face.

Most of us seek independence in life. Some people do it a couple of memorable times, while others seem to make a habit of it. Free will is our right as humans. We get to make choices and live with their consequences. Sometimes we love the consequences; other times we regret them. Sometimes we're rewarded; other times we're punished. That's life as a human being. That's life for anyone other than Jesus. At least, that's how I understand it.

For me, F-it-less living becomes so much more attainable when you have a healthy relationship with what I know as God. I believe that God is a loving and forgiving God—a parent, if you will, who loves us unconditionally and wants us to live the very best life we can, who knows we're going to F things up along the way, and who's going to forgive us for our sins and transgressions.

When I was leading one of the top real estate franchises in the country, I had many opportunities to coach and counsel my agents with regard to both personal and professional problems. We've all heard the phrase, "When it rains, it pours." Well, it's usually at that point when people finally ask for help. After listening to someone's problems, I would inevitably ask, "How would you rate your spiritual relationship on a scale from one to ten?" Anytime the person answered that question with a seven or less, I recommended that they read a proverb a day for thirty days. And almost without exception, they would report back to me that things either had gotten better or that they had gotten better at dealing with things. We tend to be better when we're connected to our source.

There's an energy and a deep-rooted sense of peace and strength that comes from having a spiritual relationship of this sort. That's because it's in our DNA, and because our heart knows more than our brain ever will. That's why we don't have to understand some things to know they exist—such as God, love, and faith. When we have enough faith to make room for God—whether through prayer, meditation, reading the Bible, or simply and consciously acknowledging our faith—things start to change for the better. Besides, sometimes the path we choose makes us feel like God is the only other person in our foxhole, and if we're going to make the choices that we need to make to live the F-it-less life we seek, trust me, it's going to be easier if we have faith. Sure, you can achieve an F-it-less-life without faith, but I think having faith makes it easier.

CHAPTER FIFTEEN
FOXHOLE

••••••••••••••••••••

Beware of those in your circle, but not in your corner.
—ANONYMOUS

••••••••••••••••••••

THERE HAVE BEEN MANY TIMES IN MY LIFE AND CAREER WHEN I've made unpopular decisions, big and small. Parents, friends, employees, my children, my ex, and my wife can attest to that. We've all been there, and if we have conviction in our choices, especially the big ones, then we need to weather the ambiguity, the confusion, the disappointment, or the disapproval no matter how much they appear to complicate matters.

Understanding that I couldn't be in two boats at the same time, in rough waters, and expect to keep afloat was an idea that stuck with me. As I said before, my feet could no longer remain in two separate canoes if I expected to get very far in my new journey. That epiphany simplified my focus. I couldn't go about making changes in my life and also control what anyone else was going to do from then on. What I could focus on was what I believed I wanted and making the choices and taking the actions that would make it a reality.

For the first time I realized that I couldn't please everyone, nor should I try. I needed to hunker down, regroup, and rethink my life's direction. In the process I created another new and very important F-word, which has since become a powerful source of comfort and perspective for me. That F-word is *Foxhole.*

> *All work and no play makes Jack a dull boy.*
> —JACK NICHOLSON AS JACK TORRANCE IN *THE SHINING*

Foxholes have been used for defensive purposes in war for centuries. They offer protection to soldiers and provide easy access to supplies that might be stored along the way during an encounter.

Whenever foxholes don't exist, soldiers have to create them using shovels, the butts of their guns, random sticks or rocks, or even their hands. The need for foxholes in battle is simply that important. Whether they're pits or trenches, they allow for strategic defensive positioning. Soldiers can't get through basic training without learning to dig and maintain a foxhole. It's been said that a foxhole is never truly done. It remains a work in progress because it must continually be improved and maintained.

The trenches I dug at the time were more for dodging bullets than firing any of my own. Going into foxhole mode was fascinating. If you've ever been in a noisy pool and have dived to the bottom, then you've experienced the same overwhelming quiet and stillness I did. It felt as if all the action above the water shifted into silent, slow motion. Everything I had been hearing before was in stereo; now it was reduced to dull white noise playing in the background. It was serene, benign, and exciting in a weird and ambiguous sort of way. I could think clearly there, away from any outside influences. If I've learned anything from Gary Keller, it's that focusing on your *one thing* (read that as your *most important thing*) is the best way to get where you want to go.

The plan for my new balanced and happy life included lots of love—sustained self-love and care, love of family, love of God, and romantic love too. Jeri and I were nurturing our relationship during this pivotal time so cocooning ourselves in the foxhole was almost instinctual. I found it a great place to duck distractions and to sort my best course of action individually and together. I believe it was the same kind of refuge for her.

Once soldiers are in their foxholes, their number-one priority is keeping their foxhole buddies alive. The key to that is trust—trust that their buddies will protect their vulnerable side and have their back. If that trust is broken, or if it even begins to waver, everyone in the foxhole becomes susceptible to outside forces. Talk to any soldier and they'll tell you the value in having a foxhole buddy—the kind of friend you make for life because of a shared emotional experience. There's a deep bond and camaraderie among those men and women who endure significant experiences together, a connection that can't be severed. Naturally, Jeri's and my feelings for each other intensified during this time.

There was no way for me to predict who else among our family, friends, colleagues, and neighbors might join us in our foxhole or how long they would stay, but those who did come solidified a place in my heart. Knowing someone has your back means everything.

Others thought that digging a foxhole was the equivalent of shrinking away from the very change I was hoping to make. But it was not. What I learned from that time in the trenches is that when you simply decide what and who is important to you, as well as what and who is *not*, you can make decisions without angst or concern for anyone or anything outside your foxhole.

Don't get me wrong—I wrestled with the egotistical pull to be wanted, needed, and appreciated like I had been for years. As I mentioned earlier, many people urged me to leave Keller Williams and start my own real estate company. They even vowed to follow me anywhere I went. But doing that would have been all about ego. Recognizing that made it easy to say no. My foxhole had no room for ego. And the funny thing about saying no is, the more you do it, the better you get at it and the easier it becomes. Foxholes don't have room for the unnecessary. They're protective survival bunkers, not luxury beachfront homes.

The true friends who joined me in the foxhole along the way understood this was about more than staking a claim in the real estate business. It was about more than selling homes. It was about building a happy one for me to spec, with all the comforts and features I had come to realize were not luxuries, but rather, downright necessities.

What's fascinating to me about a crisis is that when you're in one, it becomes crystal clear who your foxhole buddies really are. You can't help but be surprised by who shows up for the cause, and perhaps even more by who doesn't.

A friend of mine, Pat Flood, built one of the most successful mortgage companies in the real estate business. He took his company public in the early 2000s, but just seven years later, at the beginning of the economic crisis, it went under. Pat endured what many perceived to be a very public business failure, only to rise again and succeed with a new, and arguably better, company. Having survived the court of public opinion himself, Pat graciously counseled me to be prepared. He said that I was going to be unfairly judged by many people, none of whom had any right to judge anyone. He told me that I would have to find a way to ignore them. True to form, and my experience with him, Pat was right.

Another person offered similar comfort, saying that whatever people's reactions were going to be would have nothing to do with me or what I'd done; rather, it would have everything to do with them, their life story, and those personal memories or experiences my choices brought up for them. These two pieces of advice were timely for me. They provided a critical perspective that I took with me into my foxhole.

Henry David Thoreau said, "Most men lead lives of quiet desperation and die with their song still inside them."

I didn't want to be that guy. Not anymore.

During the months we were hunkered down with each other, Jeri and I grew even closer. We shared many conversations about how we felt, who we were at our core, and what we hoped the future might look like for us individually and together. We didn't share our dialogue with anyone, not even our closest confidants. Being in our foxhole together created a bond between us that will never be broken.

These conversations helped me find clarity on what I wanted—and I mean *truly* wanted—because it made me more keenly aware of the breadth of possibility that was *out* there, and *in* the foxhole, for me.

Once the toothpaste is out of the tube, there's no putting it back. And you have to be okay with that. Whatever big life change you're contemplating, starting it is the hardest step. Completing it is the second toughest. After that, it's easy. 😊 That's because you're likely going against the grain. You're doing something that isn't expected of you or that may actually be disapproved of by others in some—or *every*—way. Digging your foxhole is the only way to successfully see you through your first step, and through every step after that. Digging your foxhole is the only way to protect against the land mines laid between You 1.0 and You 2.0. So dig it. If you don't, you may just end up being other people's target practice for the rest of your life.

CHAPTER SIXTEEN
FLOAT

．．．．．．．．．．．．．．．．．．．．

Don't underestimate the value of doing nothing, of just going along, listening to all the things you can't hear, and not bothering. Doing nothing often leads to the very best something.
—Winnie the Pooh

．．．．．．．．．．．．．．．．．．．．

IT'S 6:00 A.M. AND STILL DARK OUTSIDE. I'VE ALWAYS BEEN AN early riser because, somewhere along the way, I learned that the early bird catches the worm. I'm armed with my favorite journal and a large thermos of freshly brewed coffee. As I open the door of my lake house to the dawn, the silence is broken by birds chirping to one another in the trees that surround the house. I breathe in the fresh air, filling my lungs with the promise of a new day as I head down the narrow dirt path from the house to the lake. The slow lapping of the water against my boat, moored at the wooden dock, beckons me.

I have looked forward to this moment all week.

A slow turn of the key starts the engine, and I hear the motor purr like a sports car idling in first gear. After untying the ropes and pulling up the buoys, I turn the steering wheel away from the shore, push the throttle down, and begin to accelerate, deliberately disturbing the peaceful stillness of morning. I keep pushing forward, going faster and faster, feeling the cool wind and splash of the water against my body. I love the solitude of being the only one up and at 'em at this time of day. I feel my power and potential as the boat practically vaults from one wave to the next. The *thump, thump, thump* of its hull hitting the water upon landing is the only thing I can hear as I take in the overwhelming beauty of God's early-morning artistry. Pinks, oranges, and yellows miraculously meld into the gray skies as the sun emerges above the horizon.

The throttle is now fully open, and the boat is at top speed. The cap I'm wearing is turned backward to keep from getting blown off by the wind. While the rest of the world sleeps, I feel incredibly alive.

As I approach the middle of the widest portion of the lake at full speed, I reach for the key and turn off the engine.

I don't throttle back—I just kill it.

What had just been a complete thrill ride of acceleration becomes a still, silent, utterly peaceful float.

No more noise. No more wind. No more steering.

The boat is just coasting with inertia.

No matter how many times I've been here, and as much as I've enjoyed the speed, the peace is even more intoxicating.

I lean back, prop my feet up, take a sip of my coffee, and absorb everything about this scene. It never grows old. With every breath I take in, I am calmed, comforted, and centered. The waves catch up to my still boat, gently rocking it from side to side. I feel cradled and safe. I notice a carp splash above the water to my right, while a blue heron glides toward a tree on the shore.

As much as I like to drive, there's something mesmerizing about the way I feel in the middle of this lake.

Stopped.

I move only if moved by the Universe, and only in the direction it chooses for me. I'm floating, and it feels incredibly calm, incredibly freeing. This is where I think. Where I meditate. Where I'm inspired by music or by the sheer silence. I record my hopes and dreams and all the things for which I'm thankful in my journal. I pray. I take in the rising sun and practice gratitude for all of God's great glory.

No phone, no email, no one needing me. This moment is mine.

It's a bubble.

One I sometimes wish I could bottle. I would crawl in and cocoon myself inside its peace forever.

Even at my busiest, this was my life several times a month. My lake house was my sanctuary. It was a luxury purchase that served as a great getaway from daily demands. Shutting down my engines and learning to float for a short time was a huge part of my weekend lake routine. It allowed me to recharge and renew, and then return home with all the energy and perspective I needed to handle the responsibilities and stresses to which I had become accustomed. Learning to *float*, as I came to call it, taught me to shut out the world around me for a moment. It proved to be a valuable life skill, especially in the years to come. Floating was a welcomed gift during a period of abrupt change in my life. One of the biggest complaints I used to hear from my agents was that they felt overwhelmed, overscheduled, and overcommitted. Even during their time off, they were busy going to the gym, attending social and charity events, taking their kids to sports practice, or over-engaging in social media—checking texts, emails, and Facebook posts. They were busy being busy, but not necessarily productively so. Whenever I would ask how they were doing, they would say, "I'm sick and tired of being sick and tired" or, "Things are crazy" or, "I'm swamped," which actually sent mixed messages about their desperation and pride more than anything else. Working harder is not necessarily working smarter. The fact is, most people are overloaded without realizing it. Let's face it—we all take better care of our devices than we do ourselves. Here's what I mean: Before you go to bed at night, I bet you plug in your phone and tablet to recharge their batteries. In fact, you've probably jumped out of bed more than once to make sure those things were actually plugged in. Am I right? But think about this: We wouldn't dream of going to sleep without recharging *those* batteries, and yet we rarely if ever recharge our own. We routinely deprive ourselves of a good night's sleep, a much-needed vacation, a long weekend away, or even a social media detox.

Why is that?

I've always been a big believer in the value of reflection, introspection, and time to float—the art of doing nothing.

We live in a world where the thought of being still for any period of time has become scary, unacceptable, and hard to do. And yet doing nothing may be the best thing we can do to induce a positive state of mind, nurture our creativity, and improve how we feel.

I have a good friend who says that her best ideas come to her in the shower. When you think about it, you can probably understand why: Her mind is free from all other distractions and she's able to tap into unconscious and innovative thinking.

We're living in a time of unprecedented opportunities for distraction. We're communicating like never before—across borders and time zones—on platforms, devices, computers, tablets, phones, apps, games . . . you name it. We're in contact twenty-four-seven. We're wired and wirelessly talking to, texting, tweeting, trending, and friending the other side of the room and the other side of the planet. We're spitting out the old in order to consume the new. The impact of more choices in entertainment and cyberspace is the loss of balance between action and reflection. All work and no rest make [your name here] a very frustrated and burned-out person. And it's this state of psychological burnout that gets us to a place of F-it.

I understand the plight.

Though we live in a country founded by pioneers who left their homes in search of better lives, ours is not a culture that generally encourages seemingly aimless wandering. Any type of drifting usually conjures up thoughts of idleness, trouble, and failure. Suspicious of leisure time, our culture puts a premium on quantifiable achievement, defining success as climbing the ladder one rung at a time. The options are either up or down and taking a detour could mean falling completely off. Most of us are work addicts, and our efforts are often rewarded, encouraged, and supported. Anything less is seen as lazy, unacceptable, or a waste of time. However, a multitude of studies show the negative impacts this drive can have, including mental and physical issues and lower productivity—the absolute opposite effect you might expect from all that hard work.

Most people wear hard work and exhaustion like badges of honor. They get so caught up in taking care of the world— meaning the people who matter most to them, but also, all too often, those who don't matter at all—they forget about taking care of themselves.

Everybody needs a little "me time." Some need it less than others, but most people need it more than they think they do. Many of you think you're the architect of your world, when in fact the Universe is constructing things on your behalf. If you're not doing what you need to do, the Universe will take care of it for you by closing off an old path and opening a new one. Though we tend to resist the change at first, once we can see it in the rearview mirror, we realize that this thing we thought was bad is actually the best thing that could have happened.

When I left all of my roles at Keller Williams, except that of investor, I wanted to tell the people I'd worked with and admired for years that they were wrong to judge my actions leading up to and including that decision. I went into fight-or-flight mode for sure, but I knew better than to let my emotions show in ways I would later regret. At the same time, I also felt as if a huge weight was lifted off my shoulders.

One thing I knew for sure was that I needed some time to clear my head—to collect my thoughts and think through my next steps to assess where I wanted to go with my career. Everything I was thinking and feeling needed to be reconciled.

Downtime for someone who was used to running at a hundred miles per hour wasn't going to come easy. While I'd perfected going away on vacation for a week or two without any sense of guilt or stress, this was going to be more than a quick break. This was a time for reflection, a time to pause and really think. I also needed to prepare myself for all the questions I knew people would ask—even the harmless but important ones, such as, "What are you going to do next?"

This got me thinking.

Before World War I, a university education in Germany—the privilege of men from well-to-do families—customarily included the grand European tour. The young men traveled leisurely, practicing their language skills, making useful contacts, and expanding their horizons. Typically setting out in horse-drawn carriages (and later on trains), they carried letters of introduction that opened doors for them in foreign places. This was known as a *Wanderjahr*.

With its double meaning of hiking and wandering, the *wander* portion of *Wanderjahr* suggests both a sense of purpose and the possibility of serendipity.

Maria Shriver gave a great speech at her daughter's graduation from USC on the power of the pause. She said that her daughter was struggling with the typical questions a new college graduate might get from friends and family: "What are you going to do after graduation? Do you have a job? Where will you be working? How much are they paying? Where are you going? Where will you be living?" And like many young adults, she didn't have the answers everyone was expecting; moreover, she didn't understand why she needed to. Maria encouraged her daughter and her entire graduating class to find the courage to hit the pause button instead of forcing decisions and answers that were bound to change anyway.

Try taking a break from communicating outwardly. Learn to listen to your inner voice and to communicate with yourself. Feel your strength and your vulnerability. Acknowledge your goodness; don't be afraid of it. Look at the areas in your life that aren't serving you, and then commit to understanding what got you to this place so you'll have the power to choose change. There are studies that show students who take gap years between high school and college or between college and their first professional job will often be more mature, more focused, and more aware of what they want to do.

When you give yourself the time to float, you can figure out what's important to you, discover what you love, and investigate what's real and true to you, so it can infuse and inform your work and life.

The truth is, it's okay to not always have everything perfectly figured out. It's also all right to give yourself a sabbatical. A sabbatical is an extended break from your job that gives you time to enhance your academic qualifications, reflect on your accomplishments, and decide how to prioritize your life and career. And yes, it's also okay to take an extended rest period due to professional burnout. While sabbaticals are typically a year in length, they don't need to be. They can be shorter or longer. It just depends on you. What's most important is that you use the time to get in touch with yourself, to think, reflect, heal, reframe, and repurpose your life.

There are times in life when we wobble through our decisions, but once you make them, you realize that wobbling is part of the process. The cool thing is that while you're wobbling, you're gaining a tremendous amount of freedom. This is the time to embrace the *float*—to embrace a willingness to do nothing and to let things unfold as they should instead of how you want them to.

Time is finite, but energy is always renewable.

CHAPTER SEVENTEEN
FUN

....

Just play. Have fun. Enjoy the game.
—MICHAEL JORDAN

....

WHEN MY SON NOBLE WAS A LITTLE BOY, INSTEAD OF SAYING "Have a good day," he would always say "Have a fun day!" It was cute.

Noble and my younger son, Steel, both attended Montessori school for their first three years. Jeri's boys also attended Montessori early on, and when I would see Jeri and her boys at the school, I would tell them, "Have a fun day!"

Jeri or her boys—or both—would refer to me as "Mr. Have a Fun Day Shaun," which is the name her boys first knew me as. Later, when Jeri's and my relationship became personal, it was shortened to "Mr. Have a Fun Day"; then it became "Mr. Fun Day" or "Fun Day Shaun," until finally it just became "Funday."

You can always see people trying to figure out what the boys are saying when they call me Funday in public. Regardless, I'm proud to be Funday.

If you've ever been on a Southwest Airlines flight, you've probably noticed that the flight attendants favor a fun approach to everything, even delays. It certainly beats the ho-hum practices of other airlines. A lot of businesses are starting to understand that, although their employees are working, there are many great benefits to allowing, or even inviting, some levity. Productivity goes up, morale is boosted, customers are happier, and there's a more positive overall environment.

Often, people shy away from the concepts of fun and playfulness because they believe that even the words themselves convey the wrong message, especially in the workplace. They don't want to be misperceived as placing a higher emphasis on fun than on work. But a little fun can go a long way toward offsetting all the negative noise we encounter each day.

So often successful people fail at fun. Not that they don't do things they enjoy, because most do; but if they have fun, it's usually in the course of other activities such as exercising, spending time with family, networking, supporting friends, and so on. Purposeful fun, however, can be had without any other reason.

In my opinion, fun makes the intolerable tolerable. We need fun, because sometimes life isn't. That's why having fun is a serious pursuit. Charles Darwin, Jean Piaget, Sigmund Freud, and Carl Jung have all studied the topic of fun and the value of play. In fact, in 1938, Dutch historian and theorist Johan Huizinga wrote in his book *Homo Ludens* (*Man the Player*) that "Play is older than culture, for culture . . . always presupposes human society, and animals have not waited for man to teach them their playing." If you've ever watched two puppies play together, you understand that the need to connect through fun is an inherent part of a happy existence. The absence of fun or play in one's life has been shown in countless studies to manifest a range of psychopathologies, including unhappiness, aggression, antisocial behavior, or even violence.

Fun can mean different things to different people. Think of what fun means to you. I'm not talking about doing something because it's good for you or expected of you, I'm talking about doing something because it's actually amusing, lighthearted, relaxing, and, you know, *fun*. When was the last time you had a very happy, joyful, engaging moment in your life? What were you doing to elicit this warm feeling of bliss? Camping? Playing a game? Going to see your favorite artist in concert? Visiting an amusement park? If you can't remember the last time you did something purely for the fun of it, it's definitely time to block out a day or so to pursue the real deal.

In this hectic and fast-paced life, most of us must make time for fun. We're so busy doing other things, including trying to keep others' negativity from seeping into our lives, that we forget to do the thing that came so naturally to us as kids—*play*! So make a playdate for yourself. An adult playdate. Do it now.

When did we stop believing in the merits of fun? When did it cease being so spontaneous?

What do you say to yourself to justify *not* having fun?

When did you decide you needed proof that having fun helps you maintain a better, more balanced, and healthier life?

Fun and the activity of play aren't inconsequential luxuries. They're absolute necessities for living an exceptional and F-it-less life.

History, along with recent studies, shows that the most successful and creative people engage in social play. It's a vital part of their development. Emotional control, social competency, personal resiliency, and curiosity are all skills that come from having fun, especially through normal play behavior. The best kinds of play are usually self-chosen, self-directed, not too serious, imaginative activities in which the journey is more valued than the destination. One thing everyone can connect with is a good laugh. Fun provides so many benefits to our lives, bodies, and spirits. So why, then, do we starve ourselves of something that fuels us?

Time to recharge is one of the greatest gifts you can give yourself and others. While there are those who believe that working harder and longer is more productive and increases performance, I've learned as a business leader that engaging in that type of nonstop behavior leads to unhappiness, discontent, high levels of stress, exhaustion, and feelings of being completely overwhelmed. If you don't allow yourself to renew and revitalize your mind, body, and spirit, you will eventually burn out. You have to give yourself a break from your daily stresses. Doing so refreshes you mentally and physically and gives you enough distance from the issues bogging you down to come back with a new perspective, better ideas, and better solutions. If you spend all your time focusing only on what others expect from you or what others need from you instead of what's good for you, chances are good that you're going to miss out on the benefits of all of your hard work. It's hard to *be* fun if you aren't *having* fun.

One thing fun must become is a habit—a practice that's hard to give up. Athletes call this "being in the zone." They're so laser focused on playing the game that nothing else matters. Research shows that having fun releases endorphins, the body's natural mood enhancers, which send messages of satisfaction and confidence to the brain, creating what we often refer to as a "natural high." Even the act of smiling can have this effect, because it changes your emotional state, reduces stress, and improves your ability to tolerate irritants. Even a fake smile induces this psychological response, though genuine joy is hard to top.

Psychologist Dr. Jeanne Segal has studied why play and creative learning are so beneficial to us. She suggests that people who have fun and display an overall attitude of positivity live an average of seven and a half years longer than those who have a negative outlook or who spend their life worrying and being stressed all the time. If you've gotten to a place of saying F-it in your life, chances are, the latter describes *you*. Excess stress compromises your immune system, making it easier for you to get sick. It triggers the release of cortisol in the body, setting your natural fight-or-flight response in motion, which in turn can cause all sorts of havoc, including weight gain, high blood pressure, and an increased heart rate. Cortisol comes in handy under certain circumstances—say, when you're being chased by a bear or are in other kinds of imminent danger—but contending with chronic anxiety is really hard on the body.

Taking a more carefree approach to some things will alleviate stress and help you deal better with whatever unexpected twists and turns you may face. Doing fun things, having a positive attitude, and maintaining a sense of playfulness—even when life gets hard—lowers your stress level, helps you think more clearly, and ultimately enables you to make better decisions. You can make the choice to have fun, to laugh, and to not take things too seriously, but this doesn't mean you don't recognize the challenges you're facing. You're just not allowing the proverbial Goliath to win. Think about it this way: you've survived 100 percent of the worst days you've faced so far. What can't you conquer with the right attitude? Remember, fear, more than any other emotion, holds us back from achieving our dreams.

We've all heard the saying "Work hard, play hard." And there's good reason to support that manifesto. Those who push themselves in their careers are equally driven to succeed at hobbies and leisure activities—aka, fun. What steps do you need to take to give yourself more fun? No matter how busy you are, making time for fun should be a priority. Make it a part of your weekly schedule. Put it in your calendar as an appointment you can't miss. It doesn't have to be an all-day affair; you can make it an hour if that's all the time you can carve out. The important thing is to make the commitment and to stick to it each and every week. (And if you can, try to disconnect from your electronics for that period of time.) What would you like to do? What have you dreamt about or put on your bucket list that inspires you, makes you smile, and gets you revved up? Be willing to step out of your comfort zone and try new things. If you're having a hard time answering these questions, feel free to dream big. Fantasize. (There's another F-word for you!) What does your perfect day look like? How would you spend an evening if nothing stood in your way? And, finally, be sure to let go of doing things out of obligation or because they're what others think you should do.

Now that you've got the memo, you may be asking, "How exactly do I start having fun, especially after such a long time?"

I was lucky enough to have several people reintroduce me to what was once instinctive behavior, and I promise you, it's like riding a bicycle: it'll all come back to you with a little practice.

When I was twenty-two years old, I listened to my first Tony Robbins tape. You read that right—*tape*, as in *cassette tape*, for those of you too young to know what that is. Someone gave it to me, as I recall. I remember driving up the inter- state and following dutifully along to an exercise Tony was leading on the power we have over our emotions. What he was emphasizing was the power that our physical state has on our mental and emotional states. He surmised that his listeners were likely strug- gling with something—a problem either big or small. Whatever it was, he asked that we think about it and acknowledge the feeling of anger or sadness or fear that it produced in us. Then he asked us to do something crazy: smile. And he didn't ask us to smile one of those wimpy, obligatory, get-this-picture-over- with smiles—you know, when your lips never separate and your teeth don't show. No, he asked that we smile the biggest, toothiest smile we could physically put on our face—a smile big enough to make us feel silly. And, as if he were in the car with me, he said, "If you're driving in your car while you're listening to this, even better! Take that huge smile and look around at other drivers and people on the street around you and wave at them with that big, huge, ridiculous smile. Look them in the eye and wave at them." I couldn't believe what I was doing. More important, I couldn't believe what I was *feeling*: joy. I was having fun. A smile was interrupting a perfectly sad or angry or fearful emotional moment for me. Or, more aptly, *having fun* was doing that. And then Tony told us to look ourselves in the mirror with that huge smile and try to hold on to a negative thought while maintaining

our facial posture of joy and positivity. I don't remember whether
he said it was impossible or nearly impossible, but either way, he
was right. Try it for yourself; you'll see. Fun is one of those things
in life that's often considered "not important" or "not a priority."
Many people seem to see fun as something entirely separate from
all things serious, like work or religion or certain relationships.
But it's not—or at least, in my opinion anyway, it shouldn't be.
Fun can be a part of anything, really. And what's more, fun is
only a decision or an action away! Ever listen to a great stand-up
comedian? They're the best at taking serious, real-life situations
and blowing holes in them so we can see just how ridiculously
humorous they are. The genius of comedy is that it often shines
a light on how tightly wound we tend be so we can laugh at the
absurdly funny side of life's most serious experiences, and, hence,
at ourselves. I would prescribe listening to stand-up comedy
routines in the car to anyone who wants to be happier. If you
want to have more fun, you have to start with laughter. And guess
what—there are people whose job it is to make you laugh!

I had the good fortune of being exposed to a man named Dr.
Fred. He was a mentor who taught me that if I want to achieve
big goals in my life, I have to start by creating a habit of achieving
small goals each day. After learning his methods, I taught them
to others in my real estate business for years, and I still do whenever lessons on goal-setting and achieving are warranted. Here's
how it works: Make a list of everything you can think of that
might contribute to your having a great day. Maybe it's waking
up no earlier than 8:00 a.m. Maybe it's enjoying a delicious cup
of coffee first thing in the morning, taking a walk, going to hot
yoga or SoulCycle, meditating or praying, having lunch with a
friend, making love to your spouse, hearing your children say "I

love you," watching your favorite TV show, reading a book—you get the point. What are the things you love enough to want to do on a daily basis, if you could design your life and schedule to include them? What things, if you could fit them in, would make your days more joyful?

Now, create a similar list for things you would do *weekly* because you think they'd help you have a truly great week. After that, make a list of the things that would make each *month* fantastic. Do another one for each *quarter* of the year. Then make a list of things that, if done just once or twice a year, would make your whole year incredible. Last, make a bucket list of all those things you want to do before you die. When all the lists are complete, congratulate yourself, because you've just created a plan—a plan for having more fun and more joy in your life. Dr. Fred's method works, as long as you pay attention to what I like to call the *punch line*: to achieve your goals, you've got to *hit* as many of your daily desires as you possibly can every day.

By teaching me this method of setting and achieving goals, Dr. Fred instilled in me a very important lesson: You can't achieve the big goals if you don't set and appreciate the small ones. If you want to initiate big changes and enjoy big accomplishments, you have to first create a habit of initiating small changes and enjoying small accomplishments. By focusing on all of the small things that we typically take for granted and giving them importance enough to be appreciated and celebrated as achievements in and of themselves, we train our mind to focus more naturally and more intentionally on what we want—and, even better, we begin to *expect* to succeed at whatever we're focused on.

I dare you to try this. I guarantee that you'll experience more pleasure and more fun if you do. We've all heard the saying that, "Life is 10 percent what happens to you and 90 percent how you respond." All of us have to deal with negative things and people in our lives, but just because this is true doesn't mean that we can't have fun and experience joy while doing so. Sometimes we need to step outside ourselves and our situation and try to see everything going on in our lives from above so we can put things in proper perspective. The kinds of dark-cloud people mentioned previously are sometimes unavoidable—but when they rain on our day, having some perspective and a little bit of humor give us a big, bold, colorful umbrella to happily stand under.

Years ago, two of my agents were involved in selling a professional athlete's expensive home in Atlanta. One of my agents represented the ball player, while the other represented the buyer. Something important came up for the listing agent at the last minute, and she couldn't attend the closing for the property. She asked that I go in her place, and I agreed to.

What I didn't know was that the FBI was involved in this transaction, because the buyer was one of the most wanted mortgage-fraud criminals in the country. Long story short, in the middle of the closing an entire SWAT team barged in, guns drawn, and arrested everyone present except for my agent and me. They pulled a firearm from a holster strapped to one of the buyer's legs, put everyone—including the attorney—in handcuffs, and escorted them away. It was quite a perp walk. I was dumbfounded, speechless, sad, and scared, to be honest. Never had I seen or even heard of such a thing happening.

In the hours and days that followed that event, my imagination, fueled by worry about what would come from this, began to grow and take on a life of its own. Before long, I'd practically convinced myself that I, as the broker/owner of the real estate company, was going to lose my license and go to jail. It started to consume me. This thing that started and finished inside an hour or so on a Friday afternoon had worked its way into almost every minute of my weekend. I had no sense of perspective, no logical way to stop this runaway train of thought. I remember having a conversation with Jeri about it a couple of days after it had happened. She talked me off the ledge. I can't remember exactly what she said to me, but I do remember thinking, *Yeah, I've been in this business, building a great company that does great things for people, for many, many years. There's no way I'm going to let a guy I've never even met before ruin me or everything we've worked so hard for.* That was it—that was the perspective that had eluded me for several days. And once I had it, the worrying stopped. I no longer let it take up more territory in my mind or my life than it warranted. Sure, it was an unresolved negative event, but I was able to lock it in a file drawer somewhere in my mind and move on to more important things. As the leader of my company, I had an obligation to compartmentalize the event so that I could take care of all the other agents and their business needs, which were many. And because that's what I loved to do professionally, I enjoyed the higher ground that higher thought led me to.

Compartmentalizing the difficult, scary, maddening parts of our lives in order to make room for the things and people that bring us joy is vitally important to living an F-it-less life. It's a skill that, whether habitual, top of mind, or buried beneath a pile of life's complications, is available to us all, right now and all the time. Just like Tony Robbins's instruction to simply smile a ridiculous smile or Dr. Fred's daily, weekly, monthly, yearly, lifelong goal-setting and appreciation strategy, there are simple things we can do to create more joy for ourselves today than we had yesterday. And, even better, if we can add more joy to our todays, our todays can add up to more joyful weeks, months, and years in our future.

Fun. Fun is joy. It's love. It's what we yearn for, what we seek whether we're aware of it or not. And when we've missed it or deprived ourselves of it for long enough, we regret it and crave it all the more. Peace, love, and joy are our high-water marks in life. We naturally gravitate to them. Whatever restlessness you have right now, chances are that it stems from a lack of peace, love, or joy. We were born for joy, for fun, but unless we make it a priority or a standard to protect in our lives, fun can easily get pushed lower and lower on our daily to-do list. Sadly, it's one of those things that's often forgotten as we burn the midnight oil, climb the corporate ladder, and give so much to others before ourselves. But you can't live an F-it-less life without fun. It's not possible. In fact, fun may be what life is all about. When, little by little, our experience of all things *fun* gets whittled away, compromised, or shoved in a corner, we're bound to wake up one day and wonder, "Why am I so unhappy, so frustrated? Where did all the fun in my life go?" In the same way that the foundation of a marriage crumbles when it's neglected, the foundation of your life weakens considerably when fun isn't a priority.

Unfortunately, fun is the first thing we voluntarily cut back on when something else requires our attention. Ignore it sufficiently, and pretty soon you'll have sacrificed your own happiness. You'll have developed a bad habit that inevitably leads to burnout. Don't wait until you need to be rescued. That's never pretty. Ask yourself, "What makes me happy? Who makes me happy?" Then start giving more attention and time to those people, thoughts, and activities. Make fun a priority right now, even if your first step is to wear a big, fat, stupid smile.

CHAPTER EIGHTEEN
FAMILY

· · · · · · · · · · · · · · · · · · · ·

When everything goes to hell, the people who stand
by you without flinching—they are your family.
—JIM BUTCHER

· · · · · · · · · · · · · · · · · · · ·

EVER SINCE THE IDEA FOR THIS BOOK CAME TO ME, I KNEW that Family was an F-word that had to be included, yet it's been the chapter that has challenged me the most. My personal family history has been good, if not great, for the most part. I don't feel any trailing negativity from my life's less-than-perfect parts, of which there are many. My parents divorced when I was five years old and my dad moved out of state soon thereafter, which, geographically speaking, made it tough for us to have a close relationship. My mom raised my brother and me. I spent most of my life feeling frustrated with my dad and in alignment with my mother, as we had always been so compatible. But in the year or so that preceded Dad's death in 2015, he and I became more aligned, while, as it turns out, my mom and I have increasingly drifted out of alignment, unfortunately. It's funny how life and family work. I'm always struck by the ebb and flow of it all. Regardless of this history, when I think of my family, the word *love* comes to mind first. That's because I always felt loved, and I loved in return. Sure, there are things about my family that I've hated along the way—and still do—but I know who I can count on and who I can't. Just because you're related to someone or are supposed to be able to count on someone doesn't mean that you can or should. In my experience, the quality of my life's relationships has more to do with determining who I let in and put my trust in, and who I don't. The better I am at discerning who my family members are, the better my life tends to be. I've never really had a problem with shutting out negative forces and living within a circle of positive people and energy. For whatever reason, that's something that has always been second nature to me.

Family means many things to many people. Not only are our personal life journeys different enough to formulate varying ideas about what family is but even the legal definition and recognition of what family should be has been challenged and changed and continues to be. I think that's why I love the quote at the beginning of this chapter so much. Some of us love the families we were born into; some of us don't. Some accept their families as they are; some change them along the way, for a range of reasons; and others choose to fire their God-given family, declaring their closest and most reliable friends—aka, their family of choice—to be family instead. Either way, the members of our family usually prove themselves to us through their unconditional love and support. At the end of the day, your family comprises the people who are consistently there for you no matter what.

When Jeri and I were married in October of 2015, we didn't simply become husband and wife. It was more complicated than that. Officially, we became a *blended family*. I have two sons, Noble and Steel, who were ages fourteen and eleven, respectively, at the time. Jeri has two sons as well: Jacob, who was eight then, and Andrew, who was six. She also has a daughter, Sarah, who was five. Our coming together as one family meant that all of these kids became newfound siblings. In order to foster the kind of bond we hoped would develop between them, we knew there was one significant thing we could do: we could model a consistent example of love and respect with each other and our children. This would offer our kids a perspective on marriage and on siblinghood that would hopefully make the kind of blended family we wanted a reality. Jeri and I worked together preparing home-cooked meals, we sat around the dinner table and had conversations, we held hands, we spoke with respect and gratitude, we took an interest in everyone's day, we helped with homework, we took trips together, we attended the kids' special events together, and we made sure we were always on time when we needed to be somewhere for our children. One thing was for sure: Everyone was going to have different feelings about and perspectives on our new life. These would have to be processed, interpreted, and worked through by each of them in their own time and in their own way. And we were going to be there to help through every stage.

Children are life's ultimate Rubik's Cubes. Each child requires a different set of twists and turns to best align them with their surroundings. There's no single way to solve the puzzle for them, as much as a parent may try. Sarah's perspective and needs were different from all the other kids', as were Jacob's, Andrew's, Noble's, and Steel's. Still, Jeri and I were committed to staying consistent in order to attract the acceptance and love from our children we were hoping to receive. With a little trial and error, some patience, and a sensitive touch, however, the pieces ultimately came together.

By 2018, we were going on three years of marriage and had established something of a rhythm managing our schedules and our children's needs. We were finding common ground, and the kids were more accepting of their new normal. Of course, there were days when we had to remind each other and ourselves that it would be more of a marathon than a sprint. Nevertheless, we were making progress as a family, and we could see it. A reliable schedule helped us attend everyone's extracurricular events, have home-cooked family dinners around the table, attend church on Sundays, and take a few vacations together. Jacob, who was acting in local theater productions in Atlanta, had submitted audition tapes for Broadway's *School of Rock*. In the summer of 2018, the casting agency called. They wanted to see him for a live audition in Orlando three days later. On the afternoon following his return from Orlando, they called again and asked for him to travel to New York for another live audition. Then, after nearly six weeks of silence, we received the call from *School of Rock* offering Jacob a part in the show. And just like that, he was in an Andrew Lloyd Webber musical. Jacob is Jeri's oldest child and was eleven at the time. This was an exciting opportunity, one that Jeri felt very connected to, as she, too, had acted when she was a child. She performed in *Annie* at the Burt Reynolds Jupiter Theatre with the likes of Alice Ghostley and Charles Nelson Reilly, and in various other professional productions when she was in her elementary years. Seeing her son follow in her footsteps was a dream come true for her. However, the timing was tricky. Just when the routine of our lives was starting to feel somewhat normal, it was time to pivot again as a family.

For Jacob to assume the role of James in the show, he had to be in California in twelve days to start rehearsals. Oh, and he also needed to have a parent or guardian with him on the road at all times. The national tour of the show that he was to appear in was slated to run through June of 2019. He and his guardian would be traveling to some of the nation's biggest cities, performing eight shows a week, alongside twelve other kids. That was their job.

Whoa.

I'd be lying if I said I wasn't racked with concern about how exactly we would be able to pull this off. While I recognized the opportunity that this presented for Jacob, all I could initially focus on was how incredibly hard it would be to support him without dropping the ball with the four other children whom we equally loved and needed to provide for. Our parenting schedules would have to be *flexible* (F-word!) to accommodate all the logistics involved. We'd have to come up with a travel rotation so that all our children would be properly cared for at home. Thankfully, Jeri and I had the adaptability to do this. And as it turned out, Jacob's dad and Jeri's parents were game to help out too. Together, we devised a plan to alternate turns on the road with Jacob. Gloria, our beloved nanny-turned-house manager, became an even bigger part of our family, and a rock we all relied upon to keep things running smoothly at home. All of us in this crazy family structure were about to band together for Jacob's sake. Everyone wanted him to pursue his dream and experience something that could change the trajectory of his life.

And band together we did.

Jacob's dad, a successful financial manager, was able to craft a work schedule that allowed him to spend time on the road. Jacob's grandparents pledged to be wherever we needed them whenever we needed them. It wasn't easy, but somehow it worked. Together, we figured it out.

We thought of the whole experience as a relay race. No one could leave Jacob in a city until the parent or grandparent who was tagging in had arrived. Sounds simple, but in reality, it was as stressful as an air traffic controller's job in instances. Back home, the other kids needed to get to and from school. Homework had to be done. Practice for gymnastics, soccer, and tennis required drop-offs and pickups at different times. School concerts and other activities couldn't go unnoticed or unattended, either. Jacob is an astute kid who could never possibly know all the strings that had to be pulled to enable him to make his professional acting debut because he simply wasn't there to witness them, but I'm sure he senses the collective effort made on his behalf.

Remarkably we were all able to come together to make things work for his sake. It wasn't without its hiccups, but Jacob's family showed up so he could take advantage of a dream opportunity in the world of professional theater—an opportunity that could open even more doors for him should he wish to continue along the acting path. And given the chance, we would do it all over again for him—or for any of our other children—without hesitation.

A memorable day for all of us was when we guardians attended the performance where Jacob played Freddie, the drummer in the show, together. It was the role for which he was the understudy for the first time. What we do, we do for the children, and we do it as best we can. My point is this: Your family shows up when you need them most. Whether you're related by blood or not isn't the litmus test. It's who's there when you need them that determines who your people are. Most of the time our family is a more subtle force in our lives, running quietly in the background, not needing to flex its muscles or to be recognized. It's just there. And when we need them, whether it's because we're scared, lonely, nervous, broken, angry, or about to do something courageous and just need some wind beneath our wings, the members of our family will rise up and be present. They'll pray with and for us. They'll protect, defend, and support us. The people we call *family* are the ones that we'll make room for in our foxhole. They're the people we want fighting the good fight alongside of us, and they're the people we'll fight for in return. Whatever changes we make in order to live an F-it-less life, having family we can count on, in whatever form family takes for us, will most certainly be a part of the journey.

CHAPTER NINETEEN
FREEDOM

....

*Everything can be taken from a man but one thing: the
last of the human freedoms—to choose one's attitude in
any given set of circumstances, to choose one's own way.*
—VIKTOR FRANKL

....

VIKTOR FRANKL WAS AN AUSTRIAN NEUROLOGIST AND PSYCHI-
atrist, as well as a Holocaust survivor. Prior to being captured
by the Nazis and taken to several different concentration camps
(including the death camp Auschwitz), he had begun writing
an opus about human motivation that challenged Abraham
Maslow's hierarchy of needs. Maslow had indicated that unless
your basic needs are met, you cannot do things that are transcen-
dent. As Frankl was being sent away, he hid his manuscript inside
the lining of his coat, hoping to save it, but as soon as he got to

the concentration camp, he was stripped of everything and lost his work. But it was the research and writing he'd done before his captivity that no doubt created a belief and a mindset that saved his life. In his later classic *Man's Search for Meaning*, Frankl expressed the view—further confirmed by his Holocaust experiences—that finding meaning in one's life, no matter how dire the suffering one endures, is what leads to transcendence.

Frankl was a diminutive man with a larger-than-life presence. His aura has been described by those who knew him as one who perfumed the atmosphere of being present and living totally in the moment.

His office in Vienna, where he lived after the war, was filled with twenty-nine honorary degrees, including his medical degree, his PhD in philosophy, and, oddly, a ratty certificate for solo-piloting a Cessna in San Diego when he was in his late sixties. Frankl, as you can imagine, was noted for his wisdom. When asked about the flying certificate one day, he explained that he really enjoyed hiking and mountain climbing. There were three trails outside Vienna named after him because of this passion and because he was the first to explore them. Despite this adventure seeking, he had developed an aversion to flying over the years. It wasn't until he was in his sixties that he decided he and Mrs. Frankl should learn to pilot an aircraft. His reason was simple: "There are some things about myself I don't have to tolerate."

These words really hit home for me.

And I'll bet that by now, they're pretty powerful for you too.

What things in your life do you no longer want to tolerate? What are you willing to do to change that?

Goethe said, "How can we know ourselves? Never by reflection, but only through action. Begin at once to do your duty and immediately you will know what is inside of you. And what is your duty? Whatever the day calls for."

We all know money can't buy love, and though it can make life a little easier, it doesn't really buy happiness, either. If you really want to live an F-it-less existence, I believe it's personal freedom that you're striving for. The new American dream isn't about material wealth or the accumulation of things; it's about creating a meaningful, purpose-driven life, one in which you can pursue your passions and still have time to spend with your family, help to benefit your community, and give back to the Universe for all you have. It's about value more than wealth. It's about personal freedom over affluence.

But what does that mean?

When I think of freedom, I immediately conjure up thoughts of the Fourth of July. After all, it's the day each year when Americans celebrate our freedom and independence. It's a day filled with reflection and gratitude, so it was no coincidence that I found myself once again reaching for David Hawkins's book *Letting Go* on July 4, 2016. The book deals with many topics, though it's mainly about the pathway to surrender, a simple and life-changing process whereby readers learn to release their attachments to negative, life-hindering feelings in order to achieve true personal freedom. No ideal is more fundamental to us as Americans. The concept of *freedom* is embedded in the Declaration of Independence as one of our inalienable rights. Our love of freedom is represented by many symbols, from our flag waving proudly in the wind to statues of those who have fought valiantly to preserve our freedom over the years. And though many cultures cherish freedom, we as a country are known as the Land of the Free. We are a nation founded on the premise that freedom is a basic right.

And yet freedom is often defined by its limits.

There were obvious restrictions to freedom in Colonial times, and when slave owners denied the freedom of African Americans brought here against their will, and later when women were refused the right to vote, Japanese Americans were interned in camps during World War II, Martin Luther King Jr. was compelled by the continuing poor treatment of black people to lead the civil rights movement, when the hard-fought battle for gay rights was mounted and won, and so forth.

I grew up in an era when freedom and happiness were synonymous with success. The more successful you were, the more freedom you were able to create for yourself. But in our present culture, we're experiencing a significant shift in this thinking. According to a 2016 survey by Deloitte, millennials see things very differently than I did when I entered the work-force. While I naturally accepted the notion that burning the midnight oil, clocking overtime, and working weekends were the ways to rise to the top, today's young professionals perceive a healthy work-life balance and flexibility in their schedules as marks of success. Only 13.8 percent were interested in opportunities to progress or become leaders in their field, and fewer than 10 percent stated that they wanted or expected to derive meaning from their work. What this indicates, at least to me, is that what millennials want is freedom. They want the ability to pursue work that means something to them and fits their lifestyle, and they're willing to give up fancy perks and larger salaries to have that opportunity. Happiness, as it would be measured for them, has less to do with the size of their paychecks than it does with the depth of their relationships and the value they add to the world. Financial success is no longer a driving force. It's really just a byproduct of living a desired and aligned life.

Whatever freedom looks like to you, understand that it can be created when you know how to make the right choices for yourself—when you dare to think about what you really want and make decisions accordingly. There were so many years of my life when consciously or unconsciously I thwarted my own freedom. My thoughts were my barriers. They were the gatekeepers that allowed possibility in or kept it out. The chatter inside my head that reminded me that I wasn't happy, satisfied, or content, yet offered no solutions, held me back against my better judgment. Eventually, the sound of this self-talk got so loud that I had to make a choice: fight against these thoughts or remain within their confines forever, liberate myself through active choices or continue to be constricted by passive ones. All along, the power didn't lie in my circumstances—it was mine, and I hadn't been owning it. I had the ability to make *different* choices, to choose the paths that would lead me toward my ultimate goal—freedom. Choice is always the catalyst for change. We are the culmination of all the decisions we make. Those decisions are portals to a happier and more meaningful life.

Throughout history, there have been courageous men and women known as freedom fighters who have inspired me with their bravery and fearlessness in creating great change for their beliefs, especially when it came to protecting the liberties and safety of our nation. And yet so few of us will fight for our personal freedom. I've watched so many people give away their personal power, close friends and colleagues who allow others to berate, belittle, restrict, and reduce their lives to something far less than they deserve.

So many of you have actually given your freedom away too. You've allowed others to impose their own ideologies upon you. You've given their views more credence than your own. In doing so, you've allowed doubt, disappointment, and dysfunction to impede you and interfere with your destiny. You've given in to all of the worst kind of F-words—those fractures, fears, and failures—believing they defined you. In turn, those F-words boxed you in and prevented you from focusing on what you really want in life, which is to be able to reclaim your greatest power and reach your highest potential. I know the price and the process of pursuing personal freedom, which is really the endgame in an F-it-less life.

Taking back your freedom, like everything else you do, is a choice. If you continue to live in a self-imposed prison, you will never escape from the cycle you and society have spent years creating. You don't have to give away your power anymore. No one has that much control over you. You have the ability to make different choices about what you'll tolerate. And you have the ability to determine when you'll start fighting for that change. Think about Viktor Frankl. Victory is born out of a decision to fight for the things that really matter.

Let me be absolutely clear: personal freedom takes a lot of discipline and courage to achieve, but that's not a news flash. It always has, and it's always proven to be worth the struggle to obtain. Once we accept that we cannot truly control others or let them control us, we truly begin to let go. It's in the letting go that we find freedom.

Nineteen years ago, I came across the greatest definition of freedom I'd ever heard: "True freedom is the complete lack of anxiety." For whatever reason, that struck me as incredibly profound at the time, and it continues to be a foundational thought for the architecture of my own life. It's something I genuinely wish for you too. This definition is a variation on the thinking of renowned sixth-century Zen master Seng-ts'an, who said we're free when we are "without anxiety about non-perfection." In other words, we're free when we accept our human existence and all of life exactly as it is. As I wrote earlier in chapter six, "Fix-It!," the pursuit of perfection is something our society fosters, yet it's critical to remember that imperfection is not a personal problem—it's a natural part of existing. We all get caught up in our wants and fears, we all act unconsciously, we all age, and, yes, someday we'll die. It's only when we learn to relax about our imperfections that we find freedom—that we can be and live in the moment, and experience life without any fear of being judged.

If freedom is a complete lack of anxiety, then you must understand that it's your anxiety that creates limitations in life. And if that's true, freedom also has the capacity to remove those limitations. All of us have the ability to experience this kind of freedom. And to some degree, we've all felt it from time to time. The secret—and, for me, the goal—is to experience this kind of freedom *all* the time.

Wouldn't that be great?

That is living the ultimate F-it-less life!

So, let me ask you a question: Do you have an authentic definition of freedom? I'm not talking about what everyone else has told you freedom is or means, but what it looks and feels like to you, based on what you've discovered along the way.

What does that look like? What does that feel like?

Have you ever thought about your life in these terms?

Freedom is about living your truth, on your own terms and without apologizing to anyone for that truth. It's about being in a place of self-awareness. It's about understanding that you don't need anyone else's approval to live your best life. If you've never defined it for yourself, there's no better time than now to create your very own definition of freedom.

F-It-Less Exercise: Freedom

What is your definition of freedom? Describe what this looks and feels like to you, and how living a life of freedom would impact your current life. Take a few minutes to write down your thoughts and ideas. _____

_____

_____

_____

_____

_____

_____

_____

_____

_____

_____

_____

_____

Freedom is something that ought to be protected, because it's precious and it matters. When you find your freedom, you'll be challenged—often. Old wounds, patterns, and dysfunctions will resurface and tempt you to go back to more familiar ways. That's when you have to become your own almighty protector and refuse to give in to the things that once enslaved you. You can't allow anything that was toxic back into your environment, even if it means letting go of some things, people, or places you once held dear. If you've created a clear, genuine definition of what freedom looks like to you, those old doubts are no longer welcome. If you allow anything to bump you from your path, you'll find yourself giving away one of the greatest gifts you've ever given yourself.

I've always been inspired by those who fight for a better life, a better country, a better system, a better way. Their focus, fortitude, fearlessness, and unceasing struggle paved the way for incredible change. It takes that kind of fierce determination to achieve greatness, to break out of a life of mediocrity and step into your highest personal power.

If you knocked on death's door today, could you say you lived your life being true to who you are?

Would you die happy?

Would you say you've lived a full life? Did you add value to the world?

What would you have done differently?

Imagine for a moment that you're happy with your life—I mean truly free of regret, worry, stress, judgment, and anything else that holds you back from living an F-it-less life.

What does that feel like?

What's keeping you from making that life a reality? What's standing in the way of you and *You 2.0*?

A 2016 study of over two hundred men and women in hospice care found that the number-one regret the subjects had was not having the courage to live a life that was true to themselves instead of one that conformed to the expectations of others. Clarity comes, but for some, it shows up too late. It shouldn't require facing your mortality to finally recognize this sad, late-life remorse, or any other unfulfilled dream. I can't think of anything more heartbreaking than dying knowing I could have lived a fuller, happier, freer life, and that all it would have taken was giving myself permission to make the choices that would wake me up from whatever slumber I'd been living in and help me discover that there was so much more fulfillment available for the taking.

When I look back on my life, I see that the biggest decisions I've made—the ones that I agonized over, the ones that caused me the most stress because they felt like high risk–high reward choices—were ultimately the best and most impactful decisions I ever made. Isn't that true for you too? Think about it. Maybe it was deciding where to go to college, who to marry, whether to have children, where to work, whether to have a relationship with God, or whether to pursue love or happiness over money. When you think about what it felt like on the front side of those decisions, it's probably a lot like the way you're feeling right now. I'll bet you've just forgotten what that kind of adrenaline feels like. Maybe you're rusty, or perhaps it's akin to childbirth the second time around, and you've let the memory of the pain fade so you can focus on the pleasure. The good news is that you're reading this book at just the right time. I'm here to remind you that an F-it-less life is yours for the taking, now and always. And whether the notion of having it seems easy or challenging, it is, like freedom, worth fighting for.

To be certain, choosing freedom requires courage. You're going to have to pull the trigger, make a tough call, and choose differently if you want this. There's going to be a point in your life when push comes to shove, and you'll have to make a decision about your freedom. Perhaps that point in time is now. You're limited only by the expectations you've placed on yourself. None of us really knows our full capacity; we know only what we can see, what we can feel, and what we've been brought up to believe. Your vision may change, what you want may change, your circumstances may change, and you have to believe that none of that is bad. Change is a constant in life and helps us grow bigger than we already are or ever believed we could be. Just remember: Victor Frankl was right. There are some things about yourself (and your life) that you don't have to tolerate.

CHAPTER TWENTY

FINALLY

· · · · · · · · · · · · · · · · · · · ·

We are all just walking each other home.
—RAM DASS

· · · · · · · · · · · · · · · · · · · ·

I'VE ALWAYS BEEN PASSIONATE ABOUT FINDING WAYS TO POSI-
tively contribute to the lives of others. Throughout my real
estate career, I spent countless hours helping agents realize their
goals and dreams. I've taught, trained, listened, guided, and
offered a bit of tough love whenever it was necessary. Continuing
in that vein, this project has been the most challenging and
exciting effort I've made in that direction. The need to share the
path to an F-it-less life started as a spark, and over the course of
the two years it took to write this book, it grew into a burning
flame. Regardless of what happens after these pages are printed
and their cover bound, this has been a tremendous growth

opportunity for me. And if I grew from writing this book, I know there's growth here for you too.

Presenting these concepts for living an F-it-less life became a driving passion for me, and I needed to convey them with enough vulnerability to share both my triumphs and tribulations with you, the reader. The shifts and breakthroughs that I wish for you to have as a result of walking with me through this material require that of me. In order for me and my story to connect with you enough to positively affect your narrative, I had to trust the process, open up, and put myself out there.

Generally speaking, it's easy to be happy, peaceful, calm, and loving when things are good. It's another thing entirely to be able to keep our insides *just so* when our outside world presents us with stressful people and events. It was necessary for me to make some productive adjustments so that you could hold this book in your hands. A significant portion of this story was written while Jeri and I juggled an overwhelmingly complex schedule as a result of having an eleven-year-old in the national touring company of *School of Rock*. We traveled to thirty-three cities in ten months for more than three hundred shows! I can't begin to tell you how many plane tickets were purchased and hotel rooms and Airbnbs secured only to be changed for one reason or another. Maybe it was because, in the midst of our chaos, we booked the wrong dates. Maybe it was because our flights were too early or too late to switch guardianship with Jacob's father or grandparents for the week. Maybe it was because one of our other four children had a play, a game, a recital, a meet, a graduation, or a party to attend. To say the writing process was tough for a variety of reasons is an understatement. I'm convinced these circumstances arose in order to put the material I've shared with you to the test. And tested it was. Everything about my life's structure and routine, everything that I'd designed and loved, was thrown out the window, in part to make sure that my work here was authentic and reflected the life and philosophy I strive to live by every day. But isn't that what all challenges are about—showing us by way of adversity what we're capable of? True peace and happiness come into our lives only when we can maintain them, regardless of our external circumstances. Jon Kabat-Zinn says, "You can't stop the waves, but you can learn to surf." I love that.

I'm not sure that I know anyone who has mastered true peace and happiness in their lives. That's because it's such a rare achievement. Even those of us who are committed to achieving it constantly fall short of the goal. For whatever reason, I'm better at it than most, yet not nearly as good as I want to be—or will be. Like you, I'm deeply connected to my Source and feel most inspired when I'm conscious of my peace, love, and happiness. And also like you, my external circumstances are typically far from ideal. But the F-it-less life we all seek and deserve is as much a journey as it is a destination, and the pursuit of it is most certainly a worthwhile endeavor.

We all go through things, some of them more horrible than others, some more unwanted than others. Some more unfair than others. Some more emotional than others or more painful than others. We don't always know why, particularly when we're going through them. But hopefully it becomes clear at some point. Maybe it's the passage of time; maybe it's reflection; maybe it's a person who helped us; maybe it's a song, or a seminar, or a religious service, or a book; maybe it's *this* book—whatever the impetus, sooner or later we either understand or we let it go and move on, more evolved and better equipped. Our life's setbacks and disappointments should never define us. They're not our biography, only chapters in it.

The next chapter you write is up to you. It's your choice. An F-it-less life doesn't just come to you; it's a life that must be chosen. You get to choose how you show up and what direction you take.

I hope this book has provided a perspective that empowers you to protect what you want and who you want to be. I hope it's allowed you to question what's been acceptable to you in your life and inspired you enough to raise the bar and live the kind of life you want to live. I hope it's a wake-up call. I hope it's the beginning of your F-it-less life.

Years ago, I was getting ready to fly to another city to teach a class. Before I finished packing, I ran to CVS to pick up a few items I needed. It was early on a Sunday morning. Quiet. As I got out of my car to head inside, an elderly African American woman was walking out of the store toward me. She was wearing a housecoat of sorts and walked with a slight limp. She looked like a million other people I've walked past in my lifetime. As we approached each other, I greeted her, like I often greet strangers in similar situations.

"Good morning. How are you?" I said with a friendly routineness.

Her reply was anything but routine.

Passing me, she replied, "I'm great, and I thank the Lord I met you today!"

I spun around, surprised, and said, "Well that's a little different than 'Fine.' "

I was totally taken aback. I can't begin to imagine the number of times I've exchanged the same greeting and response with people, with such consistency that it almost seems like we're following a script. And yet in one passing instant, a faceless, nameless woman in the parking lot of CVS shook me to the core and woke me up simply with the way she said hello.

"I'm great, and I thank the Lord I met you today."

Let me be clear: When someone says that to you, it changes your day. It changes your energy. It changes *you*. You never forget it. You may even up your own hello game. What if we all greeted one another with such impact, rather than with our typical, scripted "Fine" or whatever it is that you usually say?

I've thought about that woman a zillion times since that encounter. In fact, I wonder whether my exchange with her was the beginning of my quest to bring the notion of living an F-it-less life to print. If we can change the world with something as simple as how we say hello, imagine what kinds of improvements we can make in other parts of our lives.

Two years ago, Hugh, a great friend of mine, called me. He had just attended a memorial service and wanted to share a thought with me that had struck him as particularly poignant. He thought it was so awesome that he phoned me on his way home and relayed the following:

"We are all just walking each other home."

Hugh had never heard this before, and neither had I. We are all just walking each other home. We get to do this thing called life together. We're all connected as humans, as people trying to be the best version of ourselves that we can be. We give to some and receive from others. We help and are helped. No one succeeds alone. We walk with some for a while, and we walk with others for a lifetime. Together, we can make this life magnificent. Shortly after Hugh shared his aha moment with me, Jeri and I were looking for a vacation home in Florida that we could invest in and rent out when we weren't using it. We saw some lovely places, all of which were promising. However, the one that sealed the deal for us was the one that had a white-painted brick sitting on a built-in bookshelf outside the master bedroom. The brick was engraved with the phrase "We Are All Just Walking Each Other Home." Needless to say, that brick remained with the home when we purchased it. There isn't a time I walk by that brick without looking at it and being reminded that the current of the Universe is always running in the background, giving us signs both subtle and not so subtle as it moves us forward into the next chapter of our autobiography.

There's a concept called the Butterfly Effect. As I recall, it says that the wind created from the flapping of a butterfly's wings has the power to grow into a hurricane on the other side of the world. Perhaps the F-it-less approach to life can have a similar effect—it can change *your* world before becoming an even greater force that changes *the* world. Regardless of its eventual reach and impact, it has changed my life, and I hope it's begun to change yours too.

Here's to living an F-it-less life, one inspiring F-word at a time.

ACKNOWLEDGMENTS

I T'S HARD TO BELIEVE THAT A WELL-TIMED CHANCE MEETING of three people, all of whom were out of town and waiting on their dinner tables to be readied, would have turned into a whirlwind friendship and this very book, but it did. "There are no coincidences," of this I am certain. So, first and foremost, I would like to thank the Universe and all of its currents and nudges that not only made this book possible, but a reality.

Laura Morton. My co-author, my coach, my mentor, and my friend. You have curiosity, intelligence, and experience that is unrivaled. I have loved the idea and purpose of this book from the moment I woke up with it, but without you, it would have only existed in fragments and not nearly as impactful as the book in which this page is written. "Thank you" hardly seems appropriate for your guidance and contributions that took the contents of this book from good to great. Even still, "Thank you."

Thank you, Adam Mitchell, for your help with research and transcription. You are a great resource for information.

Hope Innelli, our line editor. Aside from Jeri, Laura, and myself, you were the first person to read this. I was so nervous about what you, a seasoned and successful editor of content, might think. Your enthusiasm for *"F"-It-Less!* was more freeing and inspiring than you can imagine, and more important, your insights, notes, and clarifications made this book more professional and reader-friendly. Thank you for doing what you do and specifically, for doing what you did for *me*.

Benjamin Holmes, our copy editor. My confidence soared after seeing the detailed manner in which you combed through this material. The suggestions and corrections you provided simply made this book better.

To our publisher, Jonathan Merkh. All along, Laura kept saying that she hoped this work would be something that "Jonathan" would be interested in. Frankly, not knowing anything or anyone, her words went in one ear and out the other. That is, until she called, and said, "Jonathan loves the book!" Forefront Books, along with Simon & Schuster, seems to be a lofty target of gratitude, particularly when I look at it through the lens of a simple idea that was hatched a couple of years ago. I am humbled and honored to have this work published by such accomplished companies. Thank you for embracing this work of great vulnerability and honest inspiration. Your insight, team, and professional presentation are second to none. Thank you, thank you, thank you.

To my wife, Jeri. Your trust, love, support, and patience never went unnoticed or unappreciated as this book was written. Your input along the way challenged me to be better, and therefore, this book is better because of you. You are my "foxhole buddy for life." I am awe-inspired by the capacity for love that I continue to discover for you. I could thank you for a million things, but for the purpose at hand, I thank you for the excitement, passion, and purpose you have brought out in me. Because of you, this book exists.

To Noble, Steel, Jacob, Andrew, and Sarah: I am so proud of how far we have come and how far we can go together. Thank you all for your trust and love. Thank you for challenging me to be better for you, for all of us. You taught me and Jeri more about ourselves as parents and stepparents than we even knew we needed to learn. I hope and pray that the love that Jeri and I share and F-it-lessly live is an inspiring reconciliation for our lives' paths and how they came together. And I want nothing more for each of you than to live an F-it-less life of your own.

For more information about Shaun Rawls and *"F"-It-Less,* please visit Shaunrawls.com.

Follow Shaun on Facebook:
Shaun Rawls Author

Follow Shaun on Instagram:
theshaunrawls

Follow Shaun on YouTube:
theshaunrawls

FEDERAL RULES OF APPELLATE PROCEDURE

Title I – Applicability of Rules

Rule 1. Scope of Rules; Definition; Title

(a) **Scope of Rules.**
   (1) These rules govern procedure in the United States courts of appeals.
   (2) When these rules provide for filing a motion or other document in the district court, the procedure must comply with the practice of the district court.
(b) **Definition.** In these rules, 'state' includes the District of Columbia and any United States commonwealth or territory.
(c) **Title.** These rules are to be known as the Federal Rules of Appellate Procedure.

Rule 2. Suspension of Rules

(a) **In a Particular Case.** On its own or a party's motion, a court of appeals may—to expedite its decision or for other good cause—suspend any provision of these rules in a particular case and order proceedings as it directs, except as otherwise provided in Rule 26(b).
(b) **In an Appellate Rules Emergency.**
   (1) *Conditions of Emergency.* The Judicial Conference of the United States may declare an Appellate Rules emergency if it determines that extraordinary circumstances relating to public health or safety, or affecting physical or electronic access to a court, substantially impair the court's ability to perform its functions in compliance with these rules.
   (2) *Content.* The declaration must:
      (A) designate the circuit or circuits affected; and
      (B) be limited to a stated period of no more than 90 days.
   (3) *Early Termination.* The Judicial Conference may terminate a declaration for one of more circuits before the termination date.
   (4) *Additional Declarations.* The Judicial Conference may issue additional declarations under this rule.
   (5) *Proceedings in a Rules Emergency.* When a rules emergency is declared the court may:
      (A) suspend in all or part of that circuit any provision of these rules, other than time limits imposed by statute and described in Rule 26(b)(1)-(2); and

(B) order proceedings as it directs.

Title II – Appeal from a Judgment or Order of a District Court

Rule 3. Appeal as of Right—How Taken

(a) **Filing the Notice of Appeal**.

   (1) An appeal permitted by law as of right from a district court to a court of appeals may be taken only by filing a notice of appeal with the district clerk within the time allowed by Rule 4. At the time of filing, the appellant must furnish the clerk with enough copies of the notice to enable the clerk to comply with Rule 3(d).

   (2) An appellant's failure to take any step other than the timely filing of a notice of appeal does not affect the validity of the appeal, but is ground only for the court of appeals to act as it considers appropriate, including dismissing the appeal.

   (3) An appeal from a judgment by a magistrate judge in a civil case is taken in the same way as an appeal from any other district court judgment.

   (4) An appeal by permission under 28 U.S.C. § 1292(b) or an appeal in a bankruptcy case may be taken only in the manner prescribed by Rules 5 and 6, respectively.

(b) **Joint or Consolidated Appeals**.

   (1) When two or more parties are entitled to appeal from a district court judgment or order, and their interests make joinder practicable, they may file a joint notice of appeal. They may then proceed on appeal as a single appellant.

   (2) When the parties have filed separate timely notices of appeal, the appeals may be joined or consolidated by the court of appeals.

(c) **Contents of the Notice of Appeal**.

   (1) The notice of appeal must:

      (A) specify the party or parties taking the appeal by naming each one in the caption or body of the notice, but an attorney representing more than one party may describe those parties with such terms as 'all plaintiffs,' 'the defendants,' 'the plaintiffs A, B, et al.,' or 'all defendants except X';

      (B) designate the judgment-or appealable order-from which the appeal is taken; and

      (C) name the court to which the appeal is taken.

(2) A pro se notice of appeal is considered filed on behalf of the signer and the signer's spouse and minor children (if they are parties), unless the notice clearly indicates otherwise.

(3) In a class action, whether or not the class has been certified, the notice of appeal is sufficient if it names one person qualified to bring the appeal as representative of the class.

(4) The notice of appeal encompasses all orders that, for purposes of appeal, merge into the designated judgment or appealable order. It is not necessary to designate those orders in the notice of appeal.

(5) In a civil case, a notice of appeal encompasses the final judgment, whether or not that judgment is set out in a separate document under Federal Rule of Civil Procedure 58, if the notice designates:

   (A) an order that adjudicates all remaining claims and the rights and liabilities of all remaining parties; or

   (B) an order described in Rule 4(a)(4)(A).

(6) An appellant may designate only part of a judgment or appealable order by expressly stating that the notice of appeal is so limited. Without such an express statement, specific designations do not limit the scope of the notice of appeal.

(7) An appeal must not be dismissed for informality of form or title of the notice of appeal, for failure to name a party whose intent to appeal is otherwise clear from the notice, or for failure to properly designate the judgment if the notice of appeal was filed after entry of the judgment and designates an order that merged into that judgment.

(8) Forms 1A and 1B in the Appendix of Forms are suggested forms of notices of appeal.

(d) **Serving the Notice of Appeal.**

(1) The district clerk must serve notice of the filing of a notice of appeal by sending a copy to each party's counsel of record-excluding the appellant's or, if a party is proceeding pro se, to the party's last known address. When a defendant in a criminal case appeals, the clerk must also serve a copy of the notice of appeal on the defendant. The clerk must promptly send a copy of the notice of appeal and of the docket entries–and any later docket entries–to the clerk of the court of appeals named in the notice. The district clerk must note, on each copy, the date when the notice of appeal was filed.

(2) If an inmate confined in an institution files a notice of appeal in the manner provided by Rule 4(c), the district clerk must also note the date when the clerk docketed the notice.

(3) The district clerk's failure to serve notice does not affect the validity of the appeal. The clerk must note on the docket the names of the parties to whom the clerk sends copies, with the date of sending. Service is sufficient despite the death of a party or the party's counsel.

(e) **Payment of Fees.** Upon filing a notice of appeal, the appellant must pay the district clerk all required fees. The district clerk receives the appellate docket fee on behalf of the court of appeals.

Rule 4. Appeal as of Right—When Taken

(a) **Appeal in a Civil Case.**

    (1) *Time for Filing a Notice of Appeal.*

        (A) In a civil case, except as provided in Rules 4(a)(1)(B), 4(a)(4), and 4(c), the notice of appeal required by Rule 3 must be filed with the district clerk within 30 days after entry of the judgment or order appealed from.

        (B) The notice of appeal may be filed by any party within 60 days after entry of the judgment or order appealed from if one of the parties is:

            (i) the United States;

            (ii) a United States agency;

            (iii) a United States officer or employee sued in an official capacity; or

            (iv) a current or former United States officer or employee sued in an individual capacity for an act or omission occurring in connection with duties performed on the United States' behalf—including all instances in which the United States represents that person when the judgment or order is entered or files the appeal for that person.

        (C) An appeal from an order granting or denying an application for a writ of error *coram nobis* is an appeal in a civil case for purposes of Rule 4(a).

    (2) *Filing Before Entry of Judgment.* A notice of appeal filed after the court announces a decision or order—but before the entry of the judgment or order—is treated as filed on the date of and after the entry.

    (3) *Multiple Appeals.* If one party timely files a notice of appeal, any other party may file a notice of appeal within 14 days after the date

when the first notice was filed, or within the time otherwise prescribed by this Rule 4(a), whichever period ends later.

(4) *Effect of a Motion on a Notice of Appeal.*

(A) If a party files in the district court any of the following motions under the Federal Rules of Civil Procedure—and does so within the time allowed by those rules—the time to file an appeal runs for all parties from the entry of the order disposing of the last such remaining motion:

   (i)   for judgment under Rule 50(b);

   (ii) to amend or make additional factual findings under Rule 52(b), whether or not granting the motion would alter the judgment;

   (iii) for attorney's fees under Rule 54 if the district court extends the time to appeal under Rule 58;

   (iv) to alter or amend the judgment under Rule 59;

   (v)   for a new trial under Rule 59; or

   (vi) for relief under Rule 60 if the motion is filed within the time allowed for filing a motion under Rule 59.

(B)

   (i)   If a party files a notice of appeal after the court announces or enters a judgment—but before it disposes of any motion listed in Rule 4(a)(4)(A)—the notice becomes effective to appeal a judgment or order, in whole or in part, when the order disposing of the last such remaining motion is entered.

   (ii) A party intending to challenge an order disposing of any motion listed in Rule 4(a)(4)(A), or a judgment's alteration or amendment upon such a motion, must file a notice of appeal, or an amended notice of appeal—in compliance with Rule 3(c)—within the time prescribed by this Rule measured from the entry of the order disposing of the last such remaining motion.

   (iii) No additional fee is required to file an amended notice.

(5) *Motion for Extension of Time.*

(A) The district court may extend the time to file a notice of appeal if:

   (i)   a party so moves no later than 30 days after the time prescribed by this Rule 4(a) expires; and

   (ii) regardless of whether its motion is filed before or during the 30 days after the time prescribed by this Rule 4(a) expires, that party shows excusable neglect or good cause.

(B) A motion filed before the expiration of the time prescribed in Rule 4(a)(1) or (3) may be ex parte unless the court requires otherwise. If the motion is filed after the expiration of the prescribed time, notice must be given to the other parties in accordance with local rules.

(C) No extension under this Rule 4(a)(5) may exceed 30 days after the prescribed time or 14 days after the date when the order granting the motion is entered, whichever is later.

(6) *Reopening the Time to File an Appeal.* The district court may reopen the time to file an appeal for a period of 14 days after the date when its order to reopen is entered, but only if all the following conditions are satisfied:

(A) the court finds that the moving party did not receive notice under Federal Rule of Civil Procedure 77(d) of the entry of the judgment or order sought to be appealed within 21 days after entry;

(B) the motion is filed within 180 days after the judgment or order is entered or within 14 days after the moving party receives notice under Federal Rule of Civil Procedure 77(d) of the entry, whichever is earlier; and

(C) the court finds that no party would be prejudiced.

(7) *Entry Defined.*

(A) A judgment or order is entered for purposes of this Rule 4(a):

(i) if Federal Rule of Civil Procedure 58(a) does not require a separate document, when the judgment or order is entered in the civil docket under Federal Rule of Civil Procedure 79(a); or

(ii) if Federal Rule of Civil Procedure 58(a) requires a separate document, when the judgment or order is entered in the civil docket under Federal Rule of Civil Procedure 79(a) and when the earlier of these events occurs:

- the judgment or order is set forth on a separate document, or
- 150 days have run from entry of the judgment or order in the civil docket under Federal Rule of Civil Procedure 79(a).

(B) A failure to set forth a judgment or order on a separate document when required by Federal Rule of Civil Procedure 58(a) does not affect the validity of an appeal from that judgment or order.

(b) **Appeal in a Criminal Case.**

(1) *Time for Filing a Notice of Appeal.*
  (A) In a criminal case, a defendant's notice of appeal must be filed in the district court within 14 days after the later of:
    (i) the entry of either the judgment or the order being appealed; or
    (ii) the filing of the government's notice of appeal.
  (B) When the government is entitled to appeal, its notice of appeal must be filed in the district court within 30 days after the later of:
    (i) the entry of the judgment or order being appealed; or
    (ii) the filing of a notice of appeal by any defendant.
(2) *Filing Before Entry of Judgment.* A notice of appeal filed after the court announces a decision, sentence, or order—but before the entry of the judgment or order—is treated as filed on the date of and after the entry.
(3) *Effect of a Motion on a Notice of Appeal.*
  (A) If a defendant timely makes any of the following motions under the Federal Rules of Criminal Procedure, the notice of appeal from a judgment of conviction must be filed within 14 days after the entry of the order disposing of the last such remaining motion, or within 14 days after the entry of the judgment of conviction, whichever period ends later. This provision applies to a timely motion:
    (i)   for judgment of acquittal under Rule 29;
    (ii) for a new trial under Rule 33, but if based on newly discovered evidence, only if the motion is made no later than 14 days after the entry of the judgment; or
    (iii) for arrest of judgment under Rule 34.
  (B) A notice of appeal filed after the court announces a decision, sentence, or order—but before it disposes of any of the motions referred to in Rule 4(b)(3)(A)—becomes effective upon the later of the following:
    (i) the entry of the order disposing of the last such remaining motion; or
    (ii) the entry of the judgment of conviction.
  (C) A valid notice of appeal is effective—without amendment—to appeal from an order disposing of any of the motions referred to in Rule 4(b)(3)(A).
(4) *Motion for Extension of Time.* Upon a finding of excusable neglect or good cause, the district court may—before or after the time has expired, with or without motion and notice—extend the time to file a

notice of appeal for a period not to exceed 30 days from the expiration of the time otherwise prescribed by this Rule 4(b).

(5) *Jurisdiction.* The filing of a notice of appeal under this Rule 4(b) does not divest a district court of jurisdiction to correct a sentence under Federal Rule of Criminal Procedure 35(a), nor does the filing of a motion under 35(a) affect the validity of a notice of appeal filed before entry of the order disposing of the motion. The filing of a motion under Federal Rule of Criminal Procedure 35(a) does not suspend the time for filing a notice of appeal from a judgment of conviction.

(6) *Entry Defined.* A judgment or order is entered for purposes of this Rule 4(b) when it is entered on the criminal docket.

(c) **Appeal by an Inmate Confined in an Institution.**

(1) If an institution has a system designed for legal mail, an inmate confined there must use that system to receive the benefit of this Rule 4(c)(1). If an inmate files a notice of appeal in either a civil or a criminal case, the notice is timely if it is deposited in the institution's internal mail system on or before the last day for filing and:

(A) it is accompanied by:

(i) a declaration in compliance with 28 U.S.C. § 1746—or a notarized statement—setting out the date of deposit and stating that first-class postage is being prepaid; or

(ii) evidence (such as a postmark or date stamp) showing that the notice was so deposited and that postage was prepaid; or

(B) the court of appeals exercises its discretion to permit the later filing of a declaration or notarized statement that satisfies Rule 4(c)(1)(A)(i).

(2) If an inmate files the first notice of appeal in a civil case under this Rule 4(c), the 14-day period provided in Rule 4(a)(3) for another party to file a notice of appeal runs from the date when the district court dockets the first notice.

(3) When a defendant in a criminal case files a notice of appeal under this Rule 4(c), the 30-day period for the government to file its notice of appeal runs from the entry of the judgment or order appealed from or from the district court's docketing of the defendant's notice of appeal, whichever is later.

(d) **Mistaken Filing in the Court of Appeals.** If a notice of appeal in either a civil or a criminal case is mistakenly filed in the court of appeals, the clerk of that court must note on the notice the date when it was received and send it to the district clerk. The notice is then considered filed in the district court on the date so noted.

Rule 5. Appeal by Permission

(a) **Petition for Permission to Appeal.**
    (1) To request permission to appeal when an appeal is within the court of appeals' discretion, a party must file a petition with the circuit clerk and serve it on all other parties to the district-court action.
    (2) The petition must be filed within the time specified by the statute or rule authorizing the appeal or, if no such time is specified, within the time provided by Rule 4(a) for filing a notice of appeal.
    (3) If a party cannot petition for appeal unless the district court first enters an order granting permission to do so or stating that the necessary conditions are met, the district court may amend its order, either on its own or in response to a party's motion, to include the required permission or statement. In that event, the time to petition runs from entry of the amended order.

(b) **Contents of the Petition; Answer or Cross-Petition; Oral Argument.**
    (1) The petition must include the following:
        (A) the facts necessary to understand the question presented;
        (B) the question itself;
        (C) the relief sought;
        (D) the reasons why the appeal should be allowed and is authorized by a statute or rule; and
        (E) an attached copy of:
            (i) the order, decree, or judgment complained of and any related opinion or memorandum, and
            (ii) any order stating the district court's permission to appeal or finding that the necessary conditions are met.
    (2) A party may file an answer in opposition or a cross-petition within 10 days after the petition is served.
    (3) The petition and answer will be submitted without oral argument unless the court of appeals orders otherwise.

(c) **Form of Papers; Number of Copies; Length Limits.** All papers must conform to Rule 32(c)(2). An original and 3 copies must be filed unless the court requires a different number by local rule or by order in a particular case. Except by the court's permission, and excluding the accompanying documents required by Rule 5(b)(1)(E):

(1) a paper produced using a computer must not exceed 5,200 words; and

(2) a handwritten or typewritten paper must not exceed 20 pages.

(d) **Grant of Permission; Fees; Cost Bond; Filing the Record.**

(1) Within 14 days after the entry of the order granting permission to appeal, the appellant must:

(A) pay the district clerk all required fees; and

(B) file a cost bond if required under Rule 7.

(2) A notice of appeal need not be filed. The date when the order granting permission to appeal is entered serves as the date of the notice of appeal for calculating time under these rules.

(3) The district clerk must notify the circuit clerk once the petitioner has paid the fees. Upon receiving this notice, the circuit clerk must enter the appeal on the docket. The record must be forwarded and filed in accordance with Rules 11 and 12(c).

Rule 6. Appeal in a Bankruptcy Case

(a) **Appeal From a Judgment, Order, or Decree of a District Court Exercising Original Jurisdiction in a Bankruptcy Case.** An appeal to a court of appeals from a final judgment, order, or decree of a district court exercising jurisdiction under 28 U.S.C. § 1334 is taken as any other civil appeal under these rules.

(b) **Appeal From a Judgment, Order, or Decree of a District Court or Bankruptcy Appellate Panel Exercising Appellate Jurisdiction in a Bankruptcy Case.**

(1) *Applicability of Other Rules.* These rules apply to an appeal to a court of appeals under 28 U.S.C. § 158(d)(1) from a final judgment, order, or decree of a district court or bankruptcy appellate panel exercising appellate jurisdiction under 28 U.S.C. § 158(a) or (b), but with these qualifications:

(A) Rules 4(a)(4), 4(b), 9, 10, 11, 12(c), 13-20, 22-23, and 24(b) do not apply;

(B) the reference in Rule 3(c) to 'Forms 1A and 1B in the Appendix of Forms' must be read as a reference to Form 5;

(C) when the appeal is from a bankruptcy appellate panel, 'district court,' as used in any applicable rule, means 'appellate panel'; and

(D) in Rule 12.1, 'district court' includes a bankruptcy court or bankruptcy appellate panel.

(2) *Additional Rules.* In addition to the rules made applicable by Rule 6(b)(1), the following rules apply:

(A) Motion for rehearing.

   (i) If a timely motion for rehearing under Bankruptcy Rule 8022 is filed, the time to appeal for all parties runs from the entry of the order disposing of the motion. A notice of appeal filed after the district court or bankruptcy appellate panel announces or enters a judgment, order, or decree—but before disposition of the motion for rehearing—becomes effective when the order disposing of the motion for rehearing is entered.

   (ii) If a party intends to challenge the order disposing of the motion—or the alteration or amendment of a judgment, order, or decree upon the motion—then the party, in compliance with Rules 3(c) and 6(b)(1)(B), must file a notice of appeal or amended notice of appeal. The notice or amended notice must be filed within the time prescribed by Rule 4—excluding Rules 4(a)(4) and 4(b)—measured from the entry of the order disposing of the motion.

   (iii) No additional fee is required to file an amended notice.

(B) The record on appeal.

   (i) Within 14 days after filing the notice of appeal, the appellant must file with the clerk possessing the record assembled in accordance with Bankruptcy Rule 8009—and serve on the appellee—a statement of the issues to be presented on appeal and a designation of the record to be certified and made available to the circuit clerk.

   (ii) An appellee who believes that other parts of the record are necessary must, within 14 days after being served with the appellant's designation, file with the clerk and serve on the appellant a designation of additional parts to be included.

   (iii) The record on appeal consists of:

   • the redesignated record as provided above;
   • the proceedings in the district court or bankruptcy appellate panel; and
   • a certified copy of the docket entries prepared by the clerk under Rule 3(d).

(C) Making the Record Available.

(i) When the record is complete, the district clerk or bankruptcy-appellate-panel clerk must number the documents constituting the record and promptly make it available to the circuit clerk. If the clerk makes the record available in paper form, the clerk will not send documents of unusual bulk or weight, physical exhibits other than documents, or other parts of the record designated for omission by local rule of the court of appeals, unless directed to do so by a party or the circuit clerk. If unusually bulky or heavy exhibits are to be made available in paper form, a party must arrange with the clerks in advance for their transportation and receipt.

(ii) All parties must do whatever else is necessary to enable the clerk to assemble the record and make it available. When the record is made available in paper form, the court of appeals may provide by rule or order that a certified copy of the docket entries be made available in place of the redesignated record. But any party may request at any time during the pendency of the appeal that the redesignated record be made available.

(D) Filing the record. When the district clerk or bankruptcy-appellate-panel clerk has made the record available, the circuit clerk must note that fact on the docket. The date noted on the docket serves as the filing date of the record. The circuit clerk must immediately notify all parties of the filing date.

(c) **Direct Review by Permission Under 28 U.S.C. § 158(d)(2).**

(1) *Applicability of Other Rules.* These rules apply to a direct appeal by permission under 28 U.S.C. § 158(d)(2), but with these qualifications:

(A) Rules 3-4, 5(a)(3), 6(a), 6(b), 8(a), 8(c), 9-12, 13-20, 22-23, and 24(b) do not apply;

(B) as used in any applicable rule, 'district court' or 'district clerk' includes—to the extent appropriate—a bankruptcy court or bankruptcy appellate panel or its clerk; and

(C) the reference to 'Rules 11 and 12(c)' in Rule 5(d)(3) must be read as a reference to Rules 6(c)(2)(B) and (C).

(2) *Additional Rules.* In addition, the following rules apply:

(A) The Record on Appeal. Bankruptcy Rule 8009 governs the record on appeal.

(B) Making the Record Available. Bankruptcy Rule 8010 governs completing the record and making it available.

(C) Stays Pending Appeal. Bankruptcy Rule 8007 applies to stays pending appeal.
(D) Duties of the Circuit Clerk. When the bankruptcy clerk has made the record available, the circuit clerk must note that fact on the docket. The date noted on the docket serves as the filing date of the record. The circuit clerk must immediately notify all parties of the filing date.
(E) Filing a Representation Statement. Unless the court of appeals designates another time, within 14 days after entry of the order granting permission to appeal, the attorney who sought permission must file a statement with the circuit clerk naming the parties that the attorney represents on appeal.

Rule 7. Bond for Costs on Appeal in a Civil Case

In a civil case, the district court may require an appellant to file a bond or provide other security in any form and amount necessary to ensure payment of costs on appeal. Rule 8(b) applies to a surety on a bond given under this rule.

Rule 8. Stay or Injunction Pending Appeal

(a) **Motion for Stay**.
  (1) *Initial Motion in the District Court.* A party must ordinarily move first in the district court for the following relief:
    (A) a stay of the judgment or order of a district court pending appeal;
    (B) approval of a bond or other security provided to obtain a stay of judgment; or
    (C) an order suspending, modifying, restoring, or granting an injunction while an appeal is pending.
  (2) *Motion in the Court of Appeals; Conditions on Relief.* A motion for the relief mentioned in Rule 8(a)(1) may be made to the court of appeals or to one of its judges.
    (A) The motion must:
      (i) show that moving first in the district court would be impracticable; or
      (ii) state that, a motion having been made, the district court denied the motion or failed to afford the relief requested and state any reasons given by the district court for its action.
    (B) The motion must also include:
      (i) the reasons for granting the relief requested and the facts relied on;

      (ii) originals or copies of affidavits or other sworn statements supporting facts subject to dispute; and

      (iii) relevant parts of the record.

  (C) The moving party must give reasonable notice of the motion to all parties.

  (D) A motion under this Rule 8(a)(2) must be filed with the circuit clerk and normally will be considered by a panel of the court. But in an exceptional case in which time requirements make that procedure impracticable, the motion may be made to and considered by a single judge.

  (E) The court may condition relief on a party's filing a bond or other security in the district court.

(b) **Proceeding Against a Security Provider**. If a party gives security with one or more security providers, each provider submits to the jurisdiction of the district court and irrevocably appoints the district clerk as its agent on whom any papers affecting its liability on the security may be served. On motion, a security provider's liability may be enforced in the district court without the necessity of an independent action. The motion and any notice that the district court prescribes may be served on the district clerk, who must promptly send a copy to each security provider whose address is known.

(c) **Stay in a Criminal Case**. Rule 38 of the Federal Rules of Criminal Procedure governs a stay in a criminal case.

Rule 9. Release in a Criminal Case

(a) **Release Before Judgment of Conviction**.

  (1) The district court must state in writing, or orally on the record, the reasons for an order regarding the release or detention of a defendant in a criminal case. A party appealing from the order must file with the court of appeals a copy of the district court's order and the court's statement of reasons as soon as practicable after filing the notice of appeal. An appellant who questions the factual basis for the district court's order must file a transcript of the release proceedings or an explanation of why a transcript was not obtained.

  (2) After reasonable notice to the appellee, the court of appeals must promptly determine the appeal on the basis of the papers, affidavits, and parts of the record that the parties present or the court requires. Unless the court so orders, briefs need not be filed.

(3) The court of appeals or one of its judges may order the defendant's release pending the disposition of the appeal.

(b) **Release After Judgment of Conviction**. A party entitled to do so may obtain review of a district-court order regarding release after a judgment of conviction by filing a notice of appeal from that order in the district court, or by filing a motion in the court of appeals if the party has already filed a notice of appeal from the judgment of conviction. Both the order and the review are subject to Rule 9(a). The papers filed by the party seeking review must include a copy of the judgment of conviction.

(c) **Criteria for Release**. The court must make its decision regarding release in accordance with the applicable provisions of 18 U.S.C. §§ 3142, 3143, and 3145(c).

Rule 10. The Record on Appeal

(a) **Composition of the Record on Appeal**. The following items constitute the record on appeal:

(1) the original papers and exhibits filed in the district court;

(2) the transcript of proceedings, if any; and

(3) a certified copy of the docket entries prepared by the district clerk.

(b) **The Transcript of Proceedings**.

(1) *Appellant's Duty to Order*. Within 14 days after filing the notice of appeal or entry of an order disposing of the last timely remaining motion of a type specified in Rule 4(a)(4)(A), whichever is later, the appellant must do either of the following:

(A) order from the reporter a transcript of such parts of the proceedings not already on file as the appellant considers necessary, subject to a local rule of the court of appeals and with the following qualifications:

(i) the order must be in writing;

(ii) if the cost of the transcript is to be paid by the United States under the Criminal Justice Act, the order must so state; and

(iii) the appellant must, within the same period, file a copy of the order with the district clerk; or

(B) file a certificate stating that no transcript will be ordered.

(2) *Unsupported Finding or Conclusion*. If the appellant intends to urge on appeal that a finding or conclusion is unsupported by the evidence or is contrary to the evidence, the appellant must include in the record a transcript of all evidence relevant to that finding or conclusion.

(3) *Partial Transcript*. Unless the entire transcript is ordered:

    (A) the appellant must—within the 14 days provided in Rule 10(b)(1)—file a statement of the issues that the appellant intends to present on the appeal and must serve on the appellee a copy of both the order or certificate and the statement;

    (B) if the appellee considers it necessary to have a transcript of other parts of the proceedings, the appellee must, within 14 days after the service of the order or certificate and the statement of the issues, file and serve on the appellant a designation of additional parts to be ordered; and

    (C) unless within 14 days after service of that designation the appellant has ordered all such parts, and has so notified the appellee, the appellee may within the following 14 days either order the parts or move in the district court for an order requiring the appellant to do so.

(4) *Payment.* At the time of ordering, a party must make satisfactory arrangements with the reporter for paying the cost of the transcript.

(c) **Statement of the Evidence When the Proceedings Were Not Recorded or When a Transcript Is Unavailable**. If the transcript of a hearing or trial is unavailable, the appellant may prepare a statement of the evidence or proceedings from the best available means, including the appellant's recollection. The statement must be served on the appellee, who may serve objections or proposed amendments within 14 days after being served. The statement and any objections or proposed amendments must then be submitted to the district court for settlement and approval. As settled and approved, the statement must be included by the district clerk in the record on appeal.

(d) **Agreed Statement as the Record on Appeal**. In place of the record on appeal as defined in Rule 10(a), the parties may prepare, sign, and submit to the district court a statement of the case showing how the issues presented by the appeal arose and were decided in the district court. The statement must set forth only those facts averred and proved or sought to be proved that are essential to the courts resolution of the issues. If the statement is truthful, it—together with any additions that the district court may consider necessary to a full presentation of the issues on appeal—must be approved by the district court and must then be certified to the court of appeals as the record on appeal. The district clerk must then send it to the circuit clerk within the time provided by Rule 11. A copy of the agreed statement may be filed in place of the appendix required by Rule 30.

(e) **Correction or Modification of the Record**.

(1) If any difference arises about whether the record truly discloses what occurred in the district court, the difference must be submitted to and settled by that court and the record conformed accordingly.

(2) If anything material to either party is omitted from or misstated in the record by error or accident, the omission or misstatement may be corrected and a supplemental record may be certified and forwarded:

    (A) on stipulation of the parties;

    (B) by the district court before or after the record has been forwarded; or

    (C) by the court of appeals.

(3) All other questions as to the form and content of the record must be presented to the court of appeals.

Rule 11. Forwarding the Record

(a) **Appellant's Duty**. An appellant filing a notice of appeal must comply with Rule 10(b) and must do whatever else is necessary to enable the clerk to assemble and forward the record. If there are multiple appeals from a judgment or order, the clerk must forward a single record.

(b) **Duties of Reporter and District Clerk**.

    (1) *Reporter's Duty to Prepare and File a Transcript*. The reporter must prepare and file a transcript as follows:

        (A) Upon receiving an order for a transcript, the reporter must enter at the foot of the order the date of its receipt and the expected completion date and send a copy, so endorsed, to the circuit clerk.

        (B) If the transcript cannot be completed within 30 days of the reporters receipt of the order, the reporter may request the circuit clerk to grant additional time to complete it. The clerk must note on the docket the action taken and notify the parties.

        (C) When a transcript is complete, the reporter must file it with the district clerk and notify the circuit clerk of the filing.

        (D) If the reporter fails to file the transcript on time, the circuit clerk must notify the district judge and do whatever else the court of appeals directs.

    (2) *District Clerk's Duty to Forward*. When the record is complete, the district clerk must number the documents constituting the record and send them promptly to the circuit clerk together with a list of the documents correspondingly numbered and reasonably identified. Unless directed to do so by a party or the circuit clerk, the district

clerk will not send to the court of appeals documents of unusual bulk or weight, physical exhibits other than documents, or other parts of the record designated for omission by local rule of the court of appeals. If the exhibits are unusually bulky or heavy, a party must arrange with the clerks in advance for their transportation and receipt.

(c) **Retaining the Record Temporarily in the District Court for Use in Preparing the Appeal.** The parties may stipulate, or the district court on motion may order, that the district clerk retain the record temporarily for the parties to use in preparing the papers on appeal. In that event the district clerk must certify to the circuit clerk that the record on appeal is complete. Upon receipt of the appellee's brief, or earlier if the court orders or the parties agree, the appellant must request the district clerk to forward the record.

(d) [Abrogated.]

(e) **Retaining the Record by Court Order.**

   (1) The court of appeals may, by order or local rule, provide that a certified copy of the docket entries be forwarded instead of the entire record. But a party may at any time during the appeal request that designated parts of the record be forwarded.

   (2) The district court may order the record or some part of it retained if the court needs it while the appeal is pending, subject, however, to call by the court of appeals.

   (3) If part or all of the record is ordered retained, the district clerk must send to the court of appeals a copy of the order and the docket entries together with the parts of the original record allowed by the district court and copies of any parts of the record designated by the parties.

(f) **Retaining Parts of the Record in the District Court by Stipulation of the Parties.** The parties may agree by written stipulation filed in the district court that designated parts of the record be retained in the district court subject to call by the court of appeals or request by a party. The parts of the record so designated remain a part of the record on appeal.

(g) **Record for a Preliminary Motion in the Court of Appeals.** If, before the record is forwarded, a party makes any of the following motions in the court of appeals:

   • for dismissal;
   • for release;
   • for a stay pending appeal;
   • for additional security on the bond on appeal or on a bond or other security provided to obtain a stay of judgment; or
   • for any other intermediate order—

the district clerk must send the court of appeals any parts of the record designated by any party.

Rule 12. Docketing the Appeal; Filing a Representation Statement; Filing the Record

(a) **Docketing the Appeal**. Upon receiving the copy of the notice of appeal and the docket entries from the district clerk under Rule 3(d), the circuit clerk must docket the appeal under the title of the district-court action and must identify the appellant, adding the appellant's name if necessary.

(b) **Filing a Representation Statement**. Unless the court of appeals designates another time, the attorney who filed the notice of appeal must, within 14 days after filing the notice, file a statement with the circuit clerk naming the parties that the attorney represents on appeal.

(c) **Filing the Record, Partial Record, or Certificate**. Upon receiving the record, partial record, or district clerk's certificate as provided in Rule 11, the circuit clerk must file it and immediately notify all parties of the filing date.

Rule 12.1. Remand After an Indicative Ruling by the District Court on a Motion for Relief That Is Barred by a Pending Appeal

(a) **Notice to the Court of Appeals**. If a timely motion is made in the district court for relief that it lacks authority to grant because of an appeal that has been docketed and is pending, the movant must promptly notify the circuit clerk if the district court states either that it would grant the motion or that the motion raises a substantial issue.

(b) **Remand After an Indicative Ruling**. If the district court states that it would grant the motion or that the motion raises a substantial issue, the court of appeals may remand for further proceedings but retains jurisdiction unless it expressly dismisses the appeal. If the court of appeals remands but retains jurisdiction, the parties must promptly notify the circuit clerk when the district court has decided the motion on remand.

Title III – Appeals from the United States Tax Court

Rule 13. Appeals from the Tax Court

(a) **Appeal as of Right**.
   (1) *How Obtained; Time for Filing a Notice of Appeal.*

(A) An appeal as of right from the United States Tax Court is commenced by filing a notice of appeal with the Tax Court clerk within 90 days after the entry of the Tax Court's decision. At the time of filing, the appellant must furnish the clerk with enough copies of the notice to enable the clerk to comply with Rule 3(d). If one party files a timely notice of appeal, any other party may file a notice of appeal within 120 days after the Tax Court's decision is entered.

(B) If, under Tax Court rules, a party makes a timely motion to vacate or revise the Tax Court's decision, the time to file a notice of appeal runs from the entry of the order disposing ofthe motion or from the entry of a new decision, whichever is later.

(2) *Notice of Appeal; How Filed.* The notice of appeal may be filed either at the Tax Court clerk's office in the District of Columbia or by sending it to the clerk. If sent by mail the notice is considered filed on the postmark date, subject to § 7502 of the Internal Revenue Code, as amended, and the applicable regulations.

(3) *Contents of the Notice of Appeal; Service; Effect of Filing and Service.* Rule 3 prescribes the contents of a notice of appeal, the manner of service, and the effect of its filing and service. Form 2 in the Appendix of Forms is a suggested form of a notice of appeal.*

(4) *The Record on Appeal; Forwarding; Filing.*

(A) Except as otherwise provided under Tax Court rules for the transcript of proceedings, the appeal is governed by the parts of Rules 10, 11, and 12 regarding the record on appeal from a district court, the time and manner of forwarding and filing, and the docketing in the court of appeals.

(B) If an appeal is taken to more than one court of appeals, the original record must be sent to the court named in the first notice of appeal filed. In an appeal to any other court of appeals, the appellant must apply to that other court to make provision for the record.

(b) **Appeal by Permission**. An appeal by permission is governed by Rule 5.

Rule 14. Applicability of Other Rules to Appeals from the Tax Court

All provisions of these rules, except Rules 4, 6-9, 15-20, and 22-23, apply to appeals from the Tax Court. References in any applicable rule (other than Rule

24(a)) to the district court and district clerk are to be read as referring to the Tax Court and its clerk.

Title IV – Review or Enforcement of an Order of an Administrative Agency, Board, Commission, or Officer.

Rule 15. Review or Enforcement of an Agency Order—How Obtained; Intervention

(a) **Petition for Review; Joint Petition**.
  (1) Review of an agency order is commenced by filing, within the time prescribed by law, a petition for review with the clerk of a court of appeals authorized to review the agency order. If their interests make joinder practicable, two or more persons may join in a petition to the same court to review the same order.
  (2) The petition must:
    (A) name each party seeking review either in the caption or the body of the petition—using such terms as 'et al.,' 'petitioners,' or 'respondents' does not effectively name the parties;
    (B) name the agency as a respondent (even though not named in the petition, the United States is a respondent if required by statute); and
    (C) specify the order or part thereof to be reviewed.
  (3) Form 3 in the Appendix of Forms is a suggested form of a petition for review.*
  (4) In this rule 'agency' includes an agency, board, commission, or officer; 'petition for review' includes a petition to enjoin, suspend, modify, or otherwise review, or a notice of appeal, whichever form is indicated by the applicable statute.

(b) **Application or Cross-Application to Enforce an Order; Answer; Default**.
  (1) An application to enforce an agency order must be filed with the clerk of a court of appeals authorized to enforce the order. If a petition is filed to review an agency order that the court may enforce, a party opposing the petition may file a cross-application for enforcement.
  (2) Within 21 days after the application for enforcement is filed, the respondent must serve on the applicant an answer to the application and file it with the clerk. If the respondent fails to answer in time, the court will enter judgment for the relief requested.

(3) The application must contain a concise statement of the proceedings in which the order was entered, the facts upon which venue is based, and the relief requested.

(c) **Service of the Petition or Application**. The circuit clerk must serve a copy of the petition for review, or an application or cross-application to enforce an agency order, on each respondent as prescribed by Rule 3(d), unless a different manner of service is prescribed by statute. At the time of filing, the petitioner must:

(1) serve, or have served, a copy on each party admitted to participate in the agency proceedings, except for the respondents;

(2) file with the clerk a list of those so served; and

(3) give the clerk enough copies of the petition or application to serve each respondent.

(d) **Intervention**. Unless a statute provides another method, a person who wants to intervene in a proceeding under this rule must file a motion for leave to intervene with the circuit clerk and serve a copy on all parties. The motion—or other notice of intervention authorized by statute—must be filed within 30 days after the petition for review is filed and must contain a concise statement of the interest of the moving party and the grounds for intervention.

(e) **Payment of Fees**. When filing any separate or joint petition for review in a court of appeals, the petitioner must pay the circuit clerk all required fees.

Rule 15.1. Briefs and Oral Argument in a National Labor Relations Board Proceeding

In either an enforcement or a review proceeding, a party adverse to the National Labor Relations Board proceeds first on briefing and at oral argument, unless the court orders otherwise.

Rule 16. The Record on Review or Enforcement

(a) **Composition of the Record**. The record on review or enforcement of an agency order consists of:

(1) the order involved;

(2) any findings or report on which it is based; and

(3) the pleadings, evidence, and other parts of the proceedings before the agency.

(b) **Omissions From or Misstatements in the Record**. The parties may at any time, by stipulation, supply any omission from the record or correct a misstatement, or the court may so direct. If necessary, the court may direct that a supplemental record be prepared and filed.

Rule 17. Filing the Record

(a) **Agency to File; Time for Filing; Notice of Filing**. The agency must file the record with the circuit clerk within 40 days after being served with a petition for review, unless the statute authorizing review provides otherwise, or within 40 days after it files an application for enforcement unless the respondent fails to answer or the court orders otherwise. The court may shorten or extend the time to file the record. The clerk must notify all parties of the date when the record is filed.

(b) **Filing—What Constitutes**.

    (1) The agency must file:

        (A) the original or a certified copy of the entire record or parts designated by the parties; or

        (B) a certified list adequately describing all documents, transcripts of testimony, exhibits, and other material constituting the record, or describing those parts designated by the parties.

    (2) The parties may stipulate in writing that no record or certified list be filed. The date when the stipulation is filed with the circuit clerk is treated as the date when the record is filed.

    (3) The agency must retain any portion of the record not filed with the clerk. All parts of the record retained by the agency are a part of the record on review for all purposes and, if the court or a party so requests, must be sent to the court regardless of any prior stipulation.

Rule 18. Stay Pending Review

(a) **Motion for a Stay**.

    (1) *Initial Motion Before the Agency*. A petitioner must ordinarily move first before the agency for a stay pending review of its decision or order.

    (2) *Motion in the Court of Appeals*. A motion for a stay may be made to the court of appeals or one of its judges.

        (A) The motion must:

            (i) show that moving first before the agency would be impracticable; or

            (ii) state that, a motion having been made, the agency denied the motion or failed to afford the relief requested and state any reasons given by the agency for its action.

   (B) The motion must also include:

      (i) the reasons for granting the relief requested and the facts relied on;

      (ii) originals or copies of affidavits or other sworn statements supporting facts subject to dispute; and

      (iii) relevant parts of the record.

   (C) The moving party must give reasonable notice of the motion to all parties.

   (D) The motion must be filed with the circuit clerk and normally will be considered by a panel of the court. But in an exceptional case in which time requirements make that procedure impracticable, the motion may be made to and considered by a single judge.

(b) **Bond**. The court may condition relief on the filing of a bond or other appropriate security.

Rule 19. Settlement of a Judgment Enforcing an Agency Order in Part

When the court files an opinion directing entry of judgment enforcing the agency's order in part, the agency must within 14 days file with the clerk and serve on each other party a proposed judgment conforming to the opinion. A party who disagrees with the agency's proposed judgment must within 10 days file with the clerk and serve the agency with a proposed judgment that the party believes conforms to the opinion. The court will settle the judgment and direct entry without further hearing or argument.

Rule 20. Applicability of Rules to the Review or Enforcement of an Agency Order

All provisions of these rules, except Rules 3-14 and 22-23, apply to the review or enforcement of an agency order. In these rules, 'appellant' includes a petitioner or applicant, and 'appellee' includes a respondent.

Title V – Extraordinary Writs

Rule 21. Writs of Mandamus and Prohibition, and Other Extraordinary Writs

(a) **Mandamus or Prohibition to a Court: Petition, Filing, Service, and Docketing**.

(1) A party petitioning for a writ of mandamus or prohibition directed to a court must file the petition with the circuit clerk and serve it on all parties to the proceeding in the trial court. The party must also provide a copy to the trial-court judge. All parties to the proceeding in the trial court other than the petitioner are respondents for all purposes.

(2)

    (A) The petition must be titled 'In re [name of petitioner].'

    (B) The petition must state:

        (i) the relief sought;

        (ii) the issues presented;

        (iii) the facts necessary to understand the issue presented by the petition; and

        (iv) the reasons why the writ should issue.

    (C) The petition must include a copy of any order or opinion or parts of the record that may be essential to understand the matters set forth in the petition.

(3) Upon receiving the prescribed docket fee, the clerk must docket the petition and submit it to the court.

(b) **Denial; Order Directing Answer; Briefs; Precedence**.

    (1) The court may deny the petition without an answer. Otherwise, it must order the respondent, if any, to answer within a fixed time.

    (2) The clerk must serve the order to respond on all persons directed to respond.

    (3) Two or more respondents may answer jointly.

    (4) The court of appeals may invite or order the trial-court judge to address the petition or may invite an amicus curiae to do so. The trial-court judge may request permission to address the petition but may not do so unless invited or ordered to do so by the court of appeals.

    (5) If briefing or oral argument is required, the clerk must advise the parties, and when appropriate, the trial-court judge or amicus curiae.

    (6) The proceeding must be given preference over ordinary civil cases.

    (7) The circuit clerk must send a copy of the final disposition to the trial-court judge.

(c) **Other Extraordinary Writs**. An application for an extraordinary writ other than one provided for in Rule 21(a) must be made by filing a petition with the circuit clerk and serving it on the respondents. Proceedings on the application must conform, so far as is practicable, to the procedures prescribed in Rule 21(a) and (b).

(d) **Form of Papers; Number of Copies; Length Limits**. All papers must conform to Rule 32(c)(2). An original and 3 copies must be filed unless the court requires the filing of a different number by local rule or by order in a particular case. Except by the court's permission, and excluding the accompanying documents required by Rule 21(a)(2)(C):

    (1) a paper produced using a computer must not exceed 7,800 words; and

    (2) a handwritten or typewritten paper must not exceed 30 pages.

Title VI – Habeas Corpus; Proceedings In Forma Pauperis

Rule 22. Habeas Corpus and Section 2255 Proceedings

(a) **Application for the Original Writ**. An application for a writ of habeas corpus must be made to the appropriate district court. If made to a circuit judge, the application must be transferred to the appropriate district court. If a district court denies an application made or transferred to it, renewal of the application before a circuit judge is not permitted. The applicant may, under 28 U.S.C. § 2253, appeal to the court of appeals from the district court's order denying the application.

(b) **Certificate of Appealability**.

    (1) In a habeas corpus proceeding in which the detention complained of arises from process issued by a state court, or in a 28 U.S.C. § 2255 proceeding, the applicant cannot take an appeal unless a circuit justice or a circuit or district judge issues a certificate of appealability under 28 U.S.C. §2253(c). If an applicant files a notice of appeal, the district clerk must send to the court of appeals the certificate (if any) and the statement described in Rule 11(a) of the Rules Governing Proceedings Under 28 U.S.C. §2254 or §2255 (if any), along with the notice of appeal and the file of the district-court proceedings. If the district judge has denied the certificate, the applicant may request a circuit judge to issue it.

    (2) A request addressed to the court of appeals may be considered by a circuit judge or judges, as the court prescribes. If no express request for a certificate is filed, the notice of appeal constitutes a request addressed to the judges of the court of appeals.

(3) A certificate of appealability is not required when a state or its representative or the United States or its representative appeals.

Rule 23. Custody or Release of a Prisoner in a Habeas Corpus Proceeding

(a) **Transfer of Custody Pending Review**. Pending review of a decision in a habeas corpus proceeding commenced before a court, justice, or judge of the United States for the release of a prisoner, the person having custody of the prisoner must not transfer custody to another unless a transfer is directed in accordance with this rule. When, upon application, a custodian shows the need for a transfer, the court, justice, or judge rendering the decision under review may authorize the transfer and substitute the successor custodian as a party.

(b) **Detention or Release Pending Review of Decision Not to Release**. While a decision not to release a prisoner is under review, the court or judge rendering the decision, or the court of appeals, or the Supreme Court, or a judge or justice of either court, may order that the prisoner be:

    (1) detained in the custody from which release is sought;

    (2) detained in other appropriate custody; or

    (3) released on personal recognizance, with or without surety.

(c) **Release Pending Review of Decision Ordering Release**. While a decision ordering the release of a prisoner is under review, the prisoner must—unless the court or judge rendering the decision, or the court of appeals, or the Supreme Court, or a judge or justice of either court orders otherwise—be released on personal recognizance, with or without surety.

(d) **Modification of the Initial Order on Custody**. An initial order governing the prisoner's custody or release, including any recognizance or surety, continues in effect pending review unless for special reasons shown to the court of appeals or the Supreme Court, or to a judge or justice of either court, the order is modified or an independent order regarding custody, release, or surety is issued.

Rule 24. Proceeding in Forma Pauperis

(a) **Leave to Proceed in Forma Pauperis**.

    (1) *Motion in the District Court*. Except as stated in Rule 24(a)(3), a party to a district-court action who desires to appeal in forma pauperis must file a motion in the district court. The party must attach an affidavit that:

    (A) shows in the detail prescribed by Form 4 of the Appendix of Forms the party's inability to payor to give security for fees and costs;*

    (B) claims an entitlement to redress; and

    (C) states the issues that the party intends to present on appeaL

(2) *Action on the Motion.* If the district court grants the motion, the party may proceed on appeal without prepaying or giving security for fees and costs, unless a statute provides otherwise. If the district court denies the motion, it must state its reasons in writing.

(3) *Prior Approval.* A party who was permitted to proceed in forma pauperis in the district-court action, or who was determined to be financially unable to obtain an adequate defense in a criminal case, may proceed on appeal in forma pauperis without further authorization, unless:

    (A) the district court—before or after the notice of appeal is filed—certifies that the appeal is not taken in good faith or finds that the party is not otherwise entitled to proceed in forma pauperis and states in writing its reasons for the certification or finding; or

    (B) a statute provides otherwise.

(4) *Notice of District Court's Denial.* The district clerk must immediately notify the parties and the court of appeals when the district court does any of the following:

    (A) denies a motion to proceed on appeal in forma pauperis;

    (B) certifies that the appeal is not taken in good faith; or

    (C) finds that the party is not otherwise entitled to proceed in forma pauperis.

(5) *Motion in the Court of Appeals.* A party may file a motion to proceed on appeal in forma pauperis in the court of appeals within 30 days after service of the notice prescribed in Rule 24(a)(4). The motion must include a copy of the affidavit filed in the district court and the district court's statement of reasons for its action. If no affidavit was filed in the district court, the party must include the affidavit prescribed by Rule 24(a)(l).

(b) **Leave to Proceed in Forma Pauperis on Appeal from the United States Tax Court or on Appeal or Review of an Administrative-Agency Proceeding**. A party may file in the court of appeals a motion for leave to proceed on appeal in forma pauperis with an affidavit prescribed by Rule 24(a)(l):

(1) in an appeal from the United States Tax Court; and

(2) when an appeal or review of a proceeding before an administrative agency, board, commission, or officer proceeds directly in the court of appeals.

(c) **Leave to Use Original Record**. A party allowed to proceed on appeal in forma pauperis may request that the appeal be heard on the original record without reproducing any part.

Title VII – General Provisions

Rule 25. Filing and Service

(a) **Filing**.

    (1) *Filing with the Clerk*. A paper required or permitted to be filed in a court of appeals must be filed with the clerk.

    (2) *Filing: Method and Timeliness*.

        (A) Nonelectronic Filing.

            (i) In General. For a paper not filed electronically, filing may be accomplished by mail addressed to the clerk, but filing is not timely unless the clerk receives the papers within the time fixed for filing.

            (ii) A Brief or Appendix. A brief or appendix not filed electronically is timely filed, however, if on or before the last day for filing, it is:

- mailed to the clerk by first-class mail, or other class of mail that is at least as expeditious, postage prepaid; or
- dispatched to a third-party commercial carrier for delivery to the clerk within 3 days.

            (iii) Inmate Filing. If an institution has a system designed for legal mail, an inmate confined there must use that system to receive the benefit of this Rule 25(a)(2)(A)(iii). A paper not filed electronically by an inmate is timely if it is deposited in the institution's internal mail system on or before the last day for filing and:

- it is accompanied by: a declaration in compliance with 28 U.S.C. § 1746--or a notarized statement--setting out the date of deposit and stating that first-class postage is being prepaid; or evidence (such as a postmark or date stamp) showing that the paper was so deposited and that postage was prepaid; or

- the court of appeals exercises its discretion to permit the later filing of a declaration or notarized statement that satisfies Rule 25(a)(2)(A)(iii).

(B) Electronic Filing and Signing.

    (i) By a Represented Person--Generally Required; Exceptions. A person represented by an attorney must file electronically, unless nonelectronic filing is allowed by the court for good cause or is allowed or required by local rule.

    (ii) By an Unrepresented Person--When Allowed or Required. A person not represented by an attorney:

- may file electronically only if allowed by court order or by local rule; and
- may be required to file electronically only by court order, or by a local rule that includes reasonable exceptions.

    (iii) Signing. A filing made through a person's electronic-filing account and authorized by that person, together with that person's name on a signature block, constitutes the person's signature.

    (iv) Same as a Written Paper. A paper filed electronically is a written paper for purposes of these rules.

(3) *Filing a Motion with a Judge.* If a motion requests relief that may be granted by a single judge, the judge may permit the motion to be filed with the judge; the judge must note the filing date on the motion and give it to the clerk.

(4) *Clerk's Refusal of Documents.* The clerk must not refuse to accept for filing any paper presented for that purpose solely because it is not presented in proper form as required by these rules or by any local rule or practice.

(5) *Privacy Protection.* An appeal in a case whose privacy protection was governed by Federal Rule of Bankruptcy Procedure 9037, Federal Rule of Civil Procedure 5.2, or Federal Rule of Criminal Procedure 49.1 is governed by the same rule on appeal. In all other proceedings, privacy protection is governed by Federal Rule of Civil Procedure 5.2, except that Federal Rule of Criminal Procedure 49.1 governs when an extraordinary writ is sought in a criminal case. The provisions on remote electronic access in Federal Rule of Civil Procedure 5.2(c)(1) and (2) apply in a petition for review of a benefits decision of the Railroad Retirement Board under the Railroad Retirement Act.

(6) Fed. R. App. P.25 Filing and Service [Effective December 1, 2022] (Federal Rules of Appellate Procedure (2022 Edition))

(b) **Service of All Papers Required**. Unless a rule requires service by the clerk, a party must, at or before the time of filing a paper, serve a copy on the other parties to the appeal or review. Service on a party represented by counsel must be made on the party's counsel.

(c) **Manner of Service**.

   (1) Nonelectronic service may be any of the following:

   (A) personal, including delivery to a responsible person at the office of counsel;

   (B) by mail; or

   (C) by third-party commercial carrier for delivery within 3 days.

   (2) Electronic service of a paper may be made (A) by sending it to a registered user by filing it with the court's electronic-filing system or (B) by sending it by other electronic means that the person to be served consented to in writing.

   (3) When reasonable considering such factors as the immediacy of the relief sought, distance, and cost, service on a party must be by a manner at least as expeditious as the manner used to file the paper with the court.

   (4) Service by mail or by commercial carrier is complete on mailing or delivery to the carrier. Service by electronic means is complete on filing or sending, unless the party making service is notified that the paper was not received by the party served.

(d) **Proof of Service**.

   (1) A paper presented for filing must contain either of the following if it was served other than through the court's electronic-filing system:

   (A) an acknowledgment of service by the person served; or

   (B) proof of service consisting of a statement by the person who made service certifying:

   (i)   the date and manner of service;

   (ii) the names of the persons served; and

   (iii) their mail or electronic addresses, facsimile numbers, or the addresses of the places of delivery, as appropriate for the manner of service.

   (2) When a brief or appendix is filed by mailing or dispatch in accordance with Rule 25(a)(2)(A)(ii), the proof of service must also state the date and manner by which the document was mailed or dispatched to the clerk.

   (3) Proof of service may appear on or be affixed to the papers filed.

(e) **Number of Copies**. When these rules require the filing or furnishing of a number of copies, a court may require a different number by local rule or by order in a particular case.

Rule 26. Computing and Extending Time

(a) **Computing Time**. The following rules apply in computing any time period specified in these rules, in any local rule or court order, or in any statute that does not specify a method of computing time.

    (1) *Period Stated in Days or a Longer Unit*. When the period is stated in days or a longer unit of time:

        (A) exclude the day of the event that triggers the period;

        (B) count every day, including intermediate Saturdays, Sundays, and legal holidays; and

        (C) include the last day of the period, but if the last day is a Saturday, Sunday, or legal holiday, the period continues to run until the end of the next day that is not a Saturday, Sunday, or legal holiday.

    (2) *Period Stated in Hours*. When the period is stated in hours:

        (A) begin counting immediately on the occurrence of the event that triggers the period;

        (B) count every hour, including hours during intermediate Saturdays, Sundays, and legal holidays; and

        (C) if the period would end on a Saturday, Sunday, or legal holiday, the period continues to run until the same time on the next day that is not a Saturday, Sunday, or legal holiday.

    (3) *Inaccessibility of the Clerk's Office*. Unless the court orders otherwise, if the clerk's office is inaccessible:

        (A) on the last day for filing under Rule 26(a)(1), then the time for filing is extended to the first accessible day that is not a Saturday, Sunday, or legal holiday; or

        (B) during the last hour for filing under Rule 26(a)(2), then the time for filing is extended to the same time on the first accessible day that is not a Saturday, Sunday, or legal holiday.

    (4) *'Last Day' Defined*. Unless a different time is set by a statute, local rule, or court order, the last day ends:

        (A) for electronic filing in the district court, at midnight in the court's time zone;

        (B) for electronic filing in the court of appeals, at midnight in the time zone of the circuit clerk's principal office;

- (C) for filing under Rules 4(c)(1), 25(a)(2)(A)(ii), and 25(a)(2)(A)(iii)--and filing by mail under Rule 13(a)(2)--at the latest time for the method chosen for delivery to the post office, third-party commercial carrier, or prison mailing system; and
- (D) for filing by other means, when the clerk's office is scheduled to close.
- (5) *'Next Day' Defined.* The 'next day' is determined by continuing to count forward when the period is measured after an event and backward when measured before an event.
- (6) *'Legal Holiday' Defined.* 'Legal holiday' means:
  - (A) the day set aside by statute for observing New Year's Day, Martin Luther King Jr.'s Birthday, Washington's Birthday, Memorial Day, Juneteenth National Independence Day, Independence Day, Labor Day, Columbus Day, Veterans' Day, Thanksgiving Day, or Christmas Day;
  - (B) any day declared a holiday by the President or Congress; and
  - (C) for periods that are measured after an event, any other day declared a holiday by the state where either of the following is located: the district court that rendered the challenged judgment or order, or the circuit clerk's principal office.
- (b) **Extending Time**. For good cause, the court may extend the time prescribed by these rules or by its order to perform any act, or may permit an act to be done after that time expires. But the court may not extend the time to file:
  - (1) a notice of appeal (except as authorized in Rule 4) or a petition for permission to appeal; or
  - (2) a notice of appeal from or a petition to enjoin, set aside, suspend, modify, enforce, or otherwise review an order of an administrative agency, board, commission, or officer of the United States, unless specifically authorized by law.
- (c) **Additional Time after Certain Kinds of Service**. When a party may or must act within a specified time after being served, and the paper is not served electronically on the party or delivered to the party on the date stated in the proof of service, 3 days are added after the period would otherwise expire under Rule 26(a).

Rule 26.1. Disclosure Statement

(a) **Nongovernmental Corporations**. Any nongovernmental corporation that is a party to a proceeding in a court of appeals must file a statement that identifies any parent corporation and any publicly held corporation that owns 10% or more of its stock or states that there is no such corporation. The same requirement applies to a nongovernmental corporation that seeks to intervene.

(b) **Organizational Victims in Criminal Cases**. In a criminal case, unless the government shows good cause, it must file a statement that identifies any organizational victim of the alleged criminal activity. If the organizational victim is a corporation, the statement must also disclose the information required by Rule 26.1(a) to the extent it can be obtained through due diligence.

(c) **Bankruptcy Cases**. In a bankruptcy case, the debtor, the trustee, or, if neither is a party, the appellant must file a statement that:

(1) identifies each debtor not named in the caption; and

(2) for each debtor that is a corporation, discloses the information required by Rule 26.1(a).

(d) **Time for Filing; Supplemental Filing**. The Rule 26.1 statement must:

(1) be filed with the principal brief or upon filing a motion, response, petition, or answer in the court of appeals, whichever occurs first, unless a local rule requires earlier filing;

(2) be included before the table of contents in the principal brief; and

(3) be supplemented whenever the information required under Rule 26.1 changes.

(e) **Number of Copies**. If the Rule 26.1 statement is filed before the principal brief, or if a supplemental statement is filed, an original and 3 copies must be filed unless the court requires a different number by local rule or by order in a particular case.

Rule 27. Motions

(a) **In General**.

(1) *Application for Relief.* An application for an order or other relief is made by motion unless these rules prescribe another form. A motion must be in writing unless the court permits otherwise.

(2) *Contents of a Motion.*

(A) Grounds and relief sought. A motion must state with particularity the grounds for the motion, the relief sought, and the legal argument necessary to support it.

(B) Accompanying documents.

(i) Any affidavit or other paper necessary to support a motion must be served and filed with the motion.

(ii) An affidavit must contain only factual information, not legal argument.

(iii) A motion seeking substantive relief must include a copy of the trial court's opinion or agency's decision as a separate exhibit.

(C) Documents barred or not required.

(i) A separate brief supporting or responding to a motion must not be filed.

(ii) A notice of motion is not required.

(iii) A proposed order is not required.

(3) *Response.*

(A) Time to file. Any party may file a response to a motion; Rule 27(a)(2) governs its contents. The response must be filed within 10 days after service of the motion unless the court shortens or extends the time. A motion authorized by Rules 8, 9, 18, or 41 may be granted before the 10-day period runs only if the court gives reasonable notice to the parties that it intends to act sooner.

(B) Request for affirmative relief. A response may include a motion for affirmative relief. The time to respond to the new motion, and to reply to that response, are governed by Rule 27(a)(3)(A) and (a)(4). The title of the response must alert the court to the request for relief.

(4) *Reply to Response.* Any reply to a response must be filed within 7 days after service of the response. A reply must not present matters that do not relate to the response.

(b) **Disposition of a Motion for a Procedural Order**. The court may act on a motion for a procedural order—including a motion under Rule 26(b)—at any time without awaiting a response, and may, by rule or by order in a particular case, authorize its clerk to act on specified types of procedural motions. A party adversely affected by the court's, or the clerk's, action may file a motion to reconsider, vacate, or modify that action. Timely opposition filed after the motion is granted in whole or in part does not constitute a request to reconsider, vacate, or modify the disposition; a motion requesting that relief must be filed.

(c) **Power of a Single Judge to Entertain a Motion**. A circuit judge may act alone on any motion, but may not dismiss or otherwise determine an appeal or other proceeding. A court of appeals may provide by rule or by order in a particular case that only the court may act on any motion or class of motions. The court may review the action of a single judge.

(d) **Form of Papers; Length Limits; Number of Copies**.

(1) *Format.*

    (A) Reproduction. A motion, response, or reply may be reproduced by any process that yields a clear black image on light paper. The paper must be opaque and unglazed. Only one side of the paper may be used.

    (B) Cover. A cover is not required, but there must be a caption that includes the case number, the name of the court, the title of the case, and a brief descriptive title indicating the purpose of the motion and identifying the party or parties for whom it is filed. If a cover is used, it must be white.

    (C) Binding. The document must be bound in any manner that is secure, does not obscure the text, and permits the document to lie reasonably flat when open.

    (D) Paper size, line spacing, and margins. The document must be on 8½ by 11 inch paper. The text must be double-spaced, but quotations more than two lines long may be indented and single-spaced. Headings and footnotes may be single-spaced. Margins must be at least one inch on all four sides. Page numbers may be placed in the margins, but no text may appear there.

    (E) Typeface and type styles. The document must comply with the typeface requirements of Rule 32(a)(5) and the type-style requirements of Rule 32(a)(6).

(2) *Length Limits.* Except by the court's permission, and excluding the accompanying documents authorized by Rule 27(a)(2)(B):

    (A) a motion or response to a motion produced using a computer must not exceed 5,200 words;

    (B) a handwritten or typewritten motion on or response to a motion must not exceed 20 pages;

    (C) a reply produced using a computer must not exceed 2,600 words; and

    (D) a handwritten or typewritten reply to a response must not exceed 10 pages.

(3) *Number of Copies.* An original and 3 copies must be filed unless the court requires a different number by local rule or by order in a particular case.

(e) **Oral Argument**. A motion will be decided without oral argument unless the court orders otherwise.

Rule 28. Briefs

(a) **Appellant's Brief**. The appellant's brief must contain, under appropriate headings and in the order indicated:

    (1) a disclosure statement if required by Rule 26.1;

    (2) a table of contents, with page references;

    (3) a table of authorities—cases (alphabetically arranged), statutes, and other authorities—with references to the pages of the brief where they are cited;

    (4) a jurisdictional statement, including:

        (A) the basis for the district court's or agency's subject-matter jurisdiction, with citations to applicable statutory provisions and stating relevant facts establishing jurisdiction;

        (B) the basis for the court of appeals' jurisdiction, with citations to applicable statutory provisions and stating relevant facts establishing jurisdiction;

        (C) the filing dates establishing the timeliness of the appeal or petition for review; and

        (D) an assertion that the appeal is from a final order or judgment that disposes of all parties' claims, or information establishing the court of appeals' jurisdiction on some other basis;

    (5) a statement of the issues presented for review;

    (6) a concise statement of the case setting out the facts relevant to the issues submitted for review, describing the relevant procedural history, and identifying the rulings presented for review, with appropriate references to the record (see Rule 28(e));

    (7) a summary of the argument, which must contain a succinct, clear, and accurate statement of the arguments made in the body of the brief, and which must not merely repeat the argument headings;

    (8) the argument, which must contain:

        (A) appellant's contentions and the reasons for them, with citations to the authorities and parts of the record on which the appellant relies; and

        (B) for each issue, a concise statement of the applicable standard of review (which may appear in the discussion of the issue or under a separate heading placed before the discussion of the issues);

    (9) a short conclusion stating the precise relief sought; and

    (10) the certificate of compliance, if required by Rule 32(g)(1).

(b) **Appellee's Brief**. The appellee's brief must conform to the requirements of Rule 28(a)(1)-(8) and (10), except that none of the following need appear unless the appellee is dissatisfied with the appellant's statement:

(1) the jurisdictional statement;

(2) the statement of the issues;

(3) the statement of the case; and

(4) the statement of the standard of review.

(c) **Reply Brief**. The appellant may file a brief in reply to the appellee's brief. Unless the court permits, no further briefs may be filed. A reply brief must contain a table of contents, with page references, and a table of authorities—cases (alphabetically arranged), statutes, and other authorities—with references to the pages of the reply brief where they are cited.

(d) **References to Parties**. In briefs and at oral argument, counsel should minimize use of the terms 'appellant' and 'appellee.' To make briefs clear, counsel should use the parties' actual names or the designations used in the lower court or agency proceeding, or such descriptive terms as 'the employee,' 'the injured person,' 'the taxpayer,' 'the ship,' 'the stevedore.'

(e) **References to the Record**. References to the parts of the record contained in the appendix filed with the appellant's brief must be to the pages of the appendix. If the appendix is prepared after the briefs are filed, a party referring to the record must follow one of the methods detailed in Rule 30(c). If the original record is used under Rule 30(f) and is not consecutively paginated, or if the brief refers to an unreproduced part of the record, any reference must be to the page of the original document. For example:

- Answer p. 7;
- Motion for Judgment p. 2;
- Transcript p. 231.

Only clear abbreviations may be used. A party referring to evidence whose admissibility is in controversy must cite the pages of the appendix or of the transcript at which the evidence was identified, offered, and received or rejected.

(f) **Reproduction of Statutes, Rules, Regulations, etc**. If the court's determination of the issues presented requires the study of statutes, rules, regulations, etc., the relevant parts must be set out in the brief or in an addendum at the end, or may be supplied to the court in pamphlet form.

(g) [Reserved]

(h) [Reserved]

(i) **Briefs in a Case Involving Multiple Appellants or Appellees**. In a case involving more than one appellant or appellee, including consolidated cases, any number of appellants or appellees may join in a brief, and any party may adopt by reference a part of another's brief. Parties may also join in reply briefs.

(j) **Citation of Supplemental Authorities**. If pertinent and significant authorities come to a party's attention after the party's brief has been filed—or after oral argument but before decision—a party may promptly advise the circuit clerk by letter, with a copy to all other parties, setting forth the citations. The letter must state the reasons for the supplemental citations, referring either to the page of the brief or to a point argued orally. The body of the letter must not exceed 350 words. Any response must be made promptly and must be similarly limited.

Rule 28.1. Cross-Appeals

(a) **Applicability**. This rule applies to a case in which a cross-appeal is filed. Rules 28(a)-(c), 31(a)(1), 32(a)(2), and 32(a)(7)(A)-(B) do not apply to such a case, except as otherwise provided in this rule.

(b) **Designation of Appellant**. The party who files a notice of appeal first is the appellant for the purposes of this rule and Rules 30 and 34. If notices are filed on the same day, the plaintiff in the proceeding below is the appellant. These designations may be modified by the parties' agreement or by court order.

(c) **Briefs**. In a case involving a cross-appeal:

    (1) *Appellant's Principal Brief*. The appellant must file a principal brief in the appeal. That brief must comply with Rule 28(a).

    (2) *Appellee's Principal and Response Brief*. The appellee must file a principal brief in the cross-appeal and must, in the same brief, respond to the principal brief in the appeal. That appellee's brief must comply with Rule 28(a), except that the brief need not include a statement of the case unless the appellee is dissatisfied with the appellant's statement.

    (3) *Appellant's Response and Reply Brief*. The appellant must file a brief that responds to the principal brief in the cross-appeal and may, in the same brief, reply to the response in the appeal. That brief must comply with Rule 28(a)(2)-(8) and (10), except that none of the following need appear unless the appellant is dissatisfied with the appellee's statement in the cross-appeal:

        (A) the jurisdictional statement;

      (B) the statement of the issues;

      (C) the statement of the case; and

      (D) the statement of the standard of review.

  (4) *Appellee's Reply Brief.* The appellee may file a brief in reply to the response in the cross-appeal. That brief must comply with Rule 28(a)(2)-(3) and (10) and must be limited to the issues presented by the cross-appeal.

  (5) *No Further Briefs.* Unless the court permits, no further briefs may be filed in a case involving a cross-appeal.

(d) **Cover**. Except for filings by unrepresented parties, the cover of the appellant's principal brief must be blue; the appellee's principal and response brief, red; the appellant's response and reply brief, yellow; the appellee's reply brief, gray; and intervenor's or amicus curiae's brief, green; and any supplemental brief, tan. The front cover of a brief must contain the information required by Rule 32(a)(2).

(e) **Length**.

  (1) *Page Limitation.* Unless it complies with Rule 28.1(e)(2), the appellant's principal brief must not exceed 30 pages; the appellee's principal and response brief, 35 pages; the appellant's response and reply brief, 30 pages; and the appellee's reply brief, 15 pages.

  (2) *Type-Volume Limitation.*

    (A) The appellant's principal brief or the appellant's response and reply brief is acceptable if it:

      (i) contains no more than 13,000 words; or

      (ii) uses a monospaced face and contains no more than 1,300 lines of text.

    (B) The appellee's principal and response brief is acceptable if it:

      (i) contains no more than 15,300 words; or

      (ii) uses a monospaced face and contains no more than 1,500 lines of text.

    (C) The appellee's reply brief is acceptable if it contains no more than half of the type volume specified in Rule 28.1(e)(2)(A).

(f) **Time to Serve and File a Brief**. Briefs must be served and filed as follows:

  (1) the appellant's principal brief, within 40 days after the record is filed;

  (2) the appellee's principal and response brief, within 30 days after the appellant's principal brief is served;

  (3) the appellant's response and reply brief, within 30 days after the appellee's principal and response brief is served; and

(4) the appellee's reply brief, within 21 days after the appellant's response and reply brief is served, but at least 7 days before argument unless the court, for good cause, allows a later filing.

Rule 29. Brief of an Amicus Curiae

(a) **During Initial Consideration of a Case on the Merits**.

    (1) *Applicability*. This Rule 29(a) governs amicus filings during a court's initial consideration of a case on the merits.

    (2) *When Permitted*. The United States or its officer or agency or a state may file an amicus brief without the consent of the parties or leave of court. Any other amicus curiae may file a brief only by leave of court or if the brief states that all parties have consented to its filing, but a court of appeals may prohibit the filing of or may strike an amicus brief that would result in a judge's disqualification.

    (3) *Motion for Leave to File*. The motion must be accompanied by the proposed brief and state:

        (A) the movant's interest; and

        (B) the reason why an amicus brief is desirable and why the matters asserted are relevant to the disposition of the case.

    (4) *Contents and Form*. An amicus brief must comply with Rule 32. In addition to the requirements of Rule 32, the cover must identify the party or parties supported and indicate whether the brief supports affirmance or reversal. An amicus brief need not comply with Rule 28, but must include the following:

        (A) if the amicus curiae is a corporation, a disclosure statement like that required of parties by Rule 26.1;

        (B) a table of contents, with page references;

        (C) a table of authorities--cases (alphabetically arranged), statutes, and other authorities-- with references to the pages of the brief where they are cited;

        (D) a concise statement of the identity of the amicus curiae, its interest in the case, and the source of its authority to file;

        (E) unless the amicus curiae is one listed in the first sentence of Rule 29(a)(2), a statement that indicates whether:

            (i) a party's counsel authored the brief in whole or in part;

            (ii) a party or a party's counsel contributed money that was intended to fund preparing or submitting the brief; and

            (iii) a person--other than the amicus curiae, its members, or its counsel--contributed money that was intended to fund preparing or submitting the brief and, if so, identifies each such person;

(F) an argument, which may be preceded by a summary and which need not include a statement of the applicable standard of review; and

(G) a certificate of compliance under Rule 32(g)(1), if length is computed using a word or line limit.

(5) *Length.* Except by the court's permission, an amicus brief may be no more than one-half the maximum length authorized by these rules for a party's principal brief. If the court grants a party permission to file a longer brief, that extension does not affect the length of an amicus brief.

(6) *Time for Filing.* An amicus curiae must file its brief, accompanied by a motion for filing when necessary, no later than 7 days after the principal brief of the party being supported is filed. An amicus curiae that does not support either party must file its brief no later than 7 days after the appellant's or petitioner's principal brief is filed. A court may grant leave for later filing, specifying the time within which an opposing party may answer.

(7) *Reply Brief.* Except by the court's permission, an amicus curiae may not file a reply brief.

(8) *Oral Argument.* An amicus curiae may participate in oral argument only with the court's permission.

(b) **During Consideration of Whether to Grant Rehearing.**

(1) *Applicability.* This Rule 29(b) governs amicus filings during a court's consideration of whether to grant panel rehearing or rehearing en banc, unless a local rule or order in a case provides otherwise.

(2) *When Permitted.* The United States or its officer or agency or a state may file an amicus brief without the consent of the parties or leave of court. Any other amicus curiae may file a brief only by leave of court.

(3) *Motion for Leave to File.* Rule 29(a)(3) applies to a motion for leave.

(4) *Contents, Form, and Length.* Rule 29(a)(4) applies to the amicus brief. The brief must not exceed 2,600 words.

(5) *Time for Filing.* An amicus curiae supporting the petition for rehearing or supporting neither party must file its brief, accompanied by a motion for filing when necessary, no later than 7 days after the petition is filed. An amicus curiae opposing the petition must file its brief, accompanied by a motion for filing when necessary, no later than the date set by the court for the response.

Rule 30. Appendix to the Briefs

(a) **Appellant's Responsibility**.

    (1) *Contents of the Appendix*. The appellant must prepare and file an appendix to the briefs containing:

        (A) the relevant docket entries in the proceeding below;

        (B) the relevant portions of the pleadings, charge, findings, or opinion;

        (C) the judgment, order, or decision in question; and

        (D) other parts of the record to which the parties wish to direct the court's attention.

    (2) *Excluded Material*. Memoranda of law in the district court should not be included in the appendix unless they have independent relevance. Parts of the record may be relied on by the court or the parties even though not included in the appendix.

    (3) *Time to File; Number of Copies*. Unless filing is deferred under Rule 30(c), the appellant must file 10 copies of the appendix with the brief and must serve one copy on counsel for each party separately represented. An unrepresented party proceeding in forma pauperis must file 4 legible copies with the clerk, and one copy must be served on counsel for each separately represented party. The court may by local rule or by order in a particular case require the filing or service of a different number.

(b) **All Parties' Responsibilities**.

    (1) *Determining the Contents of the Appendix*. The parties are encouraged to agree on the contents of the appendix. In the absence of an agreement, the appellant must, within 14 days after the record is filed, serve on the appellee a designation of the parts of the record the appellant intends to include in the appendix and a statement of the issues the appellant intends to present for review. The appellee may, within 14 days after receiving the designation, serve on the appellant a designation of additional parts to which it wishes to direct the court's attention. The appellant must include the designated parts in the appendix. The parties must not engage in unnecessary designation of parts of the record, because the entire record is available to the court. This paragraph applies also to a cross-appellant and a cross-appellee.

    (2) *Costs of Appendix*. Unless the parties agree otherwise, the appellant must pay the cost of the appendix. If the appellant considers parts of the record designated by the appellee to be unnecessary, the appellant

may advise the appellee, who must then advance the cost of including those parts. The cost of the appendix is a taxable cost. But if any party causes unnecessary parts of the record to be included in the appendix, the court may impose the cost of those parts on that party. Each circuit must, by local rule, provide for sanctions against attorneys who unreasonably and vexatiously increase litigation costs by including unnecessary material in the appendix.

(c) **Deferred Appendix**.

(1) *Deferral Until After Briefs Are Filed*. The court may provide by rule for classes of cases or by order in a particular case that preparation of the appendix may be deferred until after the briefs have been filed and that the appendix may be filed 21 days after the appellee's brief is served. Even though the filing of the appendix may be deferred, Rule 30(b) applies; except that a party must designate the parts of the record it wants included in the appendix when it serves its brief, and need not include a statement of the issues presented.

(2) *References to the Record*.

(A) If the deferred appendix is used, the parties may cite in their briefs the pertinent pages of the record. When the appendix is prepared, the record pages cited in the briefs must be indicated by inserting record page numbers, in brackets, at places in the appendix where those pages of the record appear.

(B) A party who wants to refer directly to pages of the appendix may serve and file copies of the brief within the time required by Rule 31(a), containing appropriate references to pertinent pages of the record. In that event, within 14 days after the appendix is filed, the party must serve and file copies of the brief, containing references to the pages of the appendix in place of or in addition to the references to the pertinent pages of the record. Except for the correction of typographical errors, no other changes may be made to the brief.

(d) **Format of the Appendix**. The appendix must begin with a table of contents identifying the page at which each part begins. The relevant docket entries must follow the table of contents. Other parts of the record must follow chronologically. When pages from the transcript of proceedings are placed in the appendix, the transcript page numbers must be shown in brackets immediately before the included pages. Omissions in the text of papers or of the transcript must be indicated by asterisks. Immaterial formal matters (captions, subscriptions, acknowledgments, etc.) should be omitted.

(e) **Reproduction of Exhibits**. Exhibits designated for inclusion in the appendix may be reproduced in a separate volume, or volumes, suitably indexed. Four copies must be filed with the appendix, and one copy must be served on counsel for each separately represented party. If a transcript of a proceeding before an administrative agency, board, commission, or officer was used in a district-court action and has been designated for inclusion in the appendix, the transcript must be placed in the appendix as an exhibit.

(f) **Appeal on the Original Record Without an Appendix**. The court may, either by rule for all cases or classes of cases or by order in a particular case, dispense with the appendix and permit an appeal to proceed on the original record with any copies of the record, or relevant parts, that the court may order the parties to file.

Rule 31. Serving and Filing Briefs

(a) **Time to Serve and File a Brief**.

    (1) The appellant must serve and file a brief within 40 days after the record is filed. The appellee must serve and file a brief within 30 days after the appellant's brief is served. The appellant may serve and file a reply brief within 21 days after service of the appellee's brief but a reply brief must be filed at least 7 days before argument, unless the court, for good cause, allows a later filing.

    (2) A court of appeals that routinely considers cases on the merits promptly after the briefs are filed may shorten the time to serve and file briefs, either by local rule or by order in a particular case.

(b) **Number of Copies**. Twenty-five copies of each brief must be filed with the clerk and 2 copies must be served on each unrepresented party and on counsel for each separately represented party. An unrepresented party proceeding in forma pauperis must file 4 legible copies with the clerk, and one copy must be served on each unrepresented party and on counsel for each separately represented party. The court may by local rule or by order in a particular case require the filing or service of a different number.

(c) **Consequence of Failure to File**. If an appellant fails to file a brief within the time provided by this rule, or within an extended time, an appellee may move to dismiss the appeal. An appellee who fails to file a brief will not be heard at oral argument unless the court grants permission.

Rule 32. Form of Briefs, Appendices, and Other Papers

(a) **Form of a Brief**.

(1) *Reproduction.*
   (A) A brief may be reproduced by any process that yields a clear black image on light paper. The paper must be opaque and unglazed. Only one side of the paper may be used.
   (B) Text must be reproduced with a clarity that equals or exceeds the output of a laser printer.
   (C) Photographs, illustrations, and tables may be reproduced by any method that results in a good copy of the original; a glossy finish is acceptable if the original is glossy.

(2) *Cover.* Except for filings by unrepresented parties, the cover of the appellant's brief must be blue; the appellee's, red; an intervenor's or amicus curiae's, green; any reply brief, gray and any supplemental brief, tan. The front cover of a brief must contain:
   (A) the number of the case centered at the top;
   (B) the name of the court;
   (C) the title of the case (see Rule 12(a));
   (D) the nature of the proceeding (e.g., Appeal, Petition for Review) and the name of the court, agency, or board below;
   (E) the title of the brief, identifying the party or parties for whom the brief is filed; and
   (F) the name, office address, and telephone number of counsel representing the party for whom the brief is filed.

(3) *Binding.* The brief must be bound in any manner that is secure, does not obscure the text, and permits the brief to lie reasonably flat when open.

(4) *Paper Size, Line Spacing, and Margins.* The brief must be on 8½ by 11 inch paper. The text must be double-spaced, but quotations more than two lines long may be indented and single-spaced. Headings and footnotes may be single-spaced. Margins must be at least one inch on all four sides. Page numbers may be placed in the margins, but no text may appear there.

(5) *Typeface.* Either a proportionally spaced or a monospaced face may be used.
   (A) A proportionally spaced face must include serifs, but sans-serif type may be used in headings and captions. A proportionally spaced face must be 14-point or larger.
   (B) A monospaced face may not contain more than 10½ characters per inch.

(6) *Type Styles.* A brief must be set in a plain, roman style, although italics or boldface may be used for emphasis. Case names must be italicized or underlined.

(7) *Length.*

    (A) Page limitation. A principal brief may not exceed 30 pages, or a reply brief 15 pages, unless it complies with Rule 32(a)(7)(B).

    (B) Type-volume limitation.

        (i) A principal brief is acceptable if it:

- contains no more than 13,000 words; or
- uses a monospaced face and contains no more than 1,300 lines of text.

        (ii) A reply brief is acceptable if it contains no more than half of the type volume specified in Rule 32(a)(7)(B)(i).

(b) **Form of an Appendix**. An appendix must comply with Rule 32(a)(1), (2), (3), and (4), with the following exceptions:

    (1) The cover of a separately bound appendix must be white.

    (2) An appendix may include a legible photocopy of any document found in the record or of a printed judicial or agency decision.

    (3) When necessary to facilitate inclusion of odd-sized documents such as technical drawings, an appendix may be a size other than 8½ by 11 inches, and need not lie reasonably flat when opened.

(c) **Form of Other Papers**.

    (1) *Motion*. The form of a motion is governed by Rule 27(d).

    (2) *Other Papers*. Any other paper, including a petition for panel rehearing and a petition for hearing or rehearing en banc, and any response to such a petition, must be reproduced in the manner prescribed by Rule 32(a), with the following exceptions:

        (A) A cover is not necessary if the caption and signature page of the paper together contain the information required by Rule 32(a)(2). If a cover is used, it must be white.

        (B) Rule 32(a)(7) does not apply.

(d) **Signature**. Every brief, motion, or other paper filed with the court must be signed by the party filing the paper or, if the party is represented, by one of the party's attorneys.

(e) **Local Variation**. Every court of appeals must accept documents that comply with the form requirements of this rule and the length limits set by these rules. By local rule or order in a particular case, a court of appeals may accept documents that do not meet all the form requirements of this rule or the length limits set by these rules.

(f) **Items Excluded from Length**. In computing any length limit, headings, footnotes, and quotations count toward the limit but the following items do not:
- cover page;
- disclosure statement;
- table of contents;
- table of citations;
- statement regarding oral argument;
- addendum containing statutes, rules, or regulations;
- certificate of counsel;
- signature block;
- proof of service; and
- any item specifically excluded by these rules or by local rule.

(g) **Certificate of Compliance**.

(1) *Briefs and Papers That Require a Certificate*. A brief submitted under Rules 28.1(e)(2), 29(b)(4), or 32(a)(7)(B)--and a paper submitted under Rules 5(c)(1), 21(d)(1), 27(d)(2)(A), 27(d)(2)(C), 35(b)(2)(A), or 40(b)(1)--must include a certificate by the attorney, or an unrepresented party, that the document complies with the type-volume limitation. The person preparing the certificate may rely on the word or line count of the word-processing system used to prepare the document. The certificate must state the number of words--or the number of lines of monospaced type--in the document.

(2) *Acceptable Form*. Form 6 in the Appendix of Forms meets the requirements for a certificate of compliance.

Rule 32.1. Citing Judicial Dispositions

(a) **Citation Permitted**. A court may not prohibit or restrict the citation of federal judicial opinions, orders, judgments, or other written dispositions that have been:

    (i) designated as 'unpublished,' 'not for publication,' 'non-precedential,' 'not precedent,' or the like; and

    (ii) issued on or after January 1, 2007.

(b) **Copies Required**. If a party cites a federal judicial opinion, order, judgment, or other written disposition that is not available in a publicly accessible electronic database, the party must file and serve a copy of that opinion, order, judgment, or disposition with the brief or other paper in which it is cited.

Rule 33. Appeal Conferences

The court may direct the attorneys—and, when appropriate, the parties—to participate in one or more conferences to address any matter that may aid in disposing of the proceedings, including simplifying the issues and discussing settlement. A judge or other person designated by the court may preside over the conference, which may be conducted in person or by telephone. Before a settlement conference, the attorneys must consult with their clients and obtain as much authority as feasible to settle the case. The court may, as a result of the conference, enter an order controlling the course of the proceedings or implementing any settlement agreement.

Rule 34. Oral Argument

(a) **In General**.
    (1) *Party's Statement*. Any party may file, or a court may require by local rule, a statement explaining why oral argument should, or need not, be permitted.
    (2) *Standards*. Oral argument must be allowed in every case unless a panel of three judges who have examined the briefs and record unanimously agrees that oral argument is unnecessary for any of the following reasons:
        (A) the appeal is frivolous;
        (B) the dispositive issue or issues have been authoritatively decided; or
        (C) the facts and legal arguments are adequately presented in the briefs and record, and the decisional process would not be significantly aided by oral argument.

(b) **Notice of Argument; Postponement**. The clerk must advise all parties whether oral argument will be scheduled, and, if so, the date, time, and place for it, and the time allowed for each side. A motion to postpone the argument or to allow longer argument must be filed reasonably in advance of the hearing date.

(c) **Order and Contents of Argument**. The appellant opens and concludes the argument. Counsel must not read at length from briefs, records, or authorities.

(d) **Cross-Appeals and Separate Appeals**. If there is a cross-appeal, Rule 28.1(b) determines which party is the appellant and which is the appellee for purposes of oral argument. Unless the court directs otherwise, a cross-appeal or separate appeal must be argued when the initial appeal is argued. Separate parties should avoid duplicative argument.

(e) **Nonappearance of a Party**. If the appellee fails to appear for argument, the court must hear appellant's argument. If the appellant fails to appear for argument, the court may hear the appellee's argument. If neither party appears, the case will be decided on the briefs, unless the court orders otherwise.

(f) **Submission on Briefs**. The parties may agree to submit a case for decision on the briefs, but the court may direct that the case be argued.

(g) **Use of Physical Exhibits at Argument; Removal**. Counsel intending to use physical exhibits other than documents at the argument must arrange to place them in the courtroom on the day of the argument before the court convenes. After the argument, counsel must remove the exhibits from the courtroom, unless the court directs otherwise. The clerk may destroy or dispose of the exhibits if counsel does not reclaim them within a reasonable time after the clerk gives notice to remove them.

Rule 35. En Banc Determination

(a) **When Hearing or Rehearing En Banc May Be Ordered**. A majority of the circuit judges who are in regular active service and who are not disqualified may order that an appeal or other proceeding be heard or reheard by the court of appeals en banc. An en banc hearing or rehearing is not favored and ordinarily will not be ordered unless:

(1) en banc consideration is necessary to secure or maintain uniformity of the court's decisions; or

(2) the proceeding involves a question of exceptional importance.

(b) **Petition for Hearing or Rehearing En Banc**. A party may petition for a hearing or rehearing en banc.

(1) The petition must begin with a statement that either:

(A) the panel decision conflicts with a decision of the United States Supreme Court or of the court to which the petition is addressed (with citation to the conflicting case or cases) and consideration by the full court is therefore necessary to secure and maintain uniformity of the court's decisions; or

(B) the proceeding involves one or more questions of exceptional importance, each of which must be concisely stated; for example, a petition may assert that a proceeding presents a question of exceptional importance if it involves an issue on which the panel decision conflicts with the authoritative decisions of other United States Courts of Appeals that have addressed the issue.

(2) Except by the court's permission:

    (A) a petition for an en banc hearing or rehearing produced using a computer must not exceed 3,900 words; and

    (B) a handwritten or typewritten petition for an en banc hearing or rehearing must not exceed 15 pages.

  (3) For purposes of the limits in Rule 35(b)(2), if a party files both a petition for panel rehearing and a petition for rehearing en banc, they are considered a single document even if they are filed separately, unless separate filing is required by local rule.

(c) **Time for Petition for Hearing or Rehearing En Banc.** A petition that an appeal be heard initially en banc must be filed by the date when the appellee's brief is due. A petition for a rehearing en banc must be filed within the time prescribed by Rule 40 for filing a petition for rehearing.

(d) **Number of Copies.** The number of copies to be filed must be prescribed by local rule and may be altered by order in a particular case.

(e) **Response.** No response may be filed to a petition for an en banc consideration unless the court orders a response. The length limits in Rule 35(b)(2) apply to a response.

(f) **Call for a Vote.** A vote need not be taken to determine whether the case will be heard or reheard en banc unless a judge calls for a vote.

Rule 36. Entry of Judgment; Notice

(a) **Entry.** A judgment is entered when it is noted on the docket. The clerk must prepare, sign, and enter the judgment:

  (1) after receiving the court's opinion-but if settlement of the judgment's form is required, after final settlement; or

  (2) if a judgment is rendered without an opinion, as the court instructs.

(b) **Notice.** On the date when judgment is entered, the clerk must serve on all parties a copy of the opinion—or the judgment, if no opinion was written—and a notice of the date when the judgment was entered.

Rule 37. Interest on Judgment

(a) **When the Court Affirms.** Unless the law provides otherwise, if a money judgment in a civil case is affirmed, whatever interest is allowed by law is payable from the date when the district court's judgment was entered.

(b) **When the Court Reverses.** If the court modifies or reverses a judgment with a direction that a money judgment be entered in the district court, the mandate must contain instructions about the allowance of interest.

Rule 38. Frivolous Appeal—Damages and Costs

If a court of appeals determines that an appeal is frivolous, it may, after a separately filed motion or notice from the court and reasonable opportunity to respond, award just damages and single or double costs to the appellee.

Rule 39. Costs

(a) **Against Whom Assessed**. The following rules apply unless the law provides or the court orders otherwise:
   (1) if an appeal is dismissed, costs are taxed against the appellant, unless the parties agree otherwise;
   (2) if a judgment is affirmed, costs are taxed against the appellant;
   (3) if a judgment is reversed, costs are taxed against the appellee;
   (4) if a judgment is affirmed in part, reversed in part, modified, or vacated, costs are taxed only as the court orders.

(b) **Costs For and Against the United States**. Costs for or against the United States, its agency, or officer will be assessed under Rule 39(a) only if authorized by law.

(c) **Costs of Copies**. Each court of appeals must, by local rule, fix the maximum rate for taxing the cost of producing necessary copies of a brief or appendix, or copies of records authorized by Rule 30(f). The rate must not exceed that generally charged for such work in the area where the clerk's office is located and should encourage economical methods of copying.

(d) **Bill of Costs: Objections; Insertion in Mandate**.
   (1) A party who wants costs taxed must—within 14 days after entry of judgment—file with the circuit clerk and serve an itemized and verified bill of costs.
   (2) Objections must be filed within 14 days after service of the bill of costs, unless the court extends the time.
   (3) The clerk must prepare and certify an itemized statement of costs for insertion in the mandate, but issuance of the mandate must not be delayed for taxing costs. If the mandate issues before costs are finally determined, the district clerk must—upon the circuit clerk's request—add the statement of costs, or any amendment of it, to the mandate.

(e) **Costs on Appeal Taxable in the District Court**. The following costs on appeal are taxable in the district court for the benefit of the party entitled to costs under this rule:
   (1) the preparation and transmission of the record;
   (2) the reporter's transcript, if needed to determine the appeal;

(3) premiums paid for a bond or other security to preserve rights pending appeal; and

(4) the fee for filing the notice of appeal.

Rule 40. Petition for Panel Rehearing

(a) **Time to File; Contents; Response; Action by the Court if Granted.**

    (1) *Time.* Unless the time is shortened or extended by order or local rule, a petition for panel rehearing may be filed within 14 days after entry of judgment. But in a civil case, unless an order shortens or extends the time, the petition may be filed by any party within 45 days after entry of judgment if one of the parties is:

        (A) the United States;

        (B) a United States agency;

        (C) a United States officer or employee sued in an official capacity; or

        (D) a current or former United States officer or employee sued in an individual capacity for an act or omission occurring in connection with duties performed on the United States' behalf— including all instances in which the United States represents that person when the court of appeals' judgment is entered or files the petition for that person.

    (2) *Contents.* The petition must state with particularity each point of law or fact that the petitioner believes the court has overlooked or misapprehended and must argue in support of the petition. Oral argument is not permitted.

    (3) *Response.* Unless the court requests, no response to a petition for panel rehearing is permitted. Ordinarily, rehearing will not be granted in the absence of such a request. If a response is requested, the requirements of Rule 40(b) apply to the response.

    (4) *Action by the Court.* If a petition for panel rehearing is granted, the court may do any of the following:

        (A) make a final disposition of the case without reargument;

        (B) restore the case to the calendar for reargument or resubmission; or

        (C) issue any other appropriate order.

(b) **Form of Petition; Length.** The petition must comply in form with Rule 32. Copies must be served and filed as Rule 31 prescribes. Except by the court's permission:

(1) a petition for panel rehearing produced using a computer must not exceed 3,900 words; and

(2) a handwritten or typewritten petition for panel rehearing must not exceed 15 pages.

Rule 41. Mandate: Contents; Issuance and Effective Date; Stay

(a) **Contents**. Unless the court directs that a formal mandate issue, the mandate consists of a certified copy of the judgment, a copy of the court's opinion, if any, and any direction about costs.

(b) **When Issued**. The court's mandate must issue 7 days after the time to file a petition for rehearing expires, or 7 days after entry of an order denying a timely petition for panel rehearing, petition for rehearing en banc, or motion for stay of mandate, whichever is later. The court may shorten or extend the time by order.

(c) **Effective Date**. The mandate is effective when issued.

(d) **Staying the Mandate Pending a Petition for Certiorari**.

(1) *Motion to Stay*. A party may move to stay the mandate pending the filing of a petition for a writ of certiorari in the Supreme Court. The motion must be served on all parties and must show that the petition would present a substantial question and that there is good cause for a stay.

(2) *Duration of Stay; Extensions*. The stay must not exceed 90 days, unless:

(A) the period is extended for good cause; or

(B) the party who obtained the stay notifies the circuit clerk in writing within the period of the stay:

(i) that the time for filing a petition has been extended, in which case the stay continues for the extended period; or

(ii) that the petition has been filed, in which case the stay continues until the Supreme Court's final disposition.

(3) *Security*. The court may require a bond or other security as a condition to granting or continuing a stay of the mandate.

(4) *Issuance of Mandate*. The court of appeals must issue the mandate immediately on receiving a copy of a Supreme Court order denying the petition, unless extraordinary circumstances exist.

Rule 42. Voluntary Dismissal

(a) **Dismissal in the District Court**. Before an appeal has been docketed by the circuit clerk, the district court may dismiss the appeal on the filing of a stipulation signed by all parties or on the appellant's motion with notice to all parties.

(b) **Dismissal in the Court of Appeals**.

    (1) *Stipulated Dismissal.* The circuit clerk must dismiss a docketed appeal if the parties file a signed dismissal agreement specifying how costs are to be paid and pay any court fees that are due.

    (2) *Appellant's Motion to Dismiss.* An appeal may be dismissed on the appellant's motion on terms agreed to by the parties or fixed by the court.

    (3) *Other Relief.* A court order is required for any relief under Rule 42(b)(1) or (2) beyond the dismissal of an appeal-including approving a settlement, vacating an action of the district court or an administrative agency, or remanding the case to either of them.

(c) **Court Approval**. This Rule 42 does not alter the legal requirements governing court approval of a settlement, payment, or other consideration.

(d) **Criminal Cases**. A court may, by local rule, impose requirements to confirm that a defendant has consented to the dismissal of an appeal in a criminal case.

Rule 43. Substitution of Parties

(a) **Death of a Party**.

    (1) *After Notice of Appeal Is Filed.* If a party dies after a notice of appeal has been filed or while a proceeding is pending in the court of appeals, the decedent's personal representative may be substituted as a party on motion filed with the circuit clerk by the representative or by any party. A party's motion must be served on the representative in accordance with Rule 25. If the decedent has no representative, any party may suggest the death on the record, and the court of appeals may then direct appropriate proceedings.

    (2) *Before Notice of Appeal Is Filed—Potential Appellant.* If a party entitled to appeal dies before filing a notice of appeal, the decedent's personal representative—or, if there is no personal representative, the decedent's attorney of record—may file a notice of appeal within the time prescribed by these rules. After the notice of appeal is filed, substitution must be in accordance with Rule 43(a)(1).

    (3) *Before Notice of Appeal Is Filed—Potential Appellee.* If a party against whom an appeal may be taken dies after entry of a judgment or order in the district court, but before a notice of appeal is filed, an appellant may proceed as if the death had not occurred. After the

notice of appeal is filed, substitution must be in accordance with Rule 43(a)(1).

(b) **Substitution for a Reason Other Than Death**. If a party needs to be substituted for any reason other than death, the procedure prescribed in Rule 43(a) applies.

(c) **Public Officer: Identification; Substitution**.

   (1) *Identification of Party*. A public officer who is a party to an appeal or other proceeding in an official capacity may be described as a party by the public officer's official title rather than by name. But the court may require the public officer's name to be added.

   (2) *Automatic Substitution of Officeholder*. When a public officer who is a party to an appeal or other proceeding in an official capacity dies, resigns, or otherwise ceases to hold office, the action does not abate. The public officer's successor is automatically substituted as a party. Proceedings following the substitution are to be in the name of the substituted party, but any misnomer that does not affect the substantial rights of the parties may be disregarded. An order of substitution may be entered at any time, but failure to enter an order does not affect the substitution.

Rule 44. Case Involving a Constitutional Question When the United States or the Relevant State is Not a Party

(a) **Constitutional Challenge to Federal Statute**. If a party questions the constitutionality of an Act of Congress in a proceeding in which the United States or its agency, officer, or employee is not a party in an official capacity, the questioning party must give written notice to the circuit clerk immediately upon the filing of the record or as soon as the question is raised in the court of appeals. The clerk must then certify that fact to the Attorney General.

(b) **Constitutional Challenge to State Statute**. If a party questions the constitutionality of a statute of a State in a proceeding in which that State or its agency, officer, or employee is not a party in an official capacity, the questioning party must give written notice to the circuit clerk immediately upon the filing of the record or as soon as the question is raised in the court of appeals. The clerk must then certify that fact to the attorney general of the State.

Rule 45. Clerk's Duties

(a) **General Provisions**.

(1) *Qualifications.* The circuit clerk must take the oath and post any bond required by law. Neither the clerk nor any deputy clerk may practice as an attorney or counselor in any court while in office.

(2) *When Court Is Open.* The court of appeals is always open for filing any paper, issuing and returning process, making a motion, and entering an order. The clerk's office with the clerk or a deputy in attendance must be open during business hours on all days except Saturdays, Sundays, and legal holidays. A court may provide by local rule or by order that the clerk's office be open for specified hours on Saturdays or on legal holidays other than New Year's Day, Martin Luther King, Jr.'s Birthday, Washington's Birthday, Memorial Day, Juneteenth National Independence Day, Independence Day, Labor Day, Columbus Day, Veterans' Day, Thanksgiving Day, and Christmas Day.

(b) **Records**.

(1) *The Docket.* The circuit clerk must maintain a docket and an index of all docketed cases in the manner prescribed by the Director of the Administrative Office of the United States Courts. The clerk must record all papers filed with the clerk and all process, orders, and judgments.

(2) *Calendar.* Under the court's direction, the clerk must prepare a calendar of cases awaiting argument. In placing cases on the calendar for argument, the clerk must give preference to appeals in criminal cases and to other proceedings and appeals entitled to preference by law.

(3) *Other Records.* The clerk must keep other books and records required by the Director of the Administrative Office of the United States Courts, with the approval of the Judicial Conference of the United States, or by the court.

(c) **Notice of an Order or Judgment**. Upon the entry of an order or judgment, the circuit clerk must immediately serve a notice of entry on each party, with a copy of any opinion, and must note the date of service on the docket. Service on a party represented by counsel must be made on counsel.

(d) **Custody of Records and Papers**. The circuit clerk has custody of the court's records and papers. Unless the court orders or instructs otherwise, the clerk must not permit an original record or paper to be taken from the clerk's office. Upon disposition of the case, original papers constituting the record on appeal or review must be returned to the court or agency from which they were received. The clerk must preserve a copy of any brief, appendix, or other paper that has been filed.

Rule 46. Attorneys

(a) **Admission to the Bar**.

    (1) *Eligibility*. An attorney is eligible for admission to the bar of a court of appeals if that attorney is of good moral and professional character and is admitted to practice before the Supreme Court of the United States, the highest court of a state, another United States court of appeals, or a United States district court (including the district courts for Guam, the Northern Mariana Islands, and the Virgin Islands).

    (2) *Application*. An applicant must file an application for admission, on a form approved by the court that contains the applicant's personal statement showing eligibility for membership. The applicant must subscribe to the following oath or affirmation:

> 'I ,_____, do solemnly swear [or affirm] that I will conduct myself as an attorney and counselor of this court, uprightly and according to law; and that I will support the Constitution of the United States.'

    (3) *Admission Procedures*. On written or oral motion of a member of the court's bar, the court will act on the application. An applicant may be admitted by oral motion in open court. But, unless the court orders otherwise, an applicant need not appear before the court to be admitted. Upon admission, an applicant must pay the clerk the fee prescribed by local rule or court order.

(b) **Suspension or Disbarment**.

    (1) *Standard*. A member of the court's bar is subject to suspension or disbarment by the court if the member:

      (A) has been suspended or disbarred from practice in any other court; or

      (B) is guilty of conduct unbecoming a member of the court's bar.

    (2) *Procedure*. The member must be given an opportunity to show good cause, within the time prescribed by the court, why the member should not be suspended or disbarred.

    (3) *Order*. The court must enter an appropriate order after the member responds and a hearing is held, if requested, or after the time prescribed for a response expires, if no response is made.

(c) **Discipline**. A court of appeals may discipline an attorney who practices before it for conduct unbecoming a member of the bar or for failure to comply with any court rule. First, however, the court must afford the attorney reasonable notice, an opportunity to show cause to the contrary, and, if requested, a hearing.

Rule 47. Local Rules by Courts of Appeals

(a) **Local Rules**.

    (1) Each court of appeals acting by a majority of its judges in regular active service may, after giving appropriate public notice and opportunity for comment, make and amend rules governing its practice. A generally applicable direction to parties or lawyers regarding practice before a court must be in a local rule rather than an internal operating procedure or standing order. A local rule must be consistent with—but not duplicative of—Acts of Congress and rules adopted under 28 U.S.C. §2072 and must conform to any uniform numbering system prescribed by the Judicial Conference of the United States. Each circuit clerk must send the Administrative Office of the United States Courts a copy of each local rule and internal operating procedure when it is promulgated or amended.

    (2) A local rule imposing a requirement of form must not be enforced in a manner that causes a party to lose rights because of a nonwillful failure to comply with the requirement.

(b) **Procedure When There Is No Controlling Law**. A court of appeals may regulate practice in a particular case in any manner consistent with federal law, these rules, and local rules of the circuit. No sanction or other disadvantage may be imposed for non-compliance with any requirement not in federal law, federal rules, or the local circuit rules unless the alleged violator has been furnished in the particular case with actual notice of the requirement.

Rule 48. Masters

(a) **Appointment; Powers**. A court of appeals may appoint a special master to hold hearings, if necessary, and to recommend factual findings and disposition in matters ancillary to proceedings in the court. Unless the order referring a matter to a master specifies or limits the master's powers, those powers include, but are not limited to, the following:

    (1) regulating all aspects of a hearing;

    (2) taking all appropriate action for the efficient performance of the master's duties under the order;

(3) requiring the production of evidence on all matters embraced in the reference; and

(4) administering oaths and examining witnesses and parties.

(b) **Compensation**. If the master is not a judge or court employee, the court must determine the master's compensation and whether the cost is to be charged to any party.

Appendix: Length Limits Stated in the Federal Rules of Appellate Procedure

This chart summarizes the length limits stated in the Federal Rules of Appellate Procedure. Please refer to the rules for precise requirements, and bear in mind the following:

- In computing these limits, you can exclude the items listed in Rule 32(f).
- If you use a word limit or a line limit (other than the word limit in Rule 28(j)), you must file the certificate required by Rule 32(g).
- For the limits in Rules 5, 21, 27, 35, and 40:
    - You must use the word limit if you produce your document on a computer; and
    - You must use the page limit if you handwrite your document or type it on a typewriter.
- For the limits in Rules 28.1, 29(a)(5), and 32:
    - You may use the word limit or page limit, regardless of how you produce the document; or
    - You may use the line limit if you type or print your document with a monospaced typeface. A typeface is monospaced when each character occupies the same amount of horizontal space.

	Rule	Document type	Word limit	Page limit	Line limit
Permission to appeal	5(c)	• Petition for permission to appeal • Answer in opposition • Cross-petition	5,200	20	Not applicable
Extraordinary writs	21(d)	• Petition for writ of mandamus or prohibition or other extraordinary writ • Answer	7,800	30	Not applicable
Motions	27(d)(2)	• Motion • Response to a motion	5,200	20	Not applicable
	27(d)(2)	• Reply to a response to a motion	2,600	10	Not applicable
Parties' briefs (where no cross-appeal)	32(a)(7)	• Principal brief	13,000	30	1,300
	32(a)(7)	• Reply brief	6,500	15	650
Parties' briefs (where cross-appeal)	28.1(e)	• Appellant's principal brief • Appellant's response and reply brief	13,000	30	1,300
	28.1(e)	• Appellee's principal and response brief	15,300	35	1,500
	28.1(e)	• Appellee's reply brief	6,500	15	650
Party's supplemental letter	28(j)	• Letter citing supplemental authorities	350	Not applicable	Not applicable

Amicus Briefs	29(a)(5)	• Amicus brief during initial consideration of case on merits	One-half the length set by the Appellate Rules for a party's principal brief	One-half the length set by the Appellate Rules for a party's principal brief	One-half the length set by the Appellate Rules for a party's principal brief
	29(b)(4)	• Amicus brief during consideration of whether to grant rehearing	2,600	Not applicable	Not Applicable
Rehearing and en banc filings	35(b)(2) & 40(b)	• Petition for rehearing en banc • Petition for panel rehearing; petition for rehearing en banc	3,900	15	Not applicable

Appendix of Forms

Form 1A. Notice of Appeal to a Court of Appeals from a Judgment or Order of a District Court

United States District Court for the _____
District of _____
File Number _____

A.B., Plaintiff v. C.D., Defendant	Notice of Appeal

_____ (name all parties taking the appeal)* appeal to the United States Court of Appeals for the _____ Circuit from the final judgment entered on _____ (state the date the decision was entered).

(s) _____
Attorney for _____
Address:_____

[*Note to inmate filers:* *If you are an inmate confined in an institution and you seek the timing benefit of Fed. R. App. P. 4(c)(1), complete Form 7 (Declaration of Inmate Filing) and file that declaration along with this Notice of Appeal.*]

* See Rule 3(c) for permissible ways of identifying appellants.

Form 1B. Notice of Appeal to a Court of Appeals from an Appealable Order of a District Court

United States District Court for the _____
District of _____
File Number _____

A.B., Plaintiff
v.
C.D., Defendant

Notice of Appeal

_____ (name all parties taking the appeal)* appeal to the United States Court of Appeals for the _____ Circuit from the order ___ (describe the order) entered on _____ (state the date the order was entered).

(s) _____
Attorney for _____
Address:_____

[*Note to inmate filers*: *If you are an inmate confined in an institution and you seek the timing benefit of Fed. R. App. P. 4(c)(1), complete Form 7 (Declaration of Inmate Filing) and file that declaration with this Notice of Appeal.*]

* See Rule 3(c) for permissible ways of identifying appellants.

Form 2. Notice of Appeal to a Court of Appeals from a Decision of the United States Tax Court

United States Tax Court
Washington, DC
Docket No. _____

A.B., Petitioner	
v.	Notice of Appeal
Commissioner of Internal Revenue, Respondent	

_____ (name all parties taking the appeal)* appeal to the United States Court of Appeals for the _____ Circuit from the decision entered on _____ (state the date the decision was entered).

(s) _____
Attorney for _____
Address:_____

* See Rule 3(c) for permissible ways of identifying appellants.

Form 3. Petition for Review of Order of an Agency, Board, Commission or Officer

United States Court of Appeals
for the
<_____> CIRCUIT

<Name of petitioner>,	)
	)
Petitioner	)
	)
v.	)
	)
<XYZ Commission>,	)
	)
Respondent	)
	)

PETITION FOR REVIEW

<Here name all parties bringing the petition> hereby petition the court for review of the Order of the <XYZ Commission> <describe the order> entered on <Date>.

Date: <Date>   <Signature of the attorney or unrepresented party>

_____
<Printed name>
<Attorney for Petitioners>
<Address>
<E-mail address>
<Telephone number>

Form 4. Affidavit Accompanying Motion for Permission to Appeal in Forma Pauperis

UNITED STATES DISTRICT COURT

for the

<_____> DISTRICT OF <_____>

<Name(s) of plaintiff(s)>,	)
	)
Plaintiff(s)	)
	)
v.	)
	) Case No. <Number>
<Name(s) of defendant(s)>,	)
	)
Defendant(s)	)
	)

**AFFIDAVIT ACCOMPANYING MOTION
FOR PERMISSION TO APPEAL IN FORMA PAUPERIS**

Affidavit in Support of Motion

    I swear or affirm under penalty of perjury that, because of my poverty, I cannot prepay the docket fees of my appeal or post a bond for them. I believe I am entitled to redress. I swear or affirm under penalty of perjury under United States laws that my answers on this form are true and correct. (28 U.S.C. § 1746; 18 U.S.C. § 1621.)

Signed:

_____

Instructions

    Complete all questions in this application and then sign it.   Do not leave any blanks: if the answer to a question is '0,' 'none,' or 'not applicable (N/A),' write in that response. If you need more space to answer a question or to explain your answer, attach a separate sheet of paper identified with your name, your case's docket number, and the question number.

Date:

_____

My issues on appeal are:

1.   *For both you and your spouse estimate the average amount of money received from each of the following sources during the past 12 months. Adjust any amount that was received weekly, biweekly, quarterly, semiannually, or annually to show the monthly rate. Use gross amounts, that is, amounts before any deductions for taxes or otherwise.*

Income source	Average monthly amount during the past 12 months		Amount expected next month	
	You	Spouse	You	Spouse
Employment	$	$	$	$
Self-employment	$	$	$	$
Income from real property (such as rental income)	$	$	$	$
Interest and dividends	$	$	$	$
Gifts	$	$	$	$
Alimony	$	$	$	$
Child support	$	$	$	$
Retirement (such as social security, pensions, annuities, insurance)	$	$	$	$
Disability (such as social security, insurance payments)	$	$	$	$
Unemployment payments	$	$	$	$
Public-assistance (such as welfare)	$	$	$	$

Other (specify):	$	$	$	$
Total monthly income:	$	$	$	$

2.   *List your employment history for the past two years, most recent employer first. (Gross monthly pay is before taxes or other deductions.)*

Employer	Address	Dates of employment	Gross monthly pay
			$
			$
			$

3.   *List your spouse's employment history for the past two years, most recent employer first. (Gross monthly pay is before taxes or other deductions.)*

Employer	Address	Dates of employment	Gross monthly pay
			$
			$
			$

4.   *How much cash do you and your spouse have? $_____*

    Below, state any money you or your spouse have in bank accounts or in any other financial institution.

Financial Institution	Type of Account	Amount you have	Amount your spouse has
		$	$
		$	$
		$	$

If you are a prisoner seeking to appeal a judgment in a civil action or proceeding, you must attach a statement certified by the appropriate institutional officer showing all receipts, expenditures, and balances during the last six months in your institutional accounts. If you have multiple accounts, perhaps because you have been in multiple institutions, attach one certified statement of each account.

5.   *List the assets, and their values, which you own or your spouse owns. Do not list clothing and ordinary household furnishings.*

Home	Other real estate	Motor vehicle #1
(Value) $	(Value) $	(Value) $
		Make and year:
		Model:
		Registration #:

Motor vehicle #2	Other assets	Other assets
(Value) $	(Value) $	(Value) $
Make and year:		
Model:		
Registration #:		

6. *State every person, business, or organization owing you or your spouse money, and the amount owed.*

Person owing you or your spouse money	Amount owed to you	Amount owed to your spouse
	$	$
	$	$
	$	$
	$	$

7. *State the persons who rely on you or your spouse for support.*

Name [or, if under 18, initials only]	Relationship	Age

8. *Estimate the average monthly expenses of you and your family. Show separately the amounts paid by your spouse. Adjust any payments that are made weekly, biweekly, quarterly, semiannually, or annually to show the monthly rate.*

	You	Your Spouse

Rent or home-mortgage payment (include lot rented for mobile home)
      Are real estate taxes included?   [ ] Yes   [ ] No
      Is property insurance included?   [ ] Yes   [ ] No
	$	$

Utilities (electricity, heating fuel, water, sewer, and telephone)	$	$
Home maintenance (repairs and upkeep)	$	$
Food	$	$
Clothing	$	$
Laundry and dry-cleaning	$	$
Medical and dental expenses	$	$
Transportation (not including motor vehicle payments)	$	$
Recreation, entertainment, newspapers, magazines, etc.	$	$
Insurance (not deducted from wages or included in mortgage payments)		
Homeowner's or renter's:	$	$
Life:	$	$
Health:	$	$
Motor vehicle:	$	$
Other:	$	$
Taxes (not deducted from wages or included in mortgage payments) (specify):	$	$
Installment payments		
Motor Vehicle:	$	$
Credit card (name):	$	$
Department store (name):	$	$
Other:	$	$
Alimony, maintenance, and support paid to others	$	$

Regular expenses for operation of business, profession, or farm (attach detailed statement)	$	$
Other (specify):	$	$
Total monthly expenses:	$	$

9. *Do you expect any major changes to your monthly income or expenses or in your assets or liabilities during the next 12 months?*

   [ ] Yes   [ ] No   If yes, describe on an attached sheet.

10. *Have you spent — or will you be spending — any money for expenses or attorney fees in connection with this lawsuit?* [ ] Yes [ ] No

   If yes, how much? $ _____

11. *Provide any other information that will help explain why you cannot pay the docket fees for your appeal.*

12. *State the city and state of your legal residence.*

   Your daytime phone number: (____) _____

   Your age: _____   Your years of schooling: _____

Form 5. Notice of Appeal to a Court of Appeals from a Judgment or Order of a District Court or a Bankruptcy Appellate Panel

United States District Court for the _____
District of _____

In re _____ , Debtor   _____ , Plaintiff v.   _____ , Defendant

File No. _____

Notice of Appeal to United States Court of Appeals for the
_____ Circuit

_____ , the plaintiff [or defendant or other party] appeals to the United States Court of Appeals for the _____ Circuit from the final judgment [or order or decree] of the district court for the district of _____ [or bankruptcy appellate panel of the _____ circuit], entered in this case on _____ , 20__ [here describe the judgment, order, or decree] _____

The parties to the judgment [or order or decree] appealed from and the names and addresses of their respective attorneys are as follows:

Dated _____
Signed _____
Attorney for Appellant
Address: _____
_____

[**Note to inmate filers:** *If you are an inmate confined in an institution and you seek the timing benefit of Fed. R. App. P. 4(c)(1), complete Form 7 (Declaration of Inmate Filing) and file that declaration along with this Notice of Appeal.*]

Form 6. Certificate of Compliance with Type–Volume Limit

Certificate of Compliance With Type-Volume Limit,
Typeface Requirements, and Type-Style Requirements

Form 6. Certificate of Compliance with Type–Volume Limit

1.   This document complies with [the type-volume limit of Fed. R. App. P. [*insert Rule citation; e.g., 32(a)(7)(B)*]] [the word limit of Fed. R. App. P. [*insert Rule citation; e.g., 5(c)(1)*]]] because, excluding the parts of the document exempted by Fed. R. App. P. 32(f) [and [*insert applicable Rule citation, if any*]]:

☐   this document contains [*state the number of*] words, **or**

☐   this brief uses a monospaced typeface and contains [*state the number of*] lines of text.

2.   This document complies with the typeface requirements of Fed. R. App. P. 32(a)(5) and the type-style requirements of Fed. R. App. P. 32(a)(6) because:

☐   this document has been prepared in a proportionally spaced typeface using [*state name and version of word-processing program*] in [*state font size and name of type style*], **or**

☐   this document has been prepared in a monospaced typeface using [*state name and version of word-processing program*] with [*state number of characters per inch and name of type style*].

(s)_____

Attorney for _____

Dated: _____

Form 7. Declaration of Inmate Filing

[*insert name of court; for example,*
United States District Court for the District of Minnesota]

A.B., Plaintiff	
v.	Case No. _____
C.D., Defendant	

I am an inmate confined in an institution. Today, _____ [*insert date*], I am depositing the _____ [*insert title of document; for example, 'notice of appeal'*] in this case in the institution's internal mail system. First-class postage is being prepaid either by me or by the institution on my behalf.

I declare under penalty of perjury that the foregoing is true and correct (see 28 U.S.C. § 1746; 18 U.S.C. § 1621).

Sign your name here_____

Signed on _____ [*insert date*]

[**Note to inmate filers:** *If your institution has a system designed for legal mail, you must use that system in order to receive the timing benefit of Fed. R. App. P. 4(c)(1) or Fed. R. App. P. 25(a)(2)(A)(iii).*]

Made in the USA
Middletown, DE
20 July 2024